The Meaning of the Universe

by <u>Christopher</u> <u>Andrus</u>

Copyright 2019

Chapter 1	*The Question That We All Need to Ask*	6
	Part 2	13
Chapter 2	*How We Got To Where We Are Today*	18
	Part 2	27
Chapter 3	*We All Believe (One Way or Another) in Order to Understand the World.*	33
	Part 2	46
Chapter 4	*Our Worldviews Are What Divide Us and "Them"*	58
Chapter 5	*Humanism's Moral Problems*	75
	Part 2	93
Chapter 6	*Humanism's Intellectual Problems*	105
	Part 2	122
Chapter 7	*Humanists' Objections to Christianity are Fallacies.*	135

PART 2

Chapter 8	*Why Christianity Is True And Approaches Which Do Not Begin With One God Fail.*	157
	Part 2	168
	Part 3	174
Chapter 9	*Why Christianity Is True And Other Approaches Which Begin With One God Fail.*	188
Chapter 10	*More Ways in which Christianity Shows its Superiority Over Other Approaches*	208
	Part 2	216
Chapter 11	*Christianity Both Defines and Promotes Freedom.*	227
	Part 2	244

Chapter 12	*Freedom, Capitalism and Socialism*	**251**
Appendix 1	*A Response to a Hindu*	**266**
Appendix 2	*Suggestions For Further Study*	**271**
Appendix 3	*Key Statements in Each Chapter*	**274**

Chapter 1
The Question That We All Need to Ask

You need to read this book.
"Really? Why?"

Because the chances are that you have never really asked yourself: "Why am I alive?" Not, "How did I come to be alive?" (which is a different question), but, "Why?"

That's a rather important question, don't you think? And to say that "My life is just an accident of Nature" and that none of our lives really has any meaning is not really an acceptable answer. Most people in the developed world today are taught that it is. But, none of us really believes that our life and the lives of others are meaningless.

Nor have most of us ever thought carefully about the basic nature of the universe, nor about the question of whether or not God exists.

And even if you have spent some time thinking about these things, it is unlikely that you have considered the perspective presented in this book. In short, this book is an invitation to think carefully and critically about the most basic questions in life. And this isn't hard at all. It's actually very easy. I promise! The problem is that most people today are never encouraged to start.[1]

---

1   *This book is about what we think and about whether or not we are right in our thinking. But it is not an introduction to Philosophy. How boring! And*

A common criticism of Christianity is that "Christians don't know how to think critically". And that is certainly true in some cases. But this is not only a problem with Christians or other religious people. The lack of careful and critical thinking is very widespread in society today. Conservatives, including many Christians often decry the lack of thought behind so many ideas which are considered "progressive" today. And on the other side, liberal writer Noam Chomsky describes the need to encourage critical thinking today:

> *"I try to encourage people to think for themselves, to question standard assumptions. Don't take assumptions for granted. Begin by taking a skeptical attitude toward anything that is conventional wisdom. Make it justify itself. It usually can't. Be willing to ask questions about what is taken for granted. Try to think things through for yourself."*[2]

I'm a Philosophy graduate! Nor is it an introduction to Theology. Most introductions to Philosophy and Theology are complicated, hard to read and, thus, quite boring. Besides, there are too many out there already.

Also, this book is not a book about Christian "Apologetics". God knows (and I mean that literally), we have enough of these already! However, it is an "Apology" for Christianity in the theological meaning of the term – A defense of Christianity against the attacks made against it and a critique of rival religions and philosophies which seeks to show their flaws. We will look at many specific failures of alternatives to Christianity (especially Humanism, which is the dominant philosophy of the developed world today). But the main reason that all non-Christian approaches fail is because they reject as their starting point The One True God, Who reveals Himself in our minds and consciences, in the world around us and, definitively, in His Word, the Bible.

2 Noam Chomsky, from a 2010 interview with Chris Hedges. However, one can't help but wonder if Chomsky will ever truly be willing to apply his own good advice to his own assumptions. Progressives (and, especially atheists) are quite prone to the hypocrisy of being critical of others' views, but quite unwilling to be critical of their own.

If you have never really thought carefully about the question: "Why am I alive?" then you are not really a careful critical thinker on the most basic and most important level, regardless of your level of education.

Why am I alive? Shouldn't this be one of the most important questions, if not <u>the</u> most important one anyone could ask? But, amazingly, most people today either haven't asked it at all or have just dismissed it as unanswerable or with the simple answer: "I have no real importance in the universe." Now, having such a perspective may seem to be humble and, even, noble. But is it correct?

Most people just accept the basic ideas which we are taught and don't think critically about them mainly because we aren't taught to do this. And we weren't taught this mainly because our teachers weren't taught to do so. For more than 50 years public education and the popular culture in most of America and most of the developed world has assumed that certain basic ideas are true. Most important among them are these three –

1) that matter-energy and mindless forces of nature and quantum fluctuation in space-time are all that exists

2) that humanity, not God, determines what is right and wrong

3) that belief in God and Christianity is outdated and incorrect

To question these ideas, while not strictly forbidden, is certainly not encouraged. But these ideas are beliefs. They are not proven facts, although many will claim that they are.[3]

---

[3] *For those of you who would claim that these ideas are not just beliefs, they're facts, consider this: It is actually logically impossible to prove that only matter-energy and mindless forces in space-time exist. This is because in making this claim one is saying that nothing else can possibly exist. But this is what is known as a negative universal claim. And such claims just aren't provable in practice. This is also true about the claim that God doesn't exist. At the least, it must always be allowed that future evidence might disprove such beliefs.*

This is where critical thinking comes in. But why is it that so many of us have never questioned and thought critically about these basic ideas, especially since they are foundations for everything else that we think and do? Part of the answer has to do with how education works. The only way we learn from others is to trust that they know better than us and also to trust that they are teaching us what is true.

Education begins with our parents or guardians or older siblings and continues when we start going to school. It even continues throughout our lives whenever it is necessary for us to learn something new. Education only works when the students are willing to accept what we are taught. Or, at least, to accept much of what we are taught. Otherwise, we could not get along in the world we live in.

But, it's not that we are completely uncritical learners by nature. Along with our necessary tendency to believe what we are taught, we also are born with a natural tendency to doubt. This, too, is necessary to protect us from believing things that would hurt us. So our mothers have said things like this to us: "If your brother told you to jump off a bridge, would you do it just because he told you to?" So we are taught to doubt and question many things in life.

But some things are presented to us as unquestionable. And for most 21st century residents in the developed world, these include the 3 basic ideas I just gave: 1) that matter-energy and mindless forces of nature and quantum fluctuation in space-time are all that exists, 2) that humanity, not God, determines what is right and wrong, and 3) that belief in God and Christianity is outdated and incorrect.

There are certainly practical reasons why questioning these ideas is discouraged, despite the fact that these ideas are only beliefs, not proven facts. They are the foundations on which a lot of other ideas are built. So, if one was to question these basic ideas it would lead us to question a lot of other things which we are supposed to learn and accept. This is considered dangerous both for individuals and for society.

Individuals who question things we aren't supposed to question will be considered weird, at best, if not dangerous. And societies in which there are disagreements on very basic ideas will have many conflicts and will be in danger of falling apart. And like it or not, this is our situation today in the developed world in the early 21st century. But this has also been true for many societies in the past.

In every society there will always be an enormous amount of pressure to accept the basic beliefs of the society and not to question them. But, sometimes the basic beliefs of societies are problematic. History is filled with examples, but Nazi Germany is perhaps the most obvious example in recent history.

We now recognize quite clearly that Nazism was evil. Quite surprisingly, though, the actual reasons why it was evil are actually unclear if one accepts the 3 basic ideas just listed, which are generally accepted today. This is mainly because of idea #2. If we alone determine what is good and evil, then how can we really know for certain when we are right or when someone else is wrong? After all, the Nazi's claimed they were right and everyone else wrong. (But more on this later)

Our understanding of Nazism today is what has been called "20-20 hindsight". It is often much easier to understand many situations later on, rather than "in the moment". This is true for our individual lives, but also for societies. People living in Germany in the 1920's, during the rise of the Nazi Party, and during the 1930's, when it took over Germany, were morally wrong to accept where their culture was going and were actually morally obligated not only to question it, but to oppose it.

However, it's a big mistake to assume that this was as clear to most Germans at that time as it is to us today. For, Germany's "Third Reich" did not spring up overnight in its fully-developed form. It was a gradual process of many steps, most of them small and easy to overlook, which occurred over many years. This is usually the way things change.

But when change happens this way, it often escapes the notice of many. It is like the often-cited example of the frog in the pot. One can take a live frog and put it in a pot of room-temperature water and begin slowly heating it. If one does it slowly enough the frog will simply stay in the water until it cooks. This is because it is unable to recognize the danger.

So, it was with most in Germany until it was too late. A very common reaction to Adolf Hitler was that he was too crazy to take seriously and it was unthinkable that he could possibly succeed with his plans. Surely it was inevitable that the decent people of Germany would eventually rise up and stop him. But, unfortunately, most Germans didn't consider that they needed to play a role in this. They assumed other people would do this. But it never happened. And as time passed it became harder and harder to oppose the Nazi's.

It's rather like cancer. When people discover strange growths on their skin, some are motivated to have it looked at, but others are afraid to do so. Of course, if it is cancerous it will not go away and will become worse and worse and may eventually be fatal. But, it may have been relatively easy and painless to deal with it in the beginning. And, more importantly, it may well have been curable.

So, Adolf Hitler could have been defeated without much difficulty if enough people had been willing to stand up to him and his thugs in the 1920's. But by the 1930's he had grown powerful enough that it had become much more dangerous and difficult to do so; too dangerous for most Germans to even think about challenging Hitler's ideas and actions.

Germany succumbed to evil mainly because it failed to question changes to some of the basic ideas accepted by society. Once those ideas became established it became very hard for people even to question them, much less fight against them. This is because another common human tendency is for us "to go along in order to get along". In other words, most people will accept things which they admit are wrong in order to avoid harm to themselves and their families. This is just an undeniable (and understandable) fact of human nature. But it is where critical thinking and courage are absolutely necessary in order to stop evil.

This is why we must always be willing to question the basic ideas of our society. Are you willing to do this with the 3 basic ideas I have listed? This is not to say that we are in the same situation that Germany was in (although a number of troubling parallels can be seen). But it would be a dangerous mistake to assume that we are immune from going down a path similar to what happened to Germany in the 1920's and 1930's. It always takes a deliberate effort to think critically because of two things which have already been mentioned: our natural tendency to accept what we are taught and also pressure coming from around us not to think critically, especially about our most basic beliefs.

But there is a third reason why we are inclined not to think critically about these ideas and to just accept them. This one comes from inside of us. It's not only because we are taught to accept these ideas. It's also because human beings have a natural tendency to resist and reject the idea that there is a God Who made us, along with everything else that exists (contrary to basic idea #1), and Who also defines what is true and good (contrary to basic idea #2). Instead, we are naturally inclined to believe other things, as if God (or, at least, the idea of God) is our Enemy. But, the Christian message is that God is only your Enemy if you treat Him as such. Rather, He wants to be your perfectly-loving Father, His Son Jesus Christ your Savior and His Holy Spirit your Guide.

Part 2

Up until about 100 years ago things were very different in the developed world than they are today. Contrary to today's 3 basic beliefs (which, again, are not proven facts), most people in Europe and the United States viewed their lives in relation to the Creator God, the same One Who is described in the Bible and Who was believed to exist by the vast majority of people. Other than a minority consisting of Jews, Atheists/Agnostics, Muslims and people of other faiths, almost everyone saw himself or herself either as a Christian or a sinner before God.[4]

But over the course of the previous century a new view had been gaining strength in intellectual circles, slowly supplanting Christianity, first in the halls of academia and, eventually, in the entire culture. This approach came to be known as Humanism and was openly admitted to be a religious alternative to Christianity and other supernatural religions in a Manifesto authored by a group of prominent teachers in the early 1930's (the first "Humanist Manifesto").

Humanism has a starkly different perspective on humanity and the universe than Christianity, rejecting the supernatural both on the personal and cosmic levels. On the cosmic side, it rejected the idea of an Almighty Creator and Lord of the universe in favor of the view that the universe was not created and consists only of matter-energy, space-time and mindless forces of Nature (which is known as the Materialism philosophy). Humanism also assumes that humanity is the source and standard of truth and morality. After all, if there is no Higher Authority, then we must determine truth and morality for ourselves.

---

4 *Of course, Jewish people, Muslims and others at that time also had a theistic or, at least, a spiritual understanding of reality, in contrast with what is taught in most of the developed world today.*

Over the past 100 years Humanism so effectively became the dominant view that it became rare that anyone would dare to question it. Those who dared to do so would tend to be viewed as odd or ignorant, at best (holding to antiquated and disproved beliefs) if not outright crazy. In American culture, the so-called "Scopes monkey trial" in 1925 was probably the clearest sign of the conquest of Humanism over the previously-dominant Christian (or Judeo-Christian) view. For, although the Humanist side lost the actual trial, it clearly won a decisive victory in the court of public opinion.

Over the following decades the Humanist view steadily supplanted the Christian view in most of the developed world. So it is that most in the U.S. and the rest of the developed world today just take the Humanist view of the universe and humanity for granted: that we are tiny specks in a vast impersonal Cosmos, mere accidents of Nature, biochemical machines which are merely the most complex product that we have found of the process of Evolution, a process governed by mindless forces.

But is the Humanist view correct? Does it explain human existence? Does it stand up to critical scrutiny? Were we correct in rejecting the old way of looking at things? Or is there another approach which may work better? That such questions are rarely asked today is, in itself, a dangerous thing. Socrates, a man who was fond of questions, is credited with saying that "An unexamined life is not worth living." Would you not agree that this is true?

It is simply not possible to examine our lives without examining our most basic beliefs about life. Sadly, most of us today have become so convinced that Humanism is correct that we have lost our ability to think critically about it and also to think about alternative views, especially about Christianity.[5]

---

5 *Since Humanism was the view which supplanted Christianity as the dominant view of the developed world, it is natural that it would be especially opposed to Christianity. And this is exactly what we see today. It is also why Humanists are almost always "secularists". Indeed, Humanism has also been called Secular Humanism in Christian circles. Secularists*

So, the goal of this book is, first, to help you take the all-important journey of examining (or re-examining) what you believe and why. Though there are hundreds (if not thousands) of belief-systems, I will suggest that there are only four that really matter today. They are Humanism (the dominant view of the developed world today), Christianity (the approach which was previously dominant in the developed world), Islam (the dominant view of the Arab world) and Hinduism & Buddhism (the dominant views among traditionalists in Asia). These four should be sufficient because it is almost certain that you will find that one of these is your view in the most important respects.[6]

The predicament of the 21st century is that we are in a "culture war" in which those on every side see those on the other sides as being seriously out-of-touch with reality and as having embraced an evil worldview and agenda. This is mainly between Humanists and Christians in the developed world, but Muslims, Hindus and (to a lesser extent) Buddhists also figure prominently in this elsewhere. The main reason that we are so divided today is because of these religious/philosophical divisions, especially that between today's dominant Humanism and Christianity (the approach which previously ruled the developed world).

It should not surprise anyone that people with very different views of reality

---

believe that only non-religious ideas should influence society. But it will be shown a little later that Humanism itself is actually a religion for all practical purposes. So there really are no non-religious people. And there really are no non-religious ideas with regard to any significant issues.

6 *If you are a person who is not affiliated with any of the major religious traditions but you believe in "New Age" spirituality, then your approach can be seen to be in line with the traditions of Hinduism and Buddhism in that your worldview and spirituality are non-theistic. In other words, both the material and spiritual aspects of existence are not seen as being the creation of an Almighty God (and, as such, distinct from Him) as both the Christian and Muslim traditions believe. But, unlike Humanists, you accept the reality of the spiritual dimension.*

and ethical authority will disagree on many issues. It also should not surprise anyone that our differences will be very passionate. For, it is quite natural to be passionate about our most basic beliefs and also highly defensive of them and very hostile to challenges by people with different basic beliefs. This is so even for people who are not very aware of their basic beliefs, working on more of a subconscious level for such people.

This is why the common idea that religions cause war is correct. But this includes Humanism, which was called "religious" in the first Humanist Manifesto, written by a group of prominent Humanists in the 1930's. Humanism is equivalent to any other religion in being a set of beliefs which cannot really be proven and are not normally questioned, beliefs which govern how one looks at one's self, the world around us and the question of whether or not there is an Almighty God, other deities or some other Higher Authority. (Substitute the term "basic philosophy" for "religion" if you wish. The point remains the same.)[7]

Thus, the issues which so passionately divide us today do so because they spring from our basic religious/philosophical differences. This can most easily be seen with issues that are clearly moral, like LGBTQ rights, abortion and the death-penalty. But it can also be seen with seemingly non-religious issues like evolution, climate-change, economics, immigration, criminal justice and the proper role of government.

The second goal of this book is to compare Christianity with the other views, especially Humanism, since it is the dominant view in the developed world

---

[7] *The first Humanist Manifesto may be found at https://americanhumanist.org/what-is-humanism/manifesto1. That later Humanist documents have stopped referring to the philosophy as religious likely reflects an awareness by Humanists that they could be accused of violating the 1st Amendment of the American Constitution insofar as they seek to establish Humanism as America's ruling philosophy. But this doesn't change the fact that Humanism is akin to a religion both in form and function. And, as the saying goes, "if it looks like a duck and quacks like a duck, then it must be a duck".*

today. It is actually surprisingly easy to show how Humanism and the other views fall into self-contradiction or other obvious absurdities or inadequacies. Christianity, on the other hand, can be seen to be the only approach which avoids this and is able to account for everything that exists and all that we know.

Of course, I admit that I am biased about this. But, so are you. We all are. I know what it is to be an anti-Christian Humanist because I was a believer in Humanism until I was 22. But in that year (1982) I embraced the Christian view, having become convinced that it succeeds and all other approaches fail. You are biased, too, whether you are already aware of this or not; or whether you are willing to admit it or not.

Most likely you have the same bias that I had until 1982, unless you have another type of belief-system (like Islam or Hinduism). We all have some sort of a belief-system that we are committed to; that is, a set of basic beliefs about ourselves, the world around us and whether or not there is a God or some other Higher Authority than us. But it is crucial to think carefully and critically about your belief-system. If you don't do this, you run the risk of making a lot of mistakes. And you also run the risk of missing the correct path.

This brings us to the final goal of this book: that it will convince you that Christianity is the True Path. I hope to do this not just because it is the right view, but because of the incomparable and immeasurable blessings of being a Christian both for our lives in this world and beyond.

Chapter 2
How We Got To Where We Are Today

Humanism has been the dominant worldview throughout most of the developed world since at least the middle of the 20th century. While this fact isn't often discussed (which is one of the main reasons for this book), it is widely-recognized, being quietly celebrated (in most cases) by those who embrace it and bemoaned by those of us who reject it, especially those of us who have rejected it in favor of the view it replaced – Christian Theism.

In chapter 1, 3 key beliefs of Humanism were identified: 1) that matter-energy and mindless forces of nature in space-time are all that exists, 2) that humanity, not God, determines what is right and wrong, and 3) that belief in God and Christianity is outdated and incorrect. It was also pointed out that these 3 key beliefs are explicit rejections of the previously-dominant view.

Despite the change in reigning worldviews and the dramatic contrast and conflict between Humanism and the Christian view, there was a tendency for many people in the developed world to want to preserve the previous Christian heritage in some fashion. This is not surprising considering how long Christianity had reigned as the dominant perspective in Europe, the British Isles and the entire Western hemisphere. Indeed, Christianity had long been seen as that which set apart "Western Civilization" from the rest of the world.

But by the time World War 2 had ended, it was clear that the Humanist perspective had won out. So, since Humanism had clearly rejected long-accepted fundamental aspects of Christianity, if one wished to keep up with the times but also retain some sense of Christianity, then it would be necessary for Christianity to be recast in a way in which it was not in conflict with the basic principles of Humanism. And this is precisely what had been occurring over the previous 150 years, first in academic circles and later in the general culture.

Humanism's conquest and its recasting of Christianity was the culmination of a process that began around 1800 A.D. (or C.E.). Prior to this, being a Christian had always meant that one truly believed that the God of the Bible was real and, therefore, that everyone was accountable to Him. And, despite many other disagreements among Christians, it was also the case that all Christians accepted that the Bible was a unique book in which God has communicated what He wanted us to have in written form. In other words, it was accepted that it was God's Word, or His definitive revelation of Himself and His will to us.

But, for the past two centuries there have been many people who have considered themselves to be Christians, yet they do not really have a meaningful belief in the God of the Bible (meaningful in the sense that their thinking about God actually has a significant impact on their lives and view of other things). Furthermore, many self-professed Christians since around 1800 A.D. have not viewed the Bible as having come from God to humanity. Rather, they have believed that the Bible was like other religious books – a book containing peoples' ideas about God.

It is the position of the writer that the rejection of these two basic beliefs that once were characteristic of all Christians – that the God of the Bible really exists and that the Bible is His Self-revelation (or His Word, not mere ideas and words of men) has destroyed the original and true meaning of being a Christian. So, my goal will be to get the readers to recognize and (hopefully) embrace both of these. But, my focus will be on the first of these.

Unlike many Christian approaches, I will not ask any reader who doesn't already believe this to presuppose that the Bible is true. Rather, my goal will be to get everyone who has not already done so to begin by accepting that the God Who makes Himself known in our minds and in the world around us must really exist. It will subsequently be shown in various ways that every human-being who has ever lived has actually presupposed the existence of this God, even though most people today deny that they do this.

But, if one gets to the point of realizing that the existence of the One True Creator God must be accepted, then it will be a simple step to see that this is the same God Who is described in the Bible and is also presented as addressing us in the Bible. And, once you have seen that this is the case, then it will be natural for one to accept that the Bible actually is what it says it is: God's unique written Revelation for us. In other words, we must first accept the existence of the God of the Bible before we can accept the Bible as what it presents itself to be.

Countless volumes of Christian literature over the past two millennia have been devoted to proving that God exists and that Christianity is true. But, amazingly, the very nature of the God described in the Bible actually makes proving His existence unnecessary.[8] This is not because the Bible says this (although it does). Rather, it is just the nature of the case that the existence of The God described in the Bible must be known and cannot be doubted.

---

8 *This is not to say that Christians shouldn't use arguments and evidence to point to this God. But we shouldn't do so as if we need to prove His existence. Rather, we do so in order to point others to "the God Who is there" (to use Christian philosopher Francis Schaeffer's term). We are simply pointing to the One Whom everyone is capable of recognizing both in their minds and in His handiwork all around them.*

We do this in order to help others do what we have already done: to stop suppressing their knowledge of God, to abandon their God-denying approaches, to accept that they live in the world that God made, having been made by Him for the purpose of being His children, and to live accordingly. Or, to put it in "A-B-C" form: We must <u>Admit</u> our sin of rejecting our Creator, <u>Believe</u> that He sent His Eternal Son into the world in order to restore us to a right relation relationship with Him as His beloved children and that He will send His Eternal Holy Spirit into our hearts in order to transform us into true disciples of His Son, and <u>Commit</u> to loving Him and all those around us.

Why is this? In short, it's because God made us so that we would all know Him. So, if He exists, then it is inevitable that we know Him.

So, does the God described in the Bible exist? He must because we know Him. So, it goes like this:

God made us to know Him → We know Him → God must exist.

This may seem like the fallacy of assuming the conclusion. But it really isn't. If the premises are true, then the conclusion logically follows. Of course, many will deny the conclusion because they deny the premises. But to deny them doesn't mean that they aren't true. People deny things that are nonetheless true all the time. To deny that God exists is like a pot saying to the potter who made it: "You don't exist.", or a child saying the same to his parents.

But knowing that God exists and having a relationship with Him are two very different things. Denial or doubt about God's existence isn't a matter of a lack of evidence or logic. It's a psychological and spiritual problem. All people know God exists, but it is a choice for all of us if we want to have a relationship with Him or not.[9]

---

9   *The approach of this book places greater weight than most on what theologians call "general revelation" (which refers to how God reveals Himself to every human-being everywhere throughout history). It is sufficient to render every human-being who has ever lived without excuse because they inevitably know The One True God, yet refuse to acknowledge Him. And every human being who has ever lived is also without excuse for not obeying Him, knowing without exception that they are under His just Judgment and wrath for their disobedience.*

   Indeed, it is the Bible that reveals this, specifically in the latter half of Romans 1. But it applies universally, regardless of whether or not one has ever been exposed to this "special revelation". This may seem to diminish the necessity of the Church and the ministry of the Word of God. Perhaps it does in the area of revealing humanity's plight before God. But, this is certainly not the case overall.

For most people, God's call to us in our minds is like a phone-call that we don't want to take; it's like a road that we don't want to take because we think it's an undesirable road and because we think the road that we are on is good enough. But do you really know where the road you are on goes? And do you really know what the road that God calls you to turn on to is like? If you are honest you must admit that the answer is "No" in both cases.

Millions of people have decided to answer God's call. And the moment you do, you will begin to see everything differently and more and more clearly.

The ministry of the Word serves to convict all humanity as sinners who are under God's wrath. But it actually does so by building on what everyone already knows. For, everyone who has ever lived has known "The Bad News" (subconsciously, at least) – that "I am under God's Judgment as a sinner." But it is precisely this Bad News which makes "The Good News" of the Biblical Gospel necessary, glorious and most to be desired.

It can be debated if God's general revelation to all also includes giving everyone an awareness of the need to ask for God's mercy and grace. I lean toward believing that it does. But, either way, recognizing the universal condemnatory role of God's general revelation only serves to further enhance the glory of the Gospel which God's special revelation, the Bible, brings to the world.

Reports are sometimes given by missionaries about people who had never previously been exposed to the Gospel but who tell them that Jesus is the Savior they have been waiting for, but Whose Name they did not know. This suggests that general revelation may be sufficient to cause people to cry out for God's mercy. But, even if this is so, it is the Bible which definitively presents His saving mercy and grace in its revelation of the atoning work of God's Eternal Son, Jesus Christ. Anyone who rejects its message of Salvation shows that they are still under God's Judgment.

Furthermore, God's written Word is needed for the process of sanctification, as the partner of God's Holy Spirit, Who comes to dwell within His redeemed children. And, finally, the witness which the Bible gives of God's Judgment of the world powerfully reinforces what general revelation has already established.

Consider the "flow-chart" below. If your answer to the question on top is found on the first or third lines, then you need to realize that these are not reasonable positions and move to the second line or, preferably, the fourth line. It's simple logic.

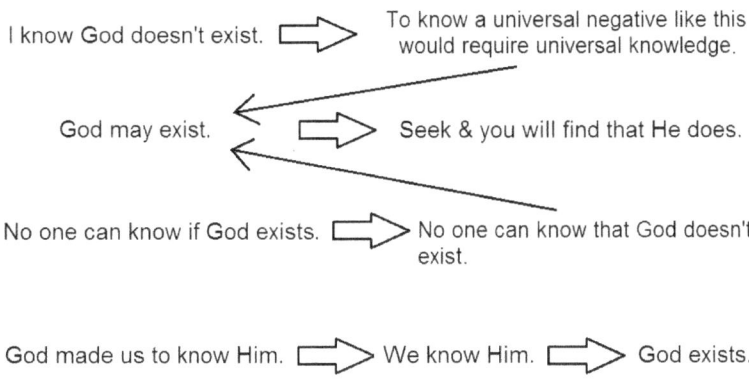

If you are not a Christian, it's not so much that you need to believe in God and Christianity. You already <u>know</u> that your Creator exists, but you have chosen to <u>disbelieve</u> this. <u>What you need to do is to suspend your disbelief in God and Christianity</u>.

Despite all of the progress in Science and technology and other areas which has occurred since Humanism took over, Christians assert that the developed world made a huge intellectual and spiritual wrong-turn about 100 years ago and needs to get back on the right road, turning back to Christianity from Humanism. This is because Humanism must ultimately be seen to be self-destructive both in principle (in destroying the true meaning of human nature and human life) and in practice over the long-run (in destroying the sanctity of life and the civility, freedom and prosperity which depend on this).

But the real reason why you and the world need to return to the point-of-view which previously reigned is because it is the only true view. And because it is, it is the only view that works in the long-run.

The very nature of the God of the Bible means that there can be no neutrality toward Him. So if this God exists, and we say that He must, then we must view everything in relation to Him. So, to fail to begin with Him, as Humanism and all other religions and philosophies do, is to make the Huge Mistake of rejecting Him.

There is no guarantee that the world will turn back to its Maker. But, every day, individuals are turning back to our Creator, The One True God, and letting Him become their loving Father, Savior, Lord and Guide. Christians want as many people as possible to do this because we have already done it and have found that it is The Greatest Thing that ever happened to us. So we want you to experience this as well. No matter what anyone may say about why Christians want to convert others, we want this because we love you and care about you and want what is best for you, too![10]

---

10   *In a You-Tube response after someone offered him a Bible (https://www.youtube.com/watch?v=6md638smQd8) well-known magician and atheist Penn Jillette has pointed out that it is wrong for people to object to Christians trying to persuade others to become Christians. This is because of what Christians believe happens to those who don't embrace Christianity. No matter how strenuously one might disagree with Christians on this, non-Christians must take seriously that Christians truly believe that those who persist in rejecting the Gospel until the end of their lives in this world will go to Hell. So, Jillette recognized that, from the Christian point-of-view, it would actually be grossly negligent if we didn't try to do all that we can to persuade others to avoid this fate! Jillette is right!*

Indeed, I wish that more Christians understood this as well as Penn Jillette does! It is rather like a situation where a motorist is speeding down a

It's regrettably true that many Christians (as well as people who claim to be Christians but really aren't) do a very poor job of "speaking the truth in love" to non-Christians. This is because we don't understand God's love for us and for you enough or because we just lose sight of this. But it's mainly because we remain sinners (although we are forgiven by God). So we will at times speak and act wrongly and badly in our efforts to appeal to others, both to fellow Christians and non-Christians. But this doesn't make us malevolent and it cannot invalidate the truth of Christianity. In fact, it actually shows why we, as well as you, need Christ.

This book is designed to work on four different levels. Level One is for those who want to skim the book in order to see the highlights. The author invites you to do this and has extracted key statements from each chapter and collected them in Appendix 3 of the book.

Level Two is the main text of the book, which should be manageable for most people today.

Level Three is in the footnotes and Appendix 1. As you may have already recognized from the notes thus far, this material will be somewhat more challenging. It is written mainly to introduce topics which are related to the main theme of the book for those who may be interested.[11]

---

mountain road in which there is a bridge that has just collapsed on the other side of an upcoming blind-turn. Wouldn't it be right to warn the motorist so that he or she can avoid plunging to their death? Indeed, such a warning may not be believed and may even be considered rude at first. But isn't such a warning actually the loving thing to do? And not making such a warning would certainly be a serious case of negligence. Of course, many believe that the danger which Christians warn about is imaginary. But we see it as real. And, even if we were wrong about this (and we aren't!), we would still be doing the loving thing from our point-of-view, not a malicious thing.

11 *It is always somewhat of a challenge to read a book with extensive footnotes. I would encourage the reader not to allow yourself to become intimidated or distracted by the notes. If they do either, just leave them alone!*

And for those who wish to go a lot deeper, Level Four will be the suggested reading list found in Appendix 2.

I have always been bothered by the fact that a lot of authors and promoters of other things want to force people into buying their books or products in order to receive what is most valuable in them. But such is not the goal of this author, nor do I believe it should be for anyone who wants to share the Christian Gospel, which by its very nature is a free gift from God. So it is that you will be able to get what the author most deeply wants you to get just by skimming through the book, if only you are open to it. This is because the basic message is actually quite simple. Yet its implications are immeasurable, endless and wonderful beyond anything that any of us can imagine.

Since this book will focus on "Big Picture" issues, it will necessarily be broad but not very deep in its treatment of various subjects (even on Level Three). There are plenty of books out there that are narrow and deep. But it is just not possible to be both as broad as possible, as this book seeks to be, and also deep. Even thousands of pages would not be sufficient. And the author had no intention of writing a book that is even several hundred pages long.

Rather, this book is intended to be a concise and simple critique of Humanism and the other major non-Christian approaches, as well as a brief introduction to the Christian worldview. So, many ideas will be expressed without being thoroughly demonstrated. It will be rather like an introductory tour of a vast country with many regions. We will make brief stops in many of the regions (though not all). Of course, if anyone wants to explore more deeply any of the regions, this is certainly welcomed.

However, many of the ideas expressed here don't really need to be demonstrated. They are credible just because they should "ring true" for all of us. And even if this is not immediately evident, the truth of many ideas here should become clear after a little reflection and, perhaps, some investigation, both of which can easily be done by anyone and are heartily encouraged. It is for this reason that the supplementary material is recommended.

Part 2

A few personal observations seem to be in order before moving on.

Like most people raised in the developed world in the 2nd half of the 20th century, I had come to accept Humanism and the Materialism philosophy (or the matter-only view of the universe) without any serious questions by the time I became a college freshman in 1978. This is because it was the worldview which I had been taught during 13 years of public education, as well as that which was assumed by most in the culture and virtually everyone I knew. So I enthusiastically embrace the Evolutionary vision of Carl Sagan when his "Cosmos" mini-series was introduced on PBS.

But, my enthusiasm would not last. For, I had a serious question pressing on my consciousness, which the evolutionary view could not answer, the same one I am asking the readers to ask yourselves: Why am I alive? The belief-system (or "worldview") that I had embraced claimed to tell me <u>how</u> it is that I am alive, but it had no answer to the question "Why?"

It's amazing how much just thinking about a simple question can sometimes change everything in your life and change it very quickly. For me, realizing that I had no answer to the question "Why am I alive?" soon put me into a state of depression and total skepticism. But, although some people seem to be content in this state (temporarily, at least), I could not remain in skepticism. I was convinced that there must be an answer to the question.

So I set out on an intellectual quest which would last about 2 years, beginning during my sophomore year at Duke University. At the end of this time I came to the inescapable conclusion that today's dominant view is what is known today as an "Epic Fail" and that the previously dominant view is in fact the correct one.

At the beginning of my quest, I believed that I was open to every possibility, but I didn't realize that I had been taught to be open to every one except Christianity. So I spent my time looking in other directions. After a while, I began gravitating toward Zen Buddhism. Zen appealed to me because it denied that there is any sort of a god and also emphasized that the world is not what it appears to be. Instead, Zen teaches that all of our experience and thinking are merely illusions and that our goal must be to see the illusions and attain the experience of *Moksha*, or liberation.

I later came to realize that I had been drawn toward Zen precisely because it agreed with Sagan's evolutionary Materialism in the two ways I just cited: in its rejection of belief in God and in the idea that what actually exists is quite different than what we perceive it to be. It seems that even though I had come to recognize that Materialism had no real answer to the question "Why?", at this point I was still somewhat loyal to the basic worldview I had been taught since youth.

But, my flirtation with Zen would not last. It wasn't long before I started asking: "Is that all there is?" (as in the popular 1970's song by Peggy Lee). For, if both Zen and modern scientists and intellectuals are correct, then all that we think and experience are merely passing fancies with only the illusion of meaning. In short, if this is the case, then we are all really the victims of a cosmic joke!

But this simply couldn't be true. For one thing, even if we are all deceived, it remains the case that we undeniably exist as the subjects of the deception. After all, only a completely insane person believes that he or she doesn't really exist. Furthermore, there are countless other things that we know to be real, as opposed to countless things we know to be unreal. It is simply impossible to function moment-by-moment without being able to make this distinction.

Being unable to accept the "Grand Illusion" view, I continued searching. But I was still too much under the sway of the Humanism and Materialism I had been taught in my public education, as well as the influence of a "post-Christian" society (to use the term popularized by Christian philosopher Francis Schaeffer) to give any real consideration to Christianity. This was so even though I had received catechism and confirmation in Catholicism as a child.

The truth is that I merely "went through the motions" of Catholicism because my parents wanted me to. I never really took seriously the teachings of the Catholic Church, much less did I actually consider them and, "Science forbid!", embrace them. I considered them outdated and irrelevant because that was what the culture I was living in told me. And even if I had been willing to consider the Catholic message, it still would have been unlikely that an hour each week over the course of several weeks could have overcome the anti-Christian Humanist indoctrination I was receiving 5 days a week and 9 months every year in a very "progressive" suburban Philadelphia school district.[12]

---

12 *Once again, we all tend to believe what we are taught every day. And to those who object to me calling my public education an "indoctrination", I would point out that all education is indoctrination because it involves the teaching of many <u>doctrines</u>. Furthermore, this will always include a set of unquestionable basic doctrines, "basic" because they are the base upon which everything else is built.*

Today's basic doctrines include things which virtually all human beings agree on, like the reliability of logic, memory and sensation in allowing us to interact successfully with the world around us (more or less). There are also moral ideas that most of us agree on (like believing murder, rape and other forms of cruelty are wrong, as well as the principle of equity: that we should do to others as we would want them to do to us, and not do to others

So I continued searching in every possible direction I could find other than Christianity. Until one day when God suddenly got my attention. Not that He spoke to me in an audible voice. Rather, He just helped me to really think for the first time about whether or not He really exists. As soon as I did, I came to an inescapable conclusion that He must truly exist and that He had made me. I was not a product of mindless forces of Nature. Rather, I was a creature who had been created by a Creator, created for a relationship with

---

as we would not want them to do to us).

But there are also basic doctrines in all of the major philosophies and religions which are clearly not shared by those in other traditions. This includes the 3 basic doctrines of Humanism: 1) that matter-energy and mindless forces of nature in space-time are all that exists, 2) that humanity, not God, determines what is right and wrong, and 3) that belief in God and Christianity is outdated and incorrect. All philosophies or religions, including both Christianity and Humanism, have their own sets of basic doctrines, which can't really be questioned in practice. After all, one simply can't go through life thinking that their most basic beliefs about themselves and the world may be wrong.

As for the relationship between the various religions and philosophies, most efforts at "inter-faith" cooperation (or ecumenism) operate on an assumption that all religions or philosophies have the same basic ideals and goals, or the same "kernel", but different peripheral notions and practices (or different "husks"). But I would suggest that the opposite is really the case. People in different religious traditions actually have very different beliefs about ourselves, God or gods and the world around us, which lead to very different values, priorities and practices, despite superficial agreements.

Serious devotees of all of the major religious traditions will also dispute the popular idea today that all religions are equally valid quests for meaning. Indeed, this view, in itself, is just one of the many basic approaches, in which it is assumed that its view: the "inclusive" view is correct and that all religions claiming exclusivity are wrong.

So, the key to "coexistence" is not to ignore the differences in what we believe and focus only on areas of agreement. Rather, while we must agree

Him.

In retrospect I consider this the day in which I became a "born-again" Christian. I had not been prompted to begin thinking about God by any person in particular, or by reading the Bible or any other book. It was simply the opening of a "vertical" connection by God to me which had not existed before. And once this happens to someone, everything changes.

Within a matter of days I became convinced that the Bible must be what it says it is: God's unique revelation of Himself. I became confident of this because, out of all ancient religious scriptures, the Bible alone presents The God Who had just made me aware of Himself.

While I had never truly been the kind of atheist who is certain that there is no God, I was what is called an "agnostic atheist", or what Christians call a "practical atheist". Though I would have never claimed certainty, I still thought and lived on the assumption that Christianity was false and that it's impossible for anyone to know for sure what ultimate reality consists of and for any one religion to be true. But all of this is just part of the belief-system which I had been taught.

Having become a true believer in the God of the Bible and the Bible, I began to describe myself as a Christian for the first time. And I now had a new and very eager desire to study the Bible so as to get to know God and His will more and more. I also began to seek the fellowship of other believers and a suitable church.

---

that we need to get along with each other in this world, we must recognize that this will be in spite of fundamental differences between us, differences which we all see as having enormous consequences both for ourselves and others. So, it is just not realistic to claim that we should give up all efforts to persuade or "proselytize" each other. We should be able to do so and to do so most spiritedly. But when we are not able to convince the other, as will commonly be the case, we must simply "agree to disagree" and do all that we can to coexist peacefully.

All true Christians should have these desires. We need to study the Bible because God will speak to us in it, as the Holy Spirit enlightens it and applies it for us. And we need Christian fellowship because we all need the encouragement and help, and, yes, sometimes the admonition of other believers in order to grow up as Christians. And we also need to do the same for our fellow believers, who are our brothers and sisters in Christ. All of this comes in the context of a congregation of believers.

So, I am a Christian not because I had been brought up as a Catholic or because I am an American, but because I had truly come to believe the message of Christianity. I had also come to see that it was the previously-dominant approach to truth and morality, Christianity (or Christian Theism), not the Humanism I had been indoctrinated in, that was actually the correct approach.

Chapter 3
We All Believe (One Way or Another) in Order to Understand the World.

You believe what you do because of your worldview. But your worldview may be right or wrong.

Is your worldview big enough? Humanism is the worldview (or philosophy) which dominates the developed world today. So, unless you were raised to be a Bible-believing Christian or a religious person in some other way (whether it's Muslim, Conservative or Orthodox Judaism, Hindu, etc.), it is almost certain that you were taught and, most likely, embraced the Humanist worldview.

As a committed believer in Humanism until the age of 22, I can certainly appreciate its appeal. The universe which Science shows us is indeed marvelous, whether we view it on the most microscopic level or on the most macroscopic level of a universe filled with countless galaxies.

But as awe-inspiring as the physical world is, is this all there is? Most people today have been convinced that it is. But there are many of us who have come to see that it isn't and have come to realize that we don't live in a universe that is ultimately impersonal. Nor are we momentary blips of life in a universe that is billions of years old, mere products of mindless forces and accidental occurrences. Rather, we have come to see that we actually live in a universe which was crafted by a Person, The Creator God, the same One Who speaks in the Bible.

This God is always present everywhere in His Creation. And, even more amazingly, He made us especially so that we would be His beloved children forever. That is, if we want to be.

Many people will say that this is just wishful thinking. But how do you know this is all it is? The truth is that you don't. And you, too, can join millions who have woken up to the much larger world that you already live in but just aren't aware of yet.

Atheists are interesting. Many of you will say that Christianity is just wishful thinking. But many of the same people will also regard it as a dreadful way of looking at the world, a plague on humanity and the ultimate enemy of freedom, truth and goodness. It's hard to see how it could be both. So, which is it? Or, are you willing to consider that it is neither?

Atheism is a belief-system that is defined by what it doesn't believe in: God or gods. First of all, this negative starting-point is really weaker than an approach that begins with a positive assertion (especially, the assertion that there is a Creator God). This is because such an approach is one that is defined in relation to the opposing position in being a rejection of that position.

Furthermore, many atheists will claim that atheism is not a belief-system. Rather, it is just a lack of belief in God or gods. But this is clearly false. While there are some things which people can no beliefs about, God or gods can't be one of them. This is because a God or gods, if they exist, are too important to be non-commital about their existence or non-existence.

This is especially the case with the God described in the Bible. For, if this God exists then this necessarily affects everything. If you begin with the assumption that there is a Creator and Lord of the universe, then you will naturally have an entirely different view of the universe and most everything in it than you will if you don't assume this.

Human-beings have always differed over countless things. But the main thing which has always divided us is that some of us live in a God-centered reality and some of us live in a no-God reality. And the latter will still be the case even if one professes to believe in God but views everything as if there is no God, or if one believes in the existence of a god or gods other than the God of the Bible. (That this is the case should become clear in what follows.)

Atheists don't lack a belief in God or gods. They <u>believe</u> that there are no gods. There are some atheists who claim certainty that there are no gods and no Supreme Being, while others leave room for doubt about this. But, either way, no one can live without a working assumption about this. So, all atheists or skeptics live based on the belief that the God described in the Bible doesn't exist.[13] Beyond this, atheists also must believe in many other

---

13   *Historically, a distinction was made between atheists and skeptics or agnostics. The first was a person who claimed certainty that no God or gods exist, while the second merely doubted that God or gods exist. The skeptical group could also be divided between those who believe it might be possible to know if there is a God or gods and those who assume it would be impossible to ever know this.*

However, the distinction between atheism and skepticism has become blurred in recent decades and the terms have come to be synonyms in many cases. People who are certain are now called "gnostic atheists", while those who aren't are called "agnostic atheists". This terminology is helpful because it points to the anti-theistic commitment which exists in either case.

It will subsequently be shown that the atheist who is certain is in the logically untenable position of asserting certainty about a universal negative claim, among other problems. On the other hand, it is logical that those who are not certain about whether or not a God or gods exist should be open to being persuaded that there is indeed a God. This is especially so of those who think it may be possible to know this.

But those who believe it would be impossible to know this are also in a logically untenable position. Skepticism of this type is self-defeating because it would have to be the case that it is impossible to know if it is impossible to know. To put it another way, if you can't know then you can't know that you can't know. Thus, it must always be possible that it is possible to know.

things which they could never prove. So, like everyone else, they have a belief-system. In most cases these are the beliefs of Humanism.

If the God described in the Bible exists (and we say that He must), then it is impossible not to know this, though it is possible to suppress this knowledge. And, in fact, suppressing this knowledge is precisely what most people do.

Most of us have heard of the expression: "the elephant in the room". This expression refers to a tendency that people sometimes have to ignore an inconvenient reality no matter how big it is. And this is what all who deny the existence of the Creator God must constantly do. This is because the Biblical God is, by nature, The Ultimate Elephant in the room. He is not only present in the room, He is present everywhere in the room. Furthermore, He is also the One Who created the room and everyone and everything in the room. And He also sustains everything and everyone in the room moment-by-moment. No one can possibly be ignorant of such a Being, assuming that He exists (again, as we say He must).

So, we say that it is logically and existentially (and, also, morally) necessary that the God described in the Bible does exist and, even, that every human being who has ever lived has known that He exists.[14] This should be seen as

---

14 *It's not only biblical but also logical to say that only a truly Supreme Being and Highest Authority for truth and morality (assuming such a Being exists) is really worthy of The Name, God. And for God to be The Supreme Being means that it is impossible to conceive of anything which can be greater than Him in any way, not even Logic and Morality as supposedly ultimate and abstract Standards.*

It will subsequently be shown that God is the Source and Ground of both logic and morality without reducing these to arbitrariness (that is, as whatever God thinks or does by definition) because He is a Real Personal God. As such, logic is simply the pattern of how His Mind works. And He always does what is good because He is a Perfectly Good God. Furthermore, God only does only what is good as a completely Free Being, otherwise He would not truly be the Supreme and Almighty God. But this

the main reason why Humanism and the other religions and philosophies both today and in the past are incorrect. But what follows will be an explanation of many other ways in which Humanism and the world's other major views fail, either by being self-defeating or leading to clear absurdities or by failing to account for all that we know and experience.

As we consider the various alternatives to Christianity the goal will be to present each view fairly and in its best possible light, not in a false and easily refutable "straw-man" fashion. Although the latter is frequently done in debates, especially against Christianity, it is not intellectually honest to do so.

Nevertheless, even when presented in their best light, it should become clear that there are numerous problems with Humanism and the other views. Moreover, these problems are simple problems that anyone should be able to understand. Furthermore, any one of these problems should be sufficient to cause one to at least question that it is the correct understanding, if not persuade you to reject it altogether and to become open to the Christian perspective. And once a person becomes open to Christianity he or she should be able to see that it must be correct and, indeed, that it is the only correct view.

But just because someone should be persuaded of something doesn't guarantee that you will. For, it will always be the case that a person must be willing to be persuaded before this can happen. If you are determined to hold on to your view then you will always look for ways to do so no matter what

---

means that it must always be possible for God to do evil. He just never chooses to do evil.

All of this shows the uniqueness of the Biblical God and of our relationship with Him, specifically in the necessity of having faith in Him. For faith is simply trust in God's Goodness so that we are confident that He won't ever lie to us and treat us unjustly. On the other hand, if God isn't trustworthy then all bets are off! In other words, we couldn't trust that we know anything.

evidence is offered against it, either by seeking to explain away what is offered or just by dismissing it. This is known as confirmation bias and it is actually done by all people with respect to our most basic beliefs.

This is because it is just not possible to go through life constantly questioning our most basic beliefs. This includes our faith in logic, the general reliability of our senses and memories and that the laws of nature will continue to work as they have until now. But it also applies to many other basic beliefs which are not commonly agreed-upon, as well as many other beliefs which flow out of our basic assumptions.[15]

Though I wasn't aware of it, I was totally-biased in favor of Humanism and against Christianity for my first 22 years. This was the case even though I had been given some basic instruction in Catholicism and had been able to "go through the motions" well enough for my Catholic faith to be officially confirmed as a young teenager. But as soon as my parents gave my sister and me the option of "sleeping-in" on Sundays, I took the option, except for Christmas and Easter. (As many Catholics know, this, in itself, is a Catholic tradition!)

This was because I had never really embraced the teachings of Catholicism. Instead, what I was really being "confirmed" in was the Humanism which

---

15 *That all people proceed according to confirmation bias is disputed by some. But the explanation should make it clear that it really is inevitable. It has also become popular to claim that confirmation bias means that all knowledge claims are relative. In other words, that there is no truth which can be known by all, there is only truth for me and truth for you. But that truth is only relative is an example of an idea that is so obviously false that it's amazing that anyone ever came up with it and even more amazing that many accept it!*

In the 21st century relativism is a hallmark of "Post-modernism". But, if relativism was true then all of us would be hopelessly isolated from everyone else, as all of our interactions with others are based on our certainty that we live in the same world and share real and universal knowledge about countless things in it.

was assumed by almost everyone I knew, including my school teachers, peers, family members and most of the "VIP's", the Very Influential People in society. It's not that Humanism is openly and directly taught in most cases. It is just assumed by most today.[16] If this hasn't already become clear to you, it should become clear in what follows.

Several years after I had stopped going to church or being involved in it in any way I took a popular Old Testament survey class as a Sophomore at Duke University because I had become somewhat curious about the religion I had drifted away from. But I was still dominated by my Humanist bias against the Bible's claims. So I read (past tense) the Bible with the assumption that it was really no different than any other book ever written. I assumed that it was merely a product of the imagination of other people, in this case people who had lived thousands of years ago in a scientifically and morally ignorant world, one filled with superstition and barbarity.

So, instead of letting the Bible speak to me, I critiqued it according to what I assumed was true. I recognized that there was some truth in it. But where the Bible conflicted with what we now know (or what I assumed that we know) I just dismissed it as a false and outdated perspective. This is just what all of

---

16 *That Humanism is normally implied and assumed rather than being explicitly taught as such is one of the main reasons why it has been so widely-embraced. This is not to suggest that this is a devious strategy consciously and deliberately adopted by our teachers in most cases. Rather, it is usually just a matter of passing on the perspective and methods that our teachers have been taught. But to inculcate people unconsciously is a very effective technique for persuading people.*

In the sales world this technique is called the "assumed close". With Humanism the basic "pitch" is this: "You will embrace these things as true because all reasonable people agree on them." This appeal is amazingly effective even though it is actually 3 fallacies at the same time: that of assuming the conclusion, the "no true Scotsman" fallacy, and that agreement by the masses determines what is true or good. The Vulcan character Spock from Star Trek appears to be correct: Humans are appallingly illogical!

us normally do. But it is not really the way to examine something fairly.

In order to understand other perspectives fairly and properly one needs to try to understand them on their own terms rather than imposing your terms on them. So, instead of reading or listening to the other view with the goal of showing how it's wrong, one should be willing to consider that it may be right even where it conflicts with one's current beliefs and thinking and to try to let the other view critique your thinking as much as you critique it. After all, isn't this the reasonable way to find out what is true and should be accepted, as opposed to what is false?[17]

So, to be fair and reasonable with regard to Christianity requires that one will be willing to think critically about your own view, whether this is Humanism or one of the other possibilities. This means being open-minded even to the possibility that your view may have fatal flaws and therefore should be rejected and replaced by another view. It also means being willing to truly think about the Christian alternative rather than being absolutely determined either to refute it or just dismiss it as ridiculous.

And this is necessary even if you are convinced that you already understand Christianity. For, how do you know that you really understand it correctly?

---

17 *It may seem that Christians are not willing to do what we ask of others: to subject our beliefs to critical thinking. But many Christians became believers precisely because we did become willing to question our previous worldviews. In other words, we already did what we ask others to do. But some will say that we should always remain willing to go back to our old view or some other view. But this belief, in itself, presupposes that relativism is true. This is the belief that it's not possible to find a view that's universally true.*

But we assert that the reason all of us know so many particular things as universally and not just relatively true (which really can't be reasonably denied) is because they are part of an overall worldview that's universally true. And once one finds universal truth, either in particular instances or in one's overall worldview, there's no reason to keep searching for it elsewhere.

The truth is that you really can't know this for sure. For it is always possible that what you think is Christianity is actually a misunderstanding or a false straw-man created by people who were prejudiced against God and Christianity.

There are two basic parts to any worldview: its view about what exists (and also: How do we know?) and its view of what is good and evil. To put it in the most simple terms, Humanism is based on these two things. First, it claims that the universe is composed only of matter-energy (which modern Physics considers to be one thing with two sides), mindless forces of Nature, space-time (which modern Physics also considers to be one thing with two sides) and quantum fluctuation.

Second, it claims that we are the ultimate determiners of what is true and good, since there is no Higher Authority that we know of. Nothing else is considered to be real. There is no Great Mind or Intelligence which created and rules over the universe. Not only that, but even our own minds and all that they do are thought to be just the chemical activity of our physical brains.

If you will only stop and think about it, most of you will realize that this is what you were taught to believe, especially if you attended secular (that is, non-religious) schools. This indoctrination has been so successful that most of you not only believe it, you accept it as unquestionable proven fact. But, how do you know that you're right in doing so? Once again, the simple truth is that you don't know this. Actually, you can't possibly know this! It's logically impossible to know that the physical world around us is all that exists. There are two simple reasons why.

First, there is the problem that this statement has two things in it: us and the world around us. We can't have perception and knowledge of the world without having both a world and perceivers/knowers of that world. Yet today's dominant understanding of the universe would reduce us to what we observe and know. This includes both our knowledge of what exists in the physical world and also in other realms, including what is true about ourselves as people and about other people, as well as what is true about history and morality.

Humanism is based on an object-only view of the universe. No subjects are allowed. But, while we may be deceived about many things, we are surely not deceived that we exist as both observers and knowers; that is, as subjects. We will return to this problem later.

But there is another very basic problem with today's approach which should be recognized from the beginning. To say that matter-energy, mindless forces, space-time and quantum fluctuation are all that exists is to say that nothing else exists. This is known as making a negative universal claim. But such claims are logically impossible to prove. To put it in the simplest terms, if you are so confident that you know all that exists, what if you find that something new shows up tomorrow? Indeed, doesn't this sort of thing often happen in our lives in a more limited way? We think we know all we need to know about some situation, but then we learn something else.

Atheist Bertrand Russell inadvertantly showed the problem of being certain about a negative universal claim when he famously compared belief in God to believing that there is a flying teapot in orbit around the earth. Russell's argument was intended to show that it is those who argue that there is a God who have the burden-of-proof, not those who doubt or deny this. But his analogy hinges on his assumption that everyone actually knows that there is not a teapot orbitting the earth, so it is not reasonable to believe that there is even though it is logically impossible to prove that there isn't.

Russell falsely presumes that the same is true with regard to belief that there is a God. As with most of the so-called "New Atheists" of the 21st century, Russell's "argument" is essentially this: "Come on people, your belief that there is a God is clearly ridiculous and should be abandoned by all reasonable people even though it can't actually be proven that He doesn't exist." The last part of this clearly shows the problem with the negative universal claim made by atheists, whether the claim is made with certainty (gnostic atheism) or not (agnostic or practical atheism). If you can't prove that something isn't true (namely, that the God described in the Bible exists), then you can't really know that it isn't true.

Besides, Russell's argument is also a clear case of the fallacy of assuming the conclusion. It's circular reasoning. The claim that a Creator God exists is not at all an inherently ridiculous proposition. Indeed, it has been believed by billions of apparently sane people.[18]

Moreover, atheists' claim that it is not a reasonable to believe that there is a God is a truth claim just as much as Christians' claim that God must exist. So atheists are just as much under a burden-of-proof for their claim as Christians. But to be certain that something doesn't exist, even orbiting teapots, but especially God, actually would require omniscience. Obviously, none of us will ever have this, though, of course, Christians say that there is One Who does.[19]

The Humanist understanding of the universe is also known as the philosophy of Materialism (or also as Physicalism). Materialists in this sense of the term are not necessarily those who value their material possessions more than

---

18 *Actually, even the claim that there is no teapot orbiting the earth isn't inherently absurd, as Russell assumed. Isn't it theoretically possible that a Russian cosmonaut may have accidently let a zero-gravity teapot escape into space when he or she went outside for a space-walk? After all, Russians are known to like tea.*

19 *Also, anyone trying to persuade atheists that God exists will quickly discover that their conviction that God doesn't exist is not really falsifiable in practice since atheists will take anything which is offered as evidence for God and seek to reinterpret it so as to fit into their presumption that the universe is God-less. Indeed, the power of human beings to practice denial being as strong as it is, it is conceivable that atheists may continue seeking other explanations even if "they see the Son of Man coming on the clouds of heaven, with power and great glory" (as Matthew 24:30 describes the return of Jesus). Indeed, a particularly honest atheist once admitted as much to me during a debate.*

anything else (another use of the term). Rather, they are those who believe that only material things exist.

Materialism is a fundamental rejection of the view that there are two aspects of reality: the physical and the spiritual (or material and immaterial). This view is known as Dualism and it was the view held by virtually everyone in the developed world (that is, in what used to be called "Western Civilization"), including virtually all intellectuals, until Materialism began to take over about 200 years ago. Dualism is represented in the diagram on the following page.

CREATOR GOD

CREATION

The Spiritual World

(Spiritual beings, including human beings, who are unique as souls housed in bodies. All human experience & knowledge are on this side and God is constantly interacting with us here.)

The Physical World

(The world around us, which is the proper domain of Science because God created the laws which it discovers and in which God only rarely intervenes. These worlds are distinct but also interactive.)

Part 2

Today's dominant view is also known as Naturalism. Whereas Materialism points to the substance of what exists, only matter (or matter-energy), Naturalism points to what governs the universe, only mindless forces of Nature. This points to the other way that Humanists reject the previously-dominant view of the universe as being under the influence both of natural and supernatural forces.[20]

---

20 *This Dualism has been described as "mind and body" or "mind and matter" or "body and soul" or "body and spirit". For our purposes, "mind", "soul" and "spirit" will be considered synonyms (although there are some theological distinctions between these three, especially between "souls" and "spirits"). "Body" and "matter" will also be considered synonyms. Also, this use of the term "Dualism" is not to be confused with the use of the same term with regard to morality.*

The Christian worldview assumes a metaphysical Dualism but strongly opposes what is known as moral Dualism. Moral Dualism sees good and evil as equally-ultimate and, usually, as balanced forces. But Christianity sees only Goodness as ultimate, as an eternal Personal quality of the Creator God. But evil is only relative to God's Goodness, as anything which is contrary to this.

Also, while it can certainly be useful to draw distinctions between Materialism, Physicalism, Naturalism, Secularism and Progressivism, our primary concern will be the fact that all of these are associated with Humanism insofar as it is opposed to the Christian worldview. For it is the conflict between Humanism and Christianity which is our primary focus. Accordingly, the primary difference between the Materialism/Physicalism/Naturalism/Secularism/Progressivism of Humanism and Christian Dualism is that the latter sees reality as consisting both of material and immaterial entities and as governed by both natural and supernatural forces.

Why do so many find it so easy to believe that matter-energy and mindless natural forces in space-time are all that really exists? One of the main reasons is the enormous faith that most people today have in Science. Not that people shouldn't have a lot of faith in Science. There is no question that the scientific method is the way to understand the physical world, which has led to the technological developments upon which the modern world relies.

But it's one thing to have a strong and proper faith in Science and quite another to assume that since the scientific method proves to be the correct way to understand the physical world, then this world must be all that exists. This just doesn't follow logically. It is a fallacy.

That the above claim is a fallacy should be easy to see. That the first part is true (that Science successfully reveals how the physical world works) doesn't make the second one true (that the physical world is all that exists). This is not to say that the second part can't be correct, just that it can't be established as being correct by the first part. (Actually, though, it will subsequently be shown that the second part must be incorrect.)

A more obvious example of the problem is seen in this example. A child who has never seen a person of a different race will naturally tend to assume that all people are the same race. Of course, this is not true. And it's false whether or not the child ever meets someone of a different race.

It is often difficult to get people to see logical fallacies today because, unfortunately, basic Logic is no longer deemed to be a subject worthy of study in most of modern education. But this only opens the door to countless logical errors. The philosopher George Santayana is famous for saying: "He who forgets the past is doomed to repeat it". But it can also be said that he who is ignorant of logic is doomed to violate it, and violate routinely.[21]

---

21 *Jason Lisle devotes 2 chapters of his excellent book, "The Ultimate Proof of Creation" to describing many common logical fallacies, especially those that relate to the case for Evolution. Though not a philosopher, Lisle's critique of the philosophy underlying Evolution is devastating.*

Another problem with trying to get people to focus on a very basic level, as I am seeking to do here, is that one's natural reaction will tend to be: "This can't be correct. How could we have made such an obvious mistake?" But it can be seen that many of the basic ideas of Humanist scientists and academics (including the previously-cited Bertrand Russell) are precisely that: mistakes that should be obvious, but are simply overlooked because they are so basic and universally-held.

This is not at all to say that Humanists are stupid. Actually, it's more accurate to say that Humanists are often too smart for their own good. Since intelligent people are usually aware of their intelligence, it is very hard in practice for them to consider that they may have been taught wrongly, especially about very basic assumptions.

Another of the key assumptions of Humanism is the belief that, until the Humanist philosophy triumphed (early in the 20th century), humanity was hopelessly mired in superstition. But is this correct?

It is true that a few isolated tribes have been found in the past century which, due to their isolation, managed to remain extremely ignorant of the laws of nature and, instead, attribute all natural phenomena to supernatural causes. But it is not accurate to say that this is characteristic of most of human civilization. These types of cultures are the exception, not the rule.

Extreme superstition (or "hyper-supernaturalism") was not universal even in the so-called "dark ages" of the Medieval period, nor in the earlier Greek and Roman empires (from which Christianity grew). On the other hand, it can be said that a type of "hyper-naturalism" (and hyper-anti-supernaturalism) does prevail today in the developed world. This is seen in the fact that people who believe in supernatural entities (God, souls, angels, Satan, devils) are commonly considered to be childishly naive, if not crazy.

Those who believe that previous generations were overwhelmingly ignorant compared to our own have a bias that's questionable at best. Such a bias is harmful because people who like to tell themselves that they are smarter, better educated and wiser than past generations will tend to underestimate the intelligence, knowledge and wisdom of their predecessors. And, as mentioned already, they will also be prone to overlooking their own mistakes, even on very basic levels.

Modern Humanists tend to regard the ancients (and, even, Christians today) as "pre-scientific" superstitious primitives with no understanding of the laws of nature. But, at the same time, they recognize examples of impressive engineering and intellectual triumphs by ancient societies and scholars. This is another contradiction. Many Humanists also refuse to recognize the education, intelligence and accomplishments of Christians of the past and the present.

Amazingly, the truth is that, unlike many scientists and intellectuals today, the ancients and most people who have ever lived up until only about 50 years ago were able to balance an understanding of the laws of nature (enough of an understanding in order to survive, at least) with recognition that the physical world is not all that exists. They were able to recognize the real existence both of ourselves and the world around us.

Sadly, many today can't distinguish between these two things in principle, although they still must in practice. So it is that many neuroscientists will claim that human consciousness is nothing more than the physical activity of our brains (that is, that "we" are only our brains). At the same time, though, they must constantly speak in the sense that we and our brains are two distinct things. (More issues with the "I am my brain." idea will be discussed shortly.)

While training in Science is necessary in order to be a scientist, it has never been necessary to be trained in Science to have a basic understanding of how the laws of nature work in our everyday lives. For example, the mechanics of gravity were not understood until the 18th century, but almost everyone knew that water flows downhill from the earliest days of human civilization.

Today's understanding of the scope of Science also goes well beyond the study of how the laws of nature work based on how we observe them today (which is its proper focus) into speculation about both the past and future and about the nature and meaning of human life, things which simply cannot be scientifically studied and established. It should be obvious that neither the unobserved past nor the future can be studied directly in the same way that we can study natural processes as they function today. Nor can our human experiences or questions of morality or meaning (the "Why?") be studied in the same way as natural phenomena, which are governed only by universal laws of nature. Such things are not phenomena that we can observe in the world or create in the lab.

Until recently, it was common to speak of the difference between the "hard Sciences" and other areas of study also labelled as sciences, like "social science", anthropology, and archaeology. It also used to be recognized that there are important differences between "operational Science" and "historical Science". But these distinctions are now denied by many. This has led to much confusion about what is really scientific and what isn't.

In fact, the term "scientific" is so widely and carelessly used today that, for many, it has become merely a synonym for what one considers rational. On the other hand, "unscientific" has become just a derogatory label on theories or conclusions which one considers irrational, regardless of how scientifically presented they are. (But, more on this problem later)

Aside from specific logical errors often made by Humanists, Humanism's bigger problem is a "Big Picture" (or worldview) problem. A good illustration of the problem with having the wrong Big Picture is jigsaw puzzles. Anyone who has ever put together jigsaw puzzles understands that in order to put one together successfully one usually must know what the completed puzzle looks like. And as one works on the puzzle one must constantly step back from examining the individual pieces and sections in order to try to discern how they fit into the entire puzzle.

Unfortunately, this is rarely done today when it comes to understanding the details of life. Indeed, many people today either have no idea about what The Big Picture is or they believe that it's unknowable or, worse yet, they have a Big Picture that is fatally-flawed, as we are seeking to show regarding the Materialist view of the universe.

But one must have a Big Picture and, indeed, the correct Big Picture in order for the details to be interpreted correctly. Without this, one will be wrong much of the time. And, even if you are right in particular instances, it will only be by accident. And if you don't know what the puzzle looks like overall, you won't have the guide that you need to complete the puzzle. So it is also with worldviews.[22]

---

22 *The analogy of a jigsaw-puzzle was previously used in the introduction of Frank Turek and Norman L. Geisler's 2004 book, "I Don't Have Enough Faith to be an Atheist". But there is a significant difference in how they apply the analogy.*

Turek and Geisler hold that unbelievers can eventually discover the "box-top" showing what the Big Picture of life really is (which for them, too, is the Biblical picture) through an honest examination of the arguments and evidence for this. However, the reality is that most unbelievers will examine the arguments and evidence for Christianity on the assumption that Christianity can't be true. They are not looking for the Christian box-top, for they believe that they already have the right box-top (either the Humanism one or one of the others). So they will never find it. Furthermore, Turek and Geisler's analogy fails to recognize that no reasonable person would try to put together a jigsaw-puzzle (other than ones made for small children with very few pieces) without having the correct box-top.

Rather, unbelievers must be willing to consider the Biblical box-top (that is, the Christian worldview) from the outset. Only in this way will they be able to view all of the pieces in their proper perspective. The primary way we can encourage them to do this is to show how their box-top fails to guide them in putting the pieces together. Showing how this is the case is the primary purpose of the first half of this book. The other main thing that

One's worldview is the intellectual equivalent of our physical eyes. It is the mental "lenses" and processor through which we view everything: ourselves, other people, the physical world, God, history, morality and values. And, make no mistake, we all have a Big Picture, or worldview that we believe in. And with regard to God, everyone has a belief about the God of the Bible, even if you deny that the God described in the the Bible exists and believe in some other Higher Authority or Authorities or reject these and consider Humanity the Ultimate Authority for truth and ethics.

As we already considered, the nature of the God described in the Bible gives us only two possible options. We can start with Him and view everything in relation to Him, and in a personal relationship <u>with</u> Him. Or we can reject Him and find another way.

But all who do the latter are making a leap of blind and false faith because you can't possibly know for certain that the Creator God described in the Bible doesn't exist. Indeed, you actually know that this God does exist (subconsciously, at least). But you are naturally-inclined to suppress this knowledge. And you are also encouraged to continue doing this by the "post-Christian" culture of today's developed world.

This is the real reason why there have been so many religions and

---

unbelievers must see is that they already know that the God of the Bible exists, but they suppress this knowledge and instead embrace a substitute worldview based on their Denial of their Creator.

Turek and Geisler also err in making the choice of worldviews a matter of probabilities, falsely claiming that the most that Christians can do is to persuade people to accept that the Christian worldview has a higher probability of being true than the Humanism view or other ones. But this neglects the clear Biblical message that every human-being who has ever lived has known that the Creator God of the Bible exists. And in knowing this everyone also knows that the correct box-top (worldview) is the one God has given us.

philosophies invented by humanity throughout history. It is quite easy to recognize that religions or philosophies develop when significant numbers of people share a preference for a particular approach which seeks to make sense of the world and they gather together and agree to develop this approach together. But the Christian perspective is that they are all substitutes made by and for people who don't want to relate to our True Creator.

Indeed, Christians see all "man-made" religions and philosophies (including Humanism) as functioning just like "the Matrix" depicted in the Sci-fi film trilogy of the same name. They are alternative perspectives designed to obscure what is really going on, made by and for people who have been convinced that it is better to suppress our knowledge of our Maker than to seek a relationship with Him.

But when one becomes a Christian it is like being set free from "the Matrix" so that one can truly see the world as it is for the very first time. Of course, some of these alternative religions and philosophies make the same claim. But this doesn't mean that they are right. Nor does it mean that no one can know the truth. In either case, this just doesn't follow logically. It must always be considered possible that there really is one True Way along with countless false ones. So, Christians call others to consider that Christianity is The One True Way.

One of the things today's Humanist cultural indoctrination does is to hide that it is an indoctrination in one particular worldview. As a result, most people will tend to think that they have the only reasonable and scientific perspective. But this is not only misleading, it is wrong. So it is that all people begin with a natural bias against God and Christianity. And most today are also reinforced in this by their culture (both in the developed world and in traditional religious cultures around the world).

So, the bad news is that many of you are self-blinded against perceiving the truth about your Creator and His ways. But this is also the good news! Since you are self-blinded you are also capable of taking your blinders off, if you are willing. God calls you to do this and will enable you to do it. <u>God is actually keeping you alive this very moment so that you will do this</u>!

But you must be willing to do it. If you are willing, God will help you remove your false perspective so that your eyes will be able to see and your ears will be able to hear the truth about God, yourself and the world clearly. As Jesus put it: "Whoever has ears, let them hear."

When one switches from one worldview to another it's amazing how much your perspective will change. This is especially true when someone switches from today's reigning Humanism or another belief-system to Christianity. When this happens many things that were previously considered ridiculous or bad will suddenly be seen as acceptable and good. Furthermore, much of what was previously prized about Humanism will actually be found to be true of Christianity, not Humanism. And much of what Humanists criticize about Christianity will actually be found to be true of Humanism, not Christianity.[23]

Moreover, Humanists and others who become Christians find that you lose nothing of value in making the switch. You only lose what isn't true and, thus, does not hold up. And you lose what is not helpful in the long run, but, rather, is destructive. This is so even though some of the things people give up when they become Christians are quite satisfying and apparently helpful for a time. But these losses aren't worthy of being compared with what we gain when we stop denying our Maker and accept God the Father as our Father (not as our condemning Judge), God the Son as our Savior and Lord,

---

23 *It is also worth noting that changing one's basic worldview from Humanism to Christianity almost always causes one to go from being a liberal (or progressive) to being a conservative. That those who go through this conversion are able to see everything in a new way allows them to see through and reject the indoctrination of today's dominant culture of Humanism, which produces a strong bias not only against Christianity but also against Conservatism and Republicans. If you believe that GOP = evil then you are under the power of this indoctrination.*

and God the Spirit as our "live-in" Counselor.

What we gain is what we have really always wanted in our hearts and, indeed, far more than we could have imagined. It is true that Christians can only promise that all of these things are true. We can't really show you that they are. As with the Matrix of the film, you have to experience it for yourself. You will only be able to know this if you make the switch yourself. But in what follows plenty of reasons will be offered for why you should make the switch.[24]

---

24 *Some may say that this is just a form of the discredited "Pascal's wager". But it isn't. We are most definitely <u>not</u> saying that people should pretend that Christianity is true and live the way Christians live, even if they don't believe in what Christianity says. Rather, we are saying that you should become real believers because you come to realize that it is true. To believe that doing the first will lead to one being saved is known as "legalism".*

The rebellion against the Roman Catholic Church which is known as the Protestant Reformation was, at its core, a rejection of this type of thinking. The Reformation began when Martin Luther became convinced that Rome had missed the true Gospel of salvation by faith and had fallen into teaching a salvation which comes by works. Luther led the way for millions to discover what the Bible actually teaches: that we are saved only by having faith in what Jesus Christ has done for us. Our good works are only the <u>result</u> of being saved, not what brings us salvation. (But more on this later)

So Pascal's wager is rightly rejected insofar as it is understood as saying this: that unbelievers should pretend that God exists and live accordingly because they will lose far more if they are wrong than if it turns out that they are right. First, this would imply that one can gain Heaven and avoid Hell just by obedience (without faith). But this is rejected by millions of us who have come to agree with Luther that the Bible is true, having come from God, and that it repudiates this false way throughout the New Testament.

Second, in verse 32 of the 15th chapter of his 1st Letter to the Corinthians, Paul says: "If the dead are not raised: 'Let us eat and drink, for tomorrow we die.'" Both the context of this verse in this part of the letter and the way Paul puts it show that the main point is this: Whether or not the Christian message is true is all-important. If Christ was not raised from the dead then we should not pretend that He was. Furthermore, if this is not true, then it

A dogmatic and intolerant "political correctness" became common in the developed world in the early 21st century by many who consider themselves "progressive" (who are almost always believers in Humanism, even if some claim to be Christians). But this is a clear case of Humanists doing exactly what they condemn Christians for. Honest Christians will admit that our forebearers were sometimes guilty of being overly dogmatic and intolerant, as are some believers today. But just by admitting this we are saying that dogmatism and intolerance are wrong and also that this is not inevitable among Christians. Rather, this is avoidable and we should always seek to avoid being this way. Besides, even in cases where Christians are wrong, does this excuse Humanists for doing the same thing? Clearly not.

Atheists will commonly react to this by saying that Christians are just falsely projecting what we are doing on them. But they are rarely willing to consider that it may be they who are doing this. In cases like this people who have been on both sides as adults (so that they can remember what is was like to be on the other side) are in the best position to tell which side is guilty of projection.[25]

There are many adults who have rejected Humanism and become Christians. Bible-believing churches across America are filled with such people. On the

---

doesn't matter how we live.

It is believed that the latter part of this verse is a quote of a contemporary saying used by people who denied that there is life after death. And, if there isn't, then we should just "live it up" while we're here. Who they were exactly doesn't really matter. It is the mindset that matters. And it's clearly the same mindset as many of today's Materialists! But, the rather surprising message of this verse is that if Materialism is correct, then we should be as unrestrained as the wildest "party-animals". But the only reason that we should not live like this is precisely because we believe they are not right.

25 *It is not surprising that people frequently and falsely project what they are doing on others. After all, we tend to assume that other people are like us in many ways. But it is also obviously true that people can be quite different, either by nature or through change.*

other hand, comparatively few adult Christians become atheists and Humanists (which usually go together). Quite a few atheists do report to being believers as children, but this faith is almost always simplistic and shallow and is thus quite easily overcome by the Humanist indoctrination from the dominant culture, which has been going on since the middle of the last century. Besides, atheists who claim that they used to be Christians tend to show by the types of arguments they use against Christianity that they never developed a mature faith. These arguments are usually ones that mature Christians will be familiar with and also have reasonable answers to.

Chapter 4
Our Worldviews Are What Divide Us And "Them"

We have already compared worldviews to jigsaw puzzles as a Big Picture which all of the "pieces" will reveal when properly put together. So worldviews determine how we view all of the details. And, of course, they also determine what we consider the Big Picture to be. They are our mental lenses, which give us perspective on everything in our lives.

Different perspectives will always lead to different views. A good illustration of this can be seen in what are called ambigrams. These are words which change when they are inverted. The following is an example.

Most people are able to read what this says. It is what we Christians want others to join us in: the "Jesus Family" as beloved children of "our Father in Heaven", with His Son Jesus as our Savior and Lord and His Holy Spirit as our Guide. But if you turn the page upside-down you will see different words. These words name the one whom those who keep refusing to accept God's loving offer to join His Family will belong to if you persist in refusing His offer until the end of your days in this world. And they also indicate how long you will belong to him.

The main goal of this book is to get you to leave the upside-down view and become part of Jesus' Family, if you haven't already! Humanism is also an upside-down perspective in that it presumes to put God and everything else under our judgment instead of letting God be the "King of Kings" that He Is. He is your Judge, but He offers to be your perfectly loving Father.

Another good example of why one needs to see the Big Picture is photo collage portraits like the one on the following page (which, of course, is also on the cover of this book).

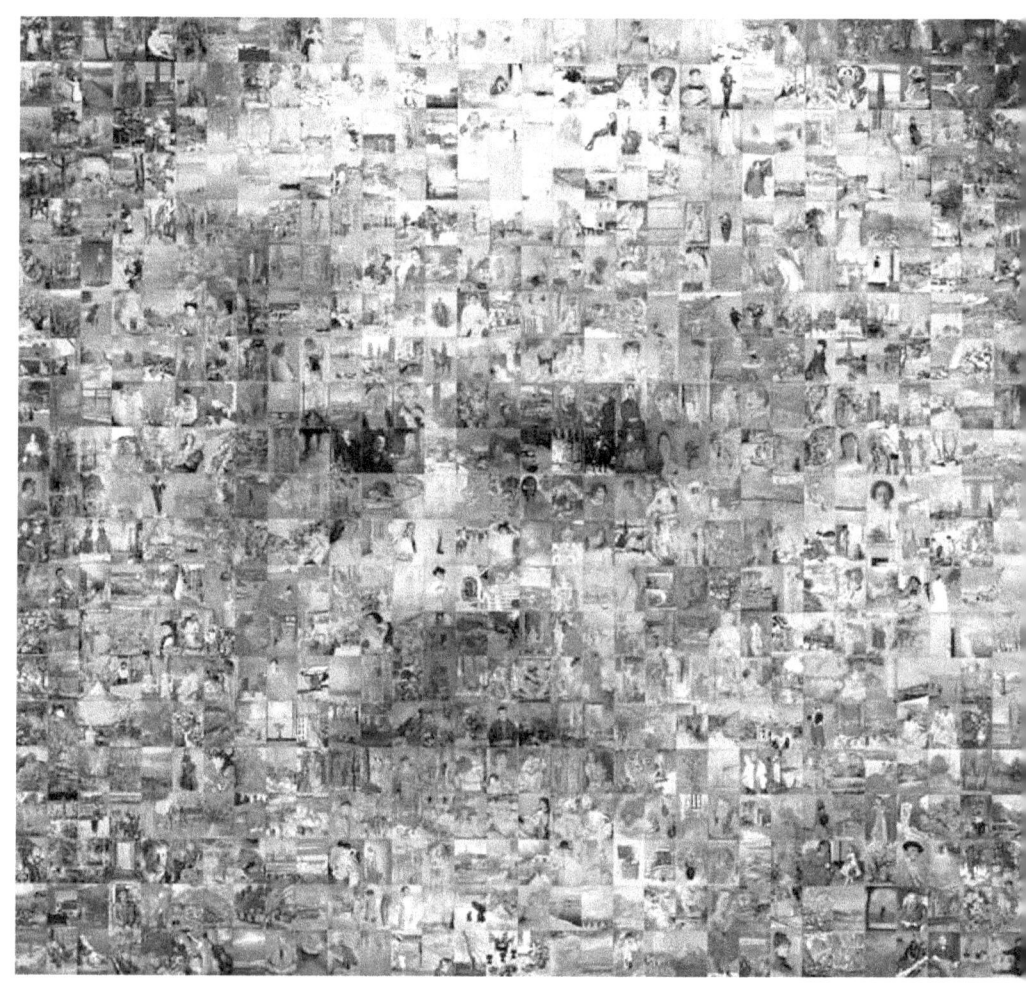

If you are too close or just focus on the individual pictures then you will miss the big picture. The Christian worldview says that when everything that we can observe in the universe is viewed properly it reveals the Creator God. But those who believe the Materialism worldview or other religious views reject this possibility. So they seek to put together the pieces differently. Now, it would take an extremely good puzzle-solver to assemble all of the pictures above properly in order to produce the correct big picture, even if the big picture is known. But it would literally be impossible if it isn't.

Another interesting illustration of the importance of perspective is tapestries. Look at the dramatic example below.

If one looks at the back side of a tapestry it may look like a random tangle of threads. But on the other side there is a beautiful picture. The Materialist view is like looking at the back side without believing there is another side. This illustration also reminds Christians to trust that God is producing a beautiful work of art both in our lives and in the entire universe despite the fact that our lives and the world around us are so often filled with details which are frustrating and confusing and seem to lack meaning. But it is also a call to those who have bought into the view that there is no Artist behind everything to reconsider this faulty assumption.

It's very easy to see that the Big Pictures of Humanists and Christians are radically different. The first views the universe as matter-only (Materialism) and denies the existence of a Creator or any supernatural entities (including human souls or minds, God or gods, angels, demons or Satan). It also assumes that we, not God or some other Higher Authority or Principle must determine what is good and evil.

Meanwhile, the Christian view says that all of history is really "His Story" and that God makes the rules. This includes all of our lives, whether or not we choose to recognize this, as well as the entire history of the universe.

The reason for the conflict between Humanism and Christianity is found in the history. Humanism, at its core, was a direct rejection of the Christian worldview which had preceded it as the dominant view of the developed world. Today's "culture war" actually began when Humanists began challenging the reigning Christian consensus around 1800 and it eventually led to the de-throning of the Christian view by around the middle of the 20th century.

However, if we look at the broader scope of history, today's tensions are just another phase in an on-going and, indeed, perennial war between those who believe in the God of the Bible and the Biblical worldview and those who reject Him and His Word. It's a war that has sometimes been "hot" and sometimes "cold".[26]

---

26 *Thankfully, it has always been a cold war in America until now. Even America's Civil War was not really a battle between conflicting worldviews. Both the North and South shared the same basic worldview, that of Christianity. But it is sobering to think about the fact that our nation is much more ideologically divided today than it was during the Civil War. The war against Christianity (along with other religions) is a hot war in many parts of the Muslim world today, as has usually been the case going back to the founding of Islam. It was also a hot war waged by Humanists against*

This war actually goes all the way back to the beginning of human history, whether or not you accept the Bible's account of the Fall of humanity due to the sin of Adam and Eve. So it should not be at all surprising that the dramatic differences between the Big Picture of Humanists and Christians (and others) are the real cause of the great polarization that characterizes 21st century society. And it's a polarization that seems to become clearer and more intense with every passing day.

The severity of the cultural war polarization comes from the fact that one's worldview influences how one views virtually everything in life, often leading people with different worldviews to draw opposite conclusions when viewing the same situations or data. It all depends on our perspective and it is our worldview which determines our perspective.

In what follows we will look at several of these differences. But the main point of showing them is not to convince anyone to change sides with any of the specific issues. Rather it is to get you to consider why you believe one way and not the other with respect to the Big Picture so that you might even be willing to change sides.

Unfortunately, a very common reaction to differences over issues today is for people to say that "I and those on my side are right and those on the other side are wrong, either because they are ignorant or bad (or both)." But this is not a satisfactory response! That anyone would think in this way in itself shows the problem of failing to think critically and carefully both about one's own views and those of others. All of us need to know why we believe what we believe and to try as hard as we can to make sure that we have valid reasons for what we believe. We also need to fight a strong tendency to assume that others don't have valid reasons for what they believe.

Christians and other religious people in the Soviet Union and its satellite nations. This is why many Christians like me pray and hope that we will not go down a similar path.

In order to do so we must be willing to consider that we may be wrong both about specific issues and, even, about our basic perspective. But this is not to say that there are no correct positions either on specific issues or worldviews. Despite its popularity today, this view, which is called "relativism", won't work. (See Chapter 3, note 17.) Critical thinking does not mean that we must doubt everything all the time. It only means that we should be willing to question what we have been taught in order so that we either confirm it to be true or prove that it is wrong.[27]

It is the goal of the writer to show that all other worldviews can be proven to be wrong, and in ways that are often surprisingly simple. But Christianity, rightly understood, cannot. Only Christianity can both explain all that we know and also avoid falling into self-contradiction or absurdity or the need to "cheat" by smuggling in things from outside which can't be accounted for within its own perspective. In other words, only Christianity can be seen to be internally consistent and also comprehensive in accounting for all human experience and knowledge.

Many people today consider the Christian worldview to be an obvious absurdity because it accepts the supposedly-impossible miracles and Creation-story described in the Bible as real events and also because of supposed factual errors and contradictions found in it, as well as teachings which are assumed to be inferior to today's supposedly more enlightened morality. But this is a prejudice which is itself part of the anti-Christian

---

27 *This process is necessary even for people who have been Christians for as long as they can recall. At some point everyone's beliefs will be put to the test, both by challenges from others and from the trials of one's own experiences. This is why the Puritans saw their children as being under God's "Covenant of Grace" and thereby expected them to believe in the Gospel and be saved. But they did not assume this was the case until they saw that their children had come to "own the Covenant" for themselves both by their professions of faith and by lives which reflect this faith. This is the real purpose for the rites of Confirmation and first communion, which should always be sought after and greatly celebrated in churches. It is also why it has been said that "God has no grandchildren, only children."*

message of Humanism. And it really is nothing other than a prejudice if the people who hold this view are not willing to consider challenges to it from the Christian side.

The most fundamental challenge is this: that all objections to what is in the Bible are based on the assumption that the God Who is described in the Bible (and is presented as speaking in it) cannot exist. But, this assumption is a negative universal claim, which cannot be proven and, thus, cannot be known for certain, as was previously pointed out. And, if the God described in the Bible actually exists, then nothing that He is described as doing or saying in it is impossible. So just having a willingness to consider that this God does exist can make everything in the Bible credible.[28]

Many people today consider that the Christian worldview is incompatible with logic, reason, Science and today's understanding of morality. Consequently, people who embrace it are irrational, anti-Scientific and/or immoral. But these are also prejudices which are part of the anti-Christian message of Humanism. And in what follows logic, reason and Science will be used to challenge many of the beliefs and moral positions of Humanism.

The extreme polarization of today's world is seen in the fact that many people today (perhaps most) will only read, watch or listen to those whom they perceive to be "on our side". Those who are identified as being on "the other side" will normally be dismissed as being either extremely ignorant or evil or both. And it's usually not hard to figure out which side others are on. There are now many issues which serve as indicators. To many Humanists, Christians have been brainwashed to believe false and evil things (even though Humanism really has no firm basis for explaining why anything is

---

28 *It is true that some apparent problems of contradictions, historical or scientific errors or moral deficiencies in the Bible are harder to overcome than others. But even in the toughest cases there are always reasonable possible resolutions. So it is not the case that there are inescapable errors in the Bible. Of course, one must want to see these answers (many of which are actually easy to see) or possible answers in order to see them. But reasonable people should be open to these.*

evil). But Christians say the same about Humanists.

So, who is right? And which side has the correct Big Picture? It is true that questions like this can never be conclusively answered by a vote, but it does seem clear that more adults tend to move from Humanism to Christianity than in the opposite direction. Although this hasn't been confirmed by scientific polling, Bible-believing churches always have large numbers of ex-atheists. On the other hand, many atheists will claim that they were originally believers. But one will find that most were only believers during childhood. Few remained so into their adult years before becoming atheists.[29]

---

29 *This is not to say that no adult believers (or, at least, those who claim to be believers) ever renounce faith, only that this is less common than adults going the other way. But there are some exceptions. So the "no true Scotsman" fallacy doesn't apply here. But the rarity of the exceptions proves the rule.*

On the other hand, the rule with atheists appears to be that most were only believers as children, if at all. And people reporting that they have never believed is becoming increasingly common. This is not surprising in our Humanism-dominated culture. While these observations would still require confirmation in the form of a scientific survey, they come from anecdotal evidence obtained in a variety of settings both in churches and among groups of atheists.

It is also important to realize that there are both explicit and implicit believers and atheists. But there really is no middle-ground between belief and unbelief. We all live either on the assumption that there is a Higher Power or on the assumption that there isn't. The assumption that God (or some other Higher Power) exists can be either a confident one (strong faith) or a tentative one (weak, unexamined and undeveloped faith). And the assumption of no God can also be either a confident one (which has been called "gnostic atheism") or a tentative one (which has been called "agnostic atheism" or "practical atheism").

It is not surprising that those who are tentative on either side would be prone to changing sides (although, again, there are notable exceptions). And the shift also tends to take one from a tentative position to a confident one...

Ironically, part of the reason that more adults go from anti-theistic Humanism to Christianity than the other way today is the successfulness of Humanist education. It has produced far more unbelieving adults than ever. I know, as I was one of them, as was almost everyone I knew when I was growing up.

Atheists like to celebrate the fact that surveys show that the percentage of adults who are not religious at all has increased in recent years. This is no mystery. It is the expected result after more than 50 years of anti-religious Humanist indoctrination in most of the developed world. If you think you are a Christian only because your family has a Christian heritage or because you received some rudimenatary religious instruction as a child, then you are either a Humanist already in your basic beliefs, or, at least, you will have no strong objection to becoming one.

But despite decades of Humanist indoctrination, surveys on religiosity continue to show that the percentages of people who believe in God and consider their religion very important to them are higher in the older age-groups.[30] Once again, this doesn't prove that religious faith is correct. But it

---

This, too, should not be surprising. For, in every case when one changes sides it represents a change of worldview, which significantly changes how one thinks and acts. So such changes are not trivial changes of opinion and they usually do not come easily. But, all things considered, it is consistently found that more adults go from unbelief to belief than the other way.

30 *A 2015 Pew Forum Religious Landscape Study showed that twice as many respondents aged 18-29 reported that religion was not important at all to them compared to respondents who said that religion was very important to them (32% versus 16%). But in the 50-64 age group the religion was very important group led the religion was not important at all group by 29% to 19%. And in the 65+ group the lead was 22% to 12%. (http://www.pewforum.org/religious-landscape-study/belief-in-god/#age-distribution).*

Perhaps more to the point, the numbers for those who reported being religious corresponded closely with the numbers for those who believe in

can be seen as evidence that points in this direction. It must be admitted that as people become older and more experienced many of them turn to God. Other reasons for this are a desire to find meaning in life which Humanism doesn't offer and, in some cases, fear of death and judgment. While atheists tend to mock the latter two fears, these fears actually reflect an intrinsic awareness that there is Someone out there and that we have a problem with Him. (Much more on this later)

Surveys also show that the percentage of people who have conservative views rather than progressive (Humanist) ones is also higher in the older age-groups. This is also not surprising in the light of the preceding trend, since strongly-religious people are far more likely to be conservative than liberal or progressive (which we will use as interchangeable terms).[31]

God with absolute certainty and the numbers for those for whom religion was not important at all to them corresponded closely with those who don't believe in God. (http://www.pewforum.org/religious-landscape-study/belief-in-god/#age-distribution)

It could be argued that the 65+ group has more believers simply because this group came of age before Humanism took over the educational establishment and began systematically discouraging faith. But the indoctrination against belief in God extends beyond one's school years through the news and entertainment media, other aspects of culture and the influence of other people in other ways. So one's faith in God must hold up against constant assaults made on it.

31 *The 2015 Pew Forum survey showed that 47% of those for whom religion was very important (a total of 18,725 respondents) described themselves as conservative and only 17% described themselves as liberal. On the other hand, among those who said that religion is not important at all for them (a total of 3966 respondents), 47% described themselves as liberal and only 14% as conservative.*
(http://www.pewforum.org/religious-landscape-study/importance-of-religion-in-ones-life/#political-ideology)

And among people who reported that they believe in God with absolute certainty 45% described themselves as conservative and only 17% as liberal. But among those who reported that they don't believe in God 50% described themselves as liberal and only 13% as conservative...

There is also another likely contributor to these trends. It has often been observed that younger people tend to be more emotionally-oriented and driven. But as people get older their experience causes many to take a more reasonable approach to things (hopefully without losing beneficial emotional sensitivities). After all, isn't this how it should be with reasonable people?

This trend is reflected in a popular saying among conservatives that: "If you are young and aren't a liberal, then you lack a heart. But if you are old and haven't become a conservative, then you lack a brain." It should be understood that this is a rather exaggerated and overly-simplified generalization. And there will always be exceptions with generalizations (especially simple ones like this one). But the general pattern of people becoming more conservative as they get older (which has been widely-recognized and measured for years) continues even in today's Humanism-dominated culture.

Another common saying (this time among liberals) is that: "A conservative is just a liberal who has had his pocket picked." So, it is thought that people become conservatives because they have been victimized. In other words, it is mainly an emotional reaction. If liberals (or progressives) see things in this way, then they appear to be projecting their more emotional orientation onto conservatives and disregarding the reasons conservatives tend to give for being conservative. At the same time, though, the saying can also be seen to reflect a reasonable conclusion that one will not tend to look at a thief as a victim if he or she is victimizing you!

It has also been said that liberals tend to "think with their hearts more than their heads". This can be seen in the fact that progressives are much more likely to participate in protests and other social causes than conservatives. It is also a likely explanation for why women are much more likely to be liberal than men, as are many artists and performers, as well as people with

---

(http://www.pewforum.org/religious-landscape-study/belief-in-god/#political-ideology).

LGBTQ tendencies. Don't get me wrong, this is not really a criticism of women and these other groups.[32]

It is very important to have emotional sensitivities and sympathies in many cases. Indeed, this is especially essential for women to be good mothers. (Although parental compassion clearly goes too far if mothers or fathers are so compassionate toward their children that they overlook or even reward their bad behavior, as often happens today.) And being emotionally sensitive and expressive is also clearly an essential part of being an artist or a compelling performer.

But being overly emotionally-driven can often lead to problems when it comes to public policy, as it can often unfairly skew one's perspective on matters of law and justice. This problem is reflected in a saying thought to have come from Aristotle that the Law should be "Reason unaffected by desire". And the belief that justice means not being overly swayed by factors which will tend to sway one's emotions is reflected in the traditional image of the woman holding the scales of justice, specifically in the fact that she is blind-folded.

For those who more emotionally-oriented, there will always be the need to mature and find balance between your emotions and your intellect. For example, sympathy and empathy are emotions which one should have for people who have legitimately been victimized. But to believe that everyone is a victim and, therefore, that even criminals should be treated sympathetically is simply not reasonable. And it doesn't help either them or society!

---

32 *However, the perspective of the author and other Bible-believing Christians on people with LGBTQ inclinations is that people with these and other deviant sexual tendencies should resist these and both can and should overcome them. Contrary to the prejudice of many today, this is not a matter of "homophobia" (that is, hateful bigotry). Rather, it is based on an honest disagreement that such behavior is natural, beneficial and unchangeable. This is further discussed in the next chapter.*

So to be sympathetic and, even, empathetic with bad people is neither "compassionate" nor loving. Rather, it is to encourage and sometimes enable or support those who are involved in behavior which is destructive to themselves, to others and, even, to society itself. This is reflected in the adage: "To be kind to the cruel is to be cruel to the kind."

On the other hand, anger and the desire for punishment is appropriate for those who are clearly evil oppressors. But these sentiments are inappropriate if extended to those who have not been conclusively shown to be evil. An example of the latter is the tendency of many progressives today to regard all rich people as evil oppressors, as was evident in the "Occupy" movement of the early 2000's. (Conveniently, though, rich progressives were usually exempted from this.)

Another example is a tendency to consider Caucasians (and, especially, males) as the chief oppressors in society, as is reflected in the focus on "white privilege" that has become popular in progressive circles in recent years. But, aside from the issue of whether this is true (which is highly-questionable in itself), this is a clearly an example of hypocrisy, in which negative stereotyping is done by people who are supposed to be against stereotypes altogether. And, no matter what views one holds, hypocrisy is never good.

We must do all that we can not to be hypocritical. And we must do all that we can not to hate the wrong people and also not to support the wrong people. The Old Testament prophet Micah criticized wayward Israel for loving the evil and hating the good (in chapter 3, verse 2 of his Old Testament prophecy). And the prophet Amos exhorted Israel to "Hate evil, love good, maintain justice in the courts." (Amos 5:15). Such advice is every bit as relevant today as it was 2500 years ago. (Christians say that this is to be expected since these words are actually from God Himself, although conveyed through human writers. The Church came to recognize that this was the case with the entire Bible. This is why it chose the books which are in it.)

In his brilliant sociological critique, "Idols for Destruction", Herbert Schlossberg cites a term used by 19th century Sociologist Max Weber to describe a powerful emotion which people will tend to have toward those whom they regard as bad (for whatever reason): "resentment". This French word describes more than what the English word "resentment" means. It is not just the feeling of resentment, it is also the desire to punish the person or group which one resents, usually in the guise of exacting "justice".[33]

But the desire to punish those whom one resents is highly-destructive if the person or group has not been conclusively shown to be guilty and, therefore, deserving of punishment (as is the case with clearly-identified oppressors, like the Nazi's in World War 2). This has certainly been a problem among conservatives at times (as has been seen in cases of clear racism, persecutions of other groups and religious divisions). But it is clearly a big problem today for many people on the political Left (progressives) when they are inclined to practice what conservatives like to call "identity politics". This refers to the practice of treating groups and the individuals in them preferentially (like LGBTQ people, racial or ethnic minorities, immigrants and women) or disparagingly (like Bible-believing Christians, "Non-Hispanic whites" and men) simply based on biases in favor of or against these groups.

But, no matter who does this, to treat any group as either good or evil in its entirety and, thus, deserving of preference or punishment across-the-board is fundamentally unjust. For this inevitably leads to the punishing of innocents in many cases, as well as to giving advantages to people who are

---

33   *In chapter 12 we will examine how this leads to the preference most progressive Humanists have for Socialism, with its ideal of "social justice". This is the desire not for equality of opportunity, but for equality of economic outcomes. In other words, it is the belief that no one should be richer than anyone else. But history has shown that whenever this has been the driving motivation of society it has led to almost everyone (the "99%") being oppressed and impoverished, except for the ruling few (the real "1%").*

undeserving. (It is admitted that there have been a few exceptions to this. For example, no one who was an active member of the Nazi Party could really be regarded as innocent. But most groups are not as thoroughly evil as this was.)

So, those who are on the progressive side often must endeavor to balance their emotions with a fair and reasonable assessment of the situations in which they find themselves. This also applies to how we assess ourselves. It is always a challenge for us to have a balanced perspective of ourselves. We must always use reason to balance the emotional responses that we will often have to our self-perception and and also to the assessments that we will often receive from others. This will be necessary in order to avoid being either overly easy or overly hard on ourselves.

On the other side, conservatives who think only with their heads and lack emotional sensitivities and sympathies are also unbalanced and need to develop emotionally. This is especially an issue for men, as we often tend to be unbalanced in the direction of "cold-hearted" reasoning at the expense of proper emotional sensitivity. Such people will often tend to be overly hard on others. They may also be overly hard on themselves, but may also be inconsistent in being hard on others, but easy on themselves. In the latter case we have the "double-standard" of hypocrisy once again.

The main point to be taken from all of this, however, is this: Since older people are more likely to be both religious believers and conservative isn't it reasonable that you should be willing to critically examine your own worldview and also become open to Christianity (unless, of course, you are already a Christian)?[34] Furthermore, those who do become believers will also find it to be emotionally-fulfilling, as well. This author will testify that

---

34 *Indeed, this is the theme of Timothy Keller's fine book, "The Reason for God" as well as the older and somewhat dated, but still very insightful "Mere Christianity" by C.S. Lewis.*

this is the case, having formerly been one of those men who was generally emotionally-inhibited in my early days, especially prior to becoming a Christian, but who is much more emotionally-free and expressive today.

In the next chapter we will briefly visit several key topics in order to show how one's worldview commonly determines how one will view the specific issues. Once again, the goal will not be to persuade you of the positions favored by the Christian side on these issues. For this rarely occurs.

Rather, the hope will be that you will better understand why Christians take the positions that we do and that you may be willing to think about or re-think why you take the positions that you do. In short, if you hold what are considered progressive positions it will usually be because you either explicitly or implicitly reject the idea that the God described in the Bible exists.[35] So you think and act for all practical purposes as though He doesn't.

What is of utmost importance is that the personal consequences of one's worldview are nothing less than life-defining. This is so no matter what point-of-view you currently have. And the worldview which one has is also (potentially, at least) of eternal consequence.

But what is also at stake is the question of why anything is right or wrong. For, in the following chapter it will be demonstrated that if the God described in the Bible did not exist then nothing could be established beyond all doubt as wrong. This includes pedophilia and genocide or anything else you may consider heinous!

---

35 *Or you assume that while God may exist, His existence has no practical significance for our daily lives. But this is clearly an untenable position. Considering the characteristics of the God described in the Bible, it would be impossible for His existence not to have an impact on everything in one's life.*

Chapter 5
Humanism's Moral Problems

Morality (along with logic and reason) is one of the main areas in which Materialists/Humanists must "smuggle in" aspects of the worldview it succeeded: Christianity. This is because morality is actually incompatible with Materialism. Here's the basic problem: If natural forces are all that exist and nature is amoral (that is, non-moral or morally neutral), then how can humanity be moral?

In a 2014 film ("Interstellar") there is a scene in which two astronauts ponder the question of whether Nature is moral or not. Both agree that it isn't. But this invites an obvious question which was not asked: How can humanity be moral if we are just a product of Nature? And how can we even speak meaningfully of good and evil, as everyone inevitably must?

To regard some things as good and others as evil is an inescapable aspect of human experience. Even the most ardent advocates of relativism (or the belief that there is no such thing as absolute truth, including right and wrong) will consider it wrong for someone to do many things to them against their will. Besides, just to say that there are no such things as absolute rights and wrongs can be seen to be a self-defeating statement.

Looking at it the other way around, if there is no such thing as an absolute wrong then it can't be absolutely wrong to think that there is such a thing as an absolute right and wrong. So, it may be right that there is such a thing as an absolute right and wrong after all. That the Materialist, or Nature-only view of reality cannot account for the undeniable existence of morality is actually enough to prove that it can't be true. But it's worth considering some other problems with today's dominant view.

Let's consider the topic of extinction. It is universally-agreed by advocates of Evolution that extinction is the way of Nature and that all species, including ours, will eventually disappear. But, at the same time, it is also commonly agreed that we should do all that we can not only to prevent our own extinction, but also the extinction of other species. This is because, presumably, extinction is bad.

Aside from the point which was made previously: that good and bad would be meaningless in a Nature-only universe, if extinction is natural and inevitable for all, how can one say that it is bad? It is important to recognize that this tension also exists with regard to our individual survival. (More on this shortly)

Concern for the ultimate destiny of one's own or other species cannot be found elsewhere in nature. Whereas symbiotic relationships are sometimes observed between species, these are only relationships which turn out to be mutually-beneficial to the particular living things involved in them. This is quite different from having a more global concern, as we do. So, in having a global concern, humanity is actually acting in a way which is inconsistent with what we observe in nature.

At the same time, though, such concern is actually consistent with the Biblical picture of mankind as having a God-given dominion over Nature. In other words, concern for the preservation of humanity and other species, as well as concern for the environment, is Biblical. But it is inconsistent with the idea that we are just another species which emerged from mindless forces in Nature.

An example of an approach which would actually be consistent with the evolutionary view is found in the film "War Games". In this film, the designer of a super-computer which is threatening to start a global thermo-nuclear war (the character Peter Falken) is content to accept that humanity may be about to make itself extinct. But, in the story this viewpoint is regarded as unacceptable by the other characters, as it no doubt will be to most of the audience as well. But the question is: Why? This is one of many cases in which most people actually view things on the basis that the Christian worldview, not the Humanist/Materialist worldview, is true, despite claiming to believe that the latter is correct.

Looking at things from an individual standpoint, virtually every culture in human history has agreed that murder, that is, the killing of another human-being (except in self-defense or the defense of others) is wrong. Yet, in nature, predatory killing runs rampant and competitive killing of other members of the same species is often observed, as well. And there are sometimes cases where one species wipes out another or wipes out its own food supply. Nevertheless, we don't regard any of this as wrong. (It is worth considering that from a Biblical perspective all of this killing in Nature is not the way things originally were, but was the result of the corruption of the original Creation coming from humanity's sinful rebellion against our Creator. So, it can be said that the violence we see in Nature is, in a certain respect, wrong, as is human violence.)

The only real reason that murder or pedophilia or genocide and many other things are rightly viewed as wrong or that any human conduct can rightly be considered good or evil is because we are more than just a part of the natural world. And the only reason that our determinations of good and evil aren't arbitrary is because there is a Higher Moral Authority than us. Humanism says that we and we alone collectively determine good and evil. But there is just no way to determine with certainty what is ultimately right and wrong if we are the ultimate authority.

In cases of moral disputes, there is always the need for something or someone higher to appeal to than the individuals involved. Otherwise, it will always be merely a matter of opinion. This is because moral claims cannot be proven like many other claims of truth. For they are not disputes over what happens, which can be objectively examined. Rather, they are disputes about the meaning of what happens, which will always be subject to interpretation. And it doesn't matter how many people might agree on a moral point. For neither might nor masses make right. If we are not moral beings who are under a Higher Authority, then it is all arbitrary.

Not only are good and evil or right and wrong arbitrary if the Materialism understanding of the universe is correct, but so are "human rights". We can easily see this when we look at how different cultures have treated people. While there are many aspects of morality which have been agreed upon across most cultures, there have also been glaring exceptions.

Hitler's Third Reich claimed that the way to preserve the human race was through the extermination of the supposedly lesser races by the supposed "Master Race" of Aryans. This goal is rightly rejected by most people for being monstrously evil. But, how do we really know for certain that the Nazi's were wrong?

If the Materialist evolutionary conception of the universe is correct, then this cannot be conclusively established, no matter how much one thinks that it can be. Indeed, the Nazi's appealed to "survival of the fittest" and other aspects of Evolution to support their programs. Furthermore, once again, if we are only material beings, the accidental product of mindless forces, then good and evil in themselves don't even exist!

In the same way, Karl Marx's collectivist ideal could not be condemned if the Materialist view was correct. Actually, Marxism is itself a product of the Materialist/Empiricist rebellion against Christianity. Thus, it is also known as "Dialectical Materialism".[36] Under the Marxist conception, individual rights and differences must yield to the common good. But, if the evolutionary picture is correct, how can it be possible to know for certain

---

36 *Empiricism is the epistemological partner of the metaphysical view known as Materialism. Epistemology is the study of how we know things, while metaphysics is the study of what exists. Materialism assumes that no immaterial entities exist because we can't observe such things with our senses or with instruments which extend the reach of our senses. Meanwhile, Empiricism says that we can only use our senses or instruments to determine what exists. So the partnership between the two is quite clear.*

what is good either for individuals or society, or, even, that there is such thing as good and evil?

Nor would it be possible to prove that capitalists who hold to a Darwinian "survival of the fittest" view of society (which has been called "Social Darwinism") are wrong. For, if the evolutionary picture is correct, then "predatory capitalism" is just natural human behavior, which is neither right nor wrong.

Serious disagreements over human rights can also be seen today between the developed world, in which Humanism reigns, and the Muslim world. The same is also true with China and other parts of the world in which traditional religious cultures still rule. But if the Materialism picture of the universe is true, then there is no Higher Authority for ethics than us. If this is so, then human rights will always and only be just a matter of human opinion.

One of the fundamental principles of freedom and American Democracy is the "rule of law". Many people today will acknowledge this. But are you really aware of what this means? To understand what the rule of law means one must realize what its alternative is: the rule of human-beings, whether it's a single human-being or a ruling few or, even, the rule of a majority. Most today would say that the last of these is desirable. But America's founders feared a "tyranny of a majority". For the rule of a ruling few was what they saw in the European societies from which many of them (or their ancestors) had fled.

It's actually very simple: if there is no Higher Authority for ethics and human rights than us then there cannot be a Higher Rule of Law, there can only be rule of people. And in this case neither might nor a majority can make something right beyond dispute (or a "right").[37]

---

37 *The fear of tyranny by a majority is why America's founders did not intend to establish a pure rule-by-majority Democracy. Rather, what they set up was a democratically-elected Constitutional Republic. As such, the Constitution was intended to be the ruling Law of the land (the rule of law*

Unlike today, virtually all 18th century Americans understood this, including those who did not believe in the Bible as God's revelation, or those who only believed parts of it. Thomas Jefferson is a famous example of the latter. Jefferson accepted the Bible's ethical teachings as having divine authority, but rejected its accounts of supernatural activity. He even produced an edited version of the Biblical Gospels in which he eliminated the latter.

---

intended to reflect universal Natural Law) under which elected representatives would make decisions on behalf of the People. Of course these include the President, Senators and House Representatives. However, most today don't realize that only the latter were popularly elected at first, with both Senators and the electors for the Presidency (the Electoral College) being chosen by the legislatures of the states.

In all cases (including the Electoral College) these representatives were not elected to execute the will of their constituencies (as many today believe). Rather, they were elected to make decisions for them in accord with what is true and good, based again on the belief that there is a Higher Standard which determines this. Fear of tyrannies by majorities or groups or a monarch is also why our founders set up a government with a separation and balance of powers.

Furthermore, while both the legislative branch (both Houses of Congress) and the executive (headed by the President) were regarded as being under the Constitution as their governing Contract, the same was also true of the judicial branch (including the Supreme Court as the highest court of appeals). Congress is charged with making the laws of the land, the Executive branch, with the President as the "Chief Executive Officer" is charged with executing these laws, and the Judiciary is responsible to make sure that these laws are consistent with the Higher Law embodied in the Constitution.

But the judicial branch was only charged with interpreting the Constitution according to its "original intent". Indeed, this is the way all contracts are supposed to be applied! So the idea that there can be a "flexible interpretation" of the Constitution fundamentally destroys its intended contractual function. The whole point of having a written contract is to preserve the original intent of those who make it!

But even those who rejected the Bible altogether as being of divine origin and, thus, as The Ultimate Standard for truth and ethics still held that that humanity was under Higher Law in the form of "Natural Law". This was the belief that the universe contains moral rules which are just as universal as the laws of nature which we discover through Science.[38]

So, in all of these ways, the Materialist/Empiricist approach shows itself to be an "Epic Fail" in the area of morality and human rights. Again, if the

> *That so many highly-educated people opt for the "flexible interpretation" view is just one of many examples of how a faulty worldview can blind people to something that should be completely obvious. This includes Constitutional lawyers who are progressive Humanists like former President Obama (who may claim to be Christians, but show by their words and actions that they have the Humanism worldview, not the Christian one).*
>
> *Of course, there is an ulterior motive for taking the "flexible interpretation" approach. It is the easiest way to change the laws of the land, without the need for Congressional approval or the intentionally-difficult process of amending the Constitution (the means for changing the document which the founders provided). But this is a gross abuse both of the powers granted to the Judiciary by the Constitution and of the principle of rule of law itself.*
>
> *Judges and justices who presume to "find" new rights and laws in the Constitution are effectively acting like tyrannical "super-legislators" ruling over all. They are most clearly asserting the "rule of man" over the rule of law. Historically, this has been done both by conservative and liberal-thinking (or progressive) members of the Judiciary, but has been much more commonly done by the latter in the past several decades.*

38 *While this idea is considered quaint by many in the developed world today, it was the view of nearly everyone in the world until quite recently, including both the Judeo-Christian tradition and the traditional Asian faiths. Believers in Natural Law in the Judeo-Christian tradition see it as having been established by the Creator God. Meanwhile, the Asian traditions see it as just being part of the order of the universe. But, with respect to the latter, it will be discussed subsequently that it is problematic to view morality as a characteristic of the universe. Rather, morality is a characteristic of moral beings.*

evolutionary understanding of humanity and the universe is correct, then the concepts of good and evil or right and wrong are meaningless. This is because this view says that all of our behavior can be explained as the product of the chemistry of our bodies. But chemistry can never be considered right or wrong. It just is. This, once again, is actually sufficient to prove that the Humanist understanding of morality, which assumes the Materialism worldview, can't be correct.

Let's consider some additional problems with the Humanist understanding of right and wrong. First, consider the problem of crime. Humanists tend to think that poverty causes crime.[39] But Christians and other traditionalists see crime mainly as a problem of human character, saying that criminals cause crime and, also, that crime causes poverty in many cases. It is not immediately obvious which side is correct. One simply must resist a common tendency to assume that their side must be correct in this and other areas. In this case both sides can support their position with statistics and other evidence and arguments.[40]

Belief in Natural Law was common both among Christians, who believe that God continues to be active in the universe, and Deists, who hold that once God created the universe He left it alone so that it unfolds on its own according to how He designed it. To this day, there are many who call themselves Christians who are really Deists in practice. This includes those who hold to "theistic evolution".

But to try to combine a Christian understanding with Evolution won't work because the Materialism worldview is assumed with the latter. So, if you want to remain consistent, if Evolution is true then you must hold that God can't work in the spiritual realm any more than He does in the physical world because the spiritual realm doesn't exist!

39 *If poverty is the cause of crime, as Humanists claim, then this doesn't explain why there are so many wealthy people who are criminals. Indeed, the evil of greedy rich people is one of the common themes of progressives. But this exposes a contradiction in their thinking about the causes of crime.*

40 *One aspect of statistics is not ambiguous, though. Studies consistently show that children raised in single-parent or no-parent households (either with other family members or with foster parents), regardless of race, have a far higher likelihood of criminal behavior than kids raised in households with*

Nevertheless, the debate over what causes crime highlights what may be the most important difference between Humanism and Christianity with regard to morality. That is the reality of <u>choice</u>. For Humanism ultimately denies choice, while Christianity affirms it. The Christian perspective is that committing crimes is always a matter of choice. Indeed there are circumstances in which there are greater enticements to commit crimes, especially in the case of a starving person stealing food. But even in this case stealing is a choice, for there are always alternatives to stealing.

One can simply ask those who have food to share theirs. In such a case the person with food would be morally-obligated to share it with those who have none. If they refused and there was no other way to get food other than taking it without the owner's permission then doing so would be morally permissible. But in this case a moral person would be willing to pay for the food later, if possible. In this case it could not reasonably be called stealing.[41]

Committing a crime is never absolutely necessary, or the only choice a person has. This is really the only reason why we hold people acccountable for crimes. Otherwise this would be unfair and we should close all of our prisons and jails. There is no middle-ground on this: either our choices are real or they aren't. But no sane person will really claim that we don't have

---

both parents. As with so many social issues, this points to the role of choices. Many, if not most of the marriage separations today could be avoided. But an emphasis on personal happiness and fulfillment rather than sacrifice for others causes many today to abandon their marriage commitments. As will be discussed in chapter 9, this is an abandonment of the call to love others; that is, to care about them more than one cares about one's self.

41 *In this and what follows many moral assessments will be made. Whether or not one agrees with them, it must be agreed that attempting to discern right and wrong is an inevitable aspect of human experience. But, as previously indicated, this is only because there is a Higher Law above all human opinion.*

real moral choices. And in doing so they point to a fatal flaw in Humanism.

We will re-visit the issue of choice a little later, as it crucial to how we view all human behavior and most critical for how we view and treat issues of mental-health and sexuality. But first we will look at the other side of the question about crime: punishment. To do so we will look at the most extreme case of punishment for crime: the death penalty.

Humanists are generally less harsh in punishing crime than Christians and others who have a Higher Standard for morality. Many oppose the death penalty. This is partly because they fear that it will be imposed on some innocent people (which will always be a risk, although modern forensics make it less of a risk than in the past) and partly because they see it as a remnant of a more barbaric age.

But Christians tend to see capital punishment as protective of the sanctity of life, in which killing convicted murderers saves many more innocent lives than it takes due to the execution of innocent people. This is because the record shows that significantly more people are killed by murderers who have been spared the penalty of death than the number of innocent people who are wrongly executed. Many Humanists won't even deny this, but they still oppose capital punishment mainly because it has always been a practice of brutal regimes. (Again, sparing innocent lives won't work as the rationale because it is clear that more innocents are killed in the absence of the death penalty, especially with today's DNA analysis and other advanced forensics.)

But saying that we shouldn't execute people because this is what brutal regimes do can be seen to be a fallacy commonly known as guilt by association. An action isn't proven to be wrong simply because other people or cultures that we don't like did it. Just because something was done by a brutal regime doesn't mean that the particular action was brutal. For example, Nazi engineers developed what became known as the Volkswagen Beetle at the request of Adolf Hitler, and Mercedes and BMW produced engines for Nazi war-planes. But, does this mean that these companies or the products they produced and produce today are evil? Obviously this is not a reasonable conclusion.

The effect of differences in worldviews is especially clear with "culture war" issues like abortion and issues of sexuality (LGBTQ). It is no mere coincidence that one's views on sexuality and sexual relations will closely correspond to whether one believes the Humanist or Christian worldview. If one believes the Christian view that God made us male and female and made us for the purpose of marital unions between one man and one woman, then he or she will naturally reject the idea that homosexual unions (or, for that matter, any other alternative types of sexual practice) are as legitimate as heterosexual marriage. And he or she will also reject the concept of "gender fluidity" (that a person can legitimately question the sex which their anatomy and chromosomes say they are). On the other hand, those with a Humanist point-of-view overwhelmingly support these things.[42]

---

42 *Until recently, abortion was probably the best barometer of one's worldview, with Humanists being almost unanimously pro-choice and Christians, as well as other traditional religious people being overwhelmingly anti-abortion. (However, one must keep in mind that there are many who would identify themselves as Christians, but who reject that the Bible is authoritative and therefore reject the Biblical worldview in favor of the Humanist understanding. I myself was once of these.) But the rise of the pro-LGBTQ movement over the past three decades or so has made it a bigger source of conflict in the culture war than the abortion issue, mainly because the attempt by LGBTQ supporters to legitimize homosexuality and desires to change one's sex affects everyone society in ways that protecting abortion does not.*

Being pro-LGBTQ and pro-choice can both be seen as being the result of embracing the Big Picture of Humanism. But the pro-LGBTQ movement is an even clearer example of the power of the Humanist worldview. In seeking to normalize homosexuals and "transgenders" Humanists have to reject what had previously been the overwhelming consensus of the world's cultures, as well as that of the scientific and medical communities until very recently (by all accounts no earlier than the 1970's).

While we are focusing issues pertaining to LGBTQ and other issues, it is

The tension between the two sides over these matters is greatly increased by the fact that Humanists commonly charge with "homophobia" or hateful bigotry all Christians and others who disagree them. But disagreeing that homosexuality is natural, healthy and unchangeable does not make one a hater!

The charge of homophobia or bigotry is unfair because it completely ignores

---

worth pointing out in passing a few key reasons why Christians and others are against abortion. One is that those who are pro-choice are inevitably selective and therefore hypocritical in this. So it is that pregnant women will consider "what" is in them either as a part of their body, of which they have the right to dispose (if they don't want the child) or as an unborn child (if they do). But that the first view is wrong is implied in the fact that those who do things which result in the death of fetuses can be charged with murder or manslaughter for this.

A child cannot be considered as such when desired, but not when he or she isn't. Unborn children are either real people deserving of protection or not. Even if this is questionable in the earliest stages of development, it is certainly the case at the point of viability, which is now seen as being prior to the 3rd trimester. And, if she is being honest, every woman who has ever been pregnant must admit that she knew from the time she learned it was there that what is inside of her is not just a part of her body, it is a distinct human-being, albeit not a fully-developed one. Besides, the Science proving that this is so is absolutely indisputable.

So, to claim an unborn child in the womb is just a part of a woman's body is just a lie and, indeed, a quite heinous lie used to justify disposing of it. It is a stunningly selfish point-of-view, but one that is sadly consistent with Humanist thinking. But not with the Christian view that human life is sacred and that we must be willing to do all that we can to protect it, even at great personal sacrifice. And it's not hard to see that regarding unborn human-beings as disposable only tends to cheapen the value of children even after they are born. That parents today can actually think that they legitimately could have aborted their children should be sufficient to show that this is so.

Furthermore, the claim by many women that they have the exclusive right to dispose of their unwanted unborn children ignores the fact that these

what the other side actually believes. Even if we are wrong (and much evidence can actually be produced to show that we are not wrong), it still should be recognized that we truly believe that LGBTQ people are harming themselves and others.

Furthermore, we believe that, like all of us, those who have homosexual or transgender inclinations always have a choice about how they will behave sexually (as well as in many other ways). It is one of the great ironies of the 21st century that those who ignore what Christians (and others) believe and assume other sinister motives for why we oppose the pro-LGBTQ movement actually are guilty of a very destructive form of prejudice and hate.[43]

---

children belong just as much to the father as the mother (which is also an indisputable fact of Science). It doesn't matter if the father doesn't care. He certainly should! So it is that both would-be mothers and fathers who would rather dispose of the results of their sexual intimacy are guilty of nothing less than child-sacrifice for the sake of their own convenience.

Even in cases of rape or incest, why does the parents' crime justify putting to death the child that is produced? Such children could be offered for adoption. And in cases of fetal deformity, who is to say that having these children won't be a great blessing rather than a terrible burden? Many parents of such children will affirm without hesitation that the former is the case. Many other arguments can and have been offered for why abortion is wrong (in most cases, at least). But these should be sufficient to show both its moral and scientific bankruptcy.

43 I am seeking to use today's "politically-correct" terminology in most cases. I do make two notable exceptions, though. I refuse to use "gender" instead of "sex" because I see the use of this term, in itself, as part of a false and destructive effort to deny that all people are born as one of two sexes: male or female. And I refuse to use the term "gay" for male homosexuals because I see it as a futile attempt to paint a smiling face on a lifestyle choice that I and many others see as ultimately leading to much misery. (Of course, it is the "G" of LGBTQ, but there is simply no practical alternative to this abbreviation.)

I also recognize that some will even object to my previous use of "lifestyle". But this only shows how ridiculously excessive "politically-correct" (or

On the other side, Christians must openly and unreservedly oppose those who really do show hatred to individuals or groups for any reason, including LGBTQ people. The "God hates fags" message of the Westboro Baptist so-called "Church" should be as offensive to us as it is to anyone else. Frankly it's so offensive to me that I was hesitant to mention it here.

Actually, such hatred should be even more offensive to Christians than to others because it is a detestable distortion of the Gospel message that "God so loved the world that He gave His Son, that whoever should believe in Him shall not perish, but have everlasting life." This is from the New Testament Gospel of John, chapter 3, verse 16. (In case you were wondering, this is the "JOHN 3:16" you may have seen on signs at sports events or other public events.) And since God has so loved us, we are also called to sacrifice ourselves to love others (including, even, our enemies).[44]

"PC") sensitivity often is. Besides, it is always one-sided: in favor of Humanist sensitivities and in complete disregard of Christian or other religious sensitivities.

It is clearly the case today that while Humanists are often offended by Christians' views and actions, few even have any awareness of when Christians are offended by things which we see or hear, much less any sympathy for this. Nevertheless, I do wish to avoid needlessly offending people on the other side with terminology. However, the real cause of offense and division between us is the dramatically different understandings of what is true and good due to our different worldviews.

44 *As an example of the extent to which Christians are called to love others, the practice of extreme Muslim jihadists of calling suicide killers "martyrs" is a detestable perversion of the uniquely Christian practice of martyrdom, in which believers, following the example of our Lord, are willing to lay down our lives to save others, not to kill them. A particularly amazing example of this was when early Christians were sometimes the only people willing to care for plague victims, often contracting and dying from the disease themselves. It seems clear that everyone else was scared-off because the risk was known. Whether or not these Christians believed that God would protect them doesn't really matter. Either way, it was an incredible act of love.*

Many Christians truly believe that pursuing same-sex relationships or bisexuality or changing one's sex are not actions which bring fulfillment in the long run. Rather, they bring much misery and destruction both to those who do these things and to those around them. Indeed, those who hold the traditional view consider involvement with all "alternative" forms of sexuality to be just as destructive, if not not more destructive than substance-abuse (whether the substance is alcohol, illegal drugs or prescription medications).[45] And this belief is not just based on the Bible.

Many today don't realize that the scientific and mental-health communities around the world were almost unanimously in agreement with the Christian point-of-view on sexuality until the 1970's. And it's not that the Science changed as a result of any significant new findings. Rather, what has changed is the political orientation of many scientists and their associations. This, in turn, reflects the underlying Humanist and Materialist worldview which most today hold. And this political bias also determines the direction of their work in many ways, in which they seek to support today's consensus view.

But Christians' firm disagreement with today's efforts to normalize homosexuality and desires to change one's sex doesn't at all mean that believers shouldn't reach out in love to those involved with these things. On the contrary, we must be willing to reach out in love to everyone who is not already on our side. No matter what others are involved in, we should be willing to appeal to them as fellow sinners, but as those who have admitted our sins and who believe that God has forgiven us on account of what He

---

45 *Christians' belief that deviant sexual behavior is especially insidious and dangerous is a reflection of the nearly 2000 year-old words of the apostle Paul in his First Letter to the Corinthians, chapter 6, verse 18: "Flee from sexual immorality. All other sins a person commits are outside the body, but whoever sins sexually sins against their own body." Sexual gratification is not only an extremely powerful and highly-addictive "drug", it is one which all normally-functioning human-beings always have easy access to.*

has done for us through The Eternal Son of God, Jesus Christ.

Christians' interactions with LGBTQ people should be very much like what the Jack Nicholson character did for the Greg Kinnear character in the film, "As Good As It Gets". (Spoiler alert) In the film Nicholson's character was initially very strongly (and quite colorfully!) against his homosexual neighbor's lifestyle. But he eventually came to his assistance when his neighbor's life went into crisis. What ensued was the development of a wonderful friendship, an excellent example of brotherly love. Sadly, this is a rarely-found and rarely-appreciated thing these days.

A Christian who really believes what the Bible says would not be able to affirm his neighbor's sexual inclination in the way Nicholson's character did at the end of the film. This is because we wouldn't want to encourage him to continue on a path which we consider as leading only to misery and harm both to him and to others in the long run. But other than this, what the Jack Nicholson character did to help his neighbor was a great example of the love that Christians should show to others. And this should not be conditioned on whether or not the other person we are helping ever comes over to our side. After all, both the Old Testament and New Testament say that we must always love our neighbors as ourselves. And Jesus said that we must do so even when our neighbors are our enemies.

You who would condemn Christians because we won't affirm the choices that LGBTQ people make are, in effect, demanding that Christians agree with your point-of-view or shut-up or be penalized. This is just as wrong as when Christians have tried to do this to others in the past. We desperately need to rediscover the original meaning of tolerance. It is the attitude reflected in a popular line from a biography of the French philosopher Voltaire: "I strongly disagree with what you say, but will defend to the death your right to say it."

Sadly, the concept of tolerance has been turned into its opposite in many circles today. Instead of allowing and protecting what is deemed offensive, tolerance is now commonly understood as to refrain from and restrain others from expressing anything which might be deemed as offensive by another individual or group. This is truly intolerance in the name of tolerance.[46]

Today's false understanding of tolerance simply doesn't work in practice and inevitably leads to hypocrisy in which only certain views are considered acceptable. This is seen more and more every day with the so-called "political correctness" which is prized by many progressive Humanists. But freedom will not survive unless we all return to revering true tolerance.

This is not only a problem on the Humanist side. Christians have often been guilty of intolerance, both in the past and still today. We must always strive to allow people the freedom to do, say and think whatever they wish so long as doing so does not take away the freedom of others to do the same or as long as it doesn't demonstrably harm others. This is why laws against what consenting adults do in private, like anti-sodomy laws, are inappropriate. But so are laws or court rulings requiring Christians to cater to same-sex weddings or forbidding Christians from counseling willing children and adults who wish to overcome unwanted sexual or trans-sexual inclinations (or so-called "change therapy").

Same-sex marriages are a tough area, though. There really is no middle-ground here. Either these marriages will be accepted by our culture as equally-legitimate to heterosexual ones or not. In either case, one side will lose and suffer for it. This ought to be recognized by both sides. Conservative Christians, who believe these are not legitimate unions must accept the fact that we may lose this debate. If so, we must accept what happens as "of the Lord" (that is, according to God's ever-wise Plan) regardless of whatever hardships this may mean for us. And we should also

---

46 *This theme has been developed in a number of recent books, including D.A. Carson's "The Intolerance of Tolerance" and Kirsten Powers' "The Silencing: How the Left is Killing Free Speech". Powers identifies herself as a liberal, but one who has become concerned with increasingly illiberal tendencies of the political Left.*

be sensitive to the frustrations which those on the other side of the issue would endure if our side were to win in this conflict.

Furthermore, even if we should lose in this conflict, Christians should not become rebels against the authorities, but are called to remain true to our consciences, come what may. So we will at times be called upon to become conscientious objectors who will say what the apostle Peter once said to the Jewish authorities when they forbid him and the other disciples from preaching or teaching in the name of Jesus Christ: "Judge for yourselves whether it is right for us to obey God or man."

Part 2

As with assembling jigsaw puzzles, having the wrong Big Picture always leads to countless other mistakes. This is especially the case with mental-health issues.

One example is today's common practice of treating alcoholism or other substance-abuse as diseases of the body, rather than as behavioral disorders which cause destruction to the body. Even a spiritually-based program like Alcoholics' Anonymous has come to accept the "disease-model" of alcoholism. But in doing so AA has rejected the body and soul Dualism, which was part of its original Christian foundation and has embraced today's dominant (but faulty) Materialist view.

As we have already seen, a fatal flaw with the Materialist view of Humanists is that it denies the reality of choice.[47] So, to be consistent with this view all behavior would have to be regarded as being determined only by our physiology and the mindless forces that govern it. Of course, there are certainly many real diseases due to problems with the function of our bodies, which are not brought on by any choices that we make. (However, even with real physiological diseases, our choices often have a significant effect on whether or not there is healing.) But, with alcoholism or other substance-abuse it is clear that the main problem is one of behavioral choices.

Even if it is the case that some people are genetically pre-disposed to

---

[47] *Some Materialists do recognize that there is a serious problem in explaining how real human freedom and choice can exist in a universe governed only by mindless and unvarying laws of nature. Accordingly, it has been suggested that choice is accounted for by the uncertainties of Quantum Mechanics. This is clever, but it is also an argument from ignorance because no one has even begun to explain how this could work. Nor is it clear if this is even possible. Besides, this suggestion would still do nothing to eliminate many other problems with the matter-only view shown here.*

alcoholism, such people would still not become alchoholics if they simply refused to start drinking. And it's simply absurd to claim that it is ever physically necessary for anyone to do this. To deny or underemphasize this is to do a huge disservice to people struggling with substance-abuse issues.[48]

The role of choice is also dangerously under-estimated (if not denied altogether) in other areas of mental-health treatment. Depression used to be treated as mainly a cognitive disorder. But today it is treated primarily as a problem with our brain-chemistry, with medication being considered the primary need.

But an integrated body and soul (or mind and body) approach takes into account the inter-relationship of our minds and our brains. It recognizes that our repeated choices actually "re-wire" our brains constantly, as we are increasingly able to see with today's steady advances in neurological studies. This includes our choices of actions and also what we choose to think about and how we choose to think about these things. We can either choose to think and act in ways that promote health or in ways that are self-destructive.

It is probably not possible to heal other parts of our bodies by what we think (not directly, at least). But it is becoming increasingly clear that we can extensively control and, perhaps, heal our brains in this way. Furthermore, it should also be clear that having a proper attitude helps with most any human problem, even real physiological ones!

Today's approach to so-called "eating disorders" is another example of how the role of our choices has been foolishly and destructively minimized or even denied altogether due to the almost-universal embrace of the disease model, a model which is based on the false Materialist notion that we are

---

48 *It will always be questionable whether tendencies to alcoholism, depression, suicide or other mental/behavioral issues in families are a matter of nature (real genetic factors) or nurture (or learned behavior). The identification of genetic markers doesn't determine that it's nature rather than nurture. There would still be the question: "Which came first, the chicken or the egg?"*

just machines.[49] It is not our brains that make us eat too much or eat too little or eat unhealthy things! Rather, if we have these inclinations it can be seen that they are patterns of behavior which have been established as a result of repeated real choices we have made. Such repeated choices do change our brains over time. But it is the choices that are both the start of the pathology and also what keep it going.

But contrary to what most of us today have been taught, this is good news! What we have done to ourselves can also be un-done. And, in many cases, we don't need "med's". What we mainly need is a commitment to making healthy choices instead of unhealthy ones. Medication is sometimes helpful in this, but it should only be used (on a temporary basis) if it is clear that people are unable to change on their own.

This will no doubt seem both overly simplistic and harsh to many today, after decades of contrary claims by so-called "experts". But the truth of this assessment really can't be refuted. And in our hearts we actually know that these things are true. No one doubts that we can change our physiques if we decide to start working-out. But it is now possible to observe that we can change our brains, too, by the choices that we make. It has even been said that the brain is like a muscle. If so, then our brain is our most important muscle. And like our other muscles we can re-train them to work better for us.[50]

Another good example of the problem is "Panic Disorder". Until recently "panic attacks" or anxiety attacks were viewed as a psychological problem

---

49 *Even the name "eating disorder" itself shows the tendency to view the problem as a physical disorder, which should be treated with medication. Another term commonly used for the same purpose is to call a problem a "syndrome". The proliferation of "disorders" and "syndromes" these days is quite troubling, as it reflects an increasing tendency to deny the role of choice for our actions and the responsibility which comes from this.*

50 *We will discuss the relationship of us and our brains further in the next chapter. It's another area in which there is an amazing amount of basic confusion today.*

and treated using cognitive behavioral techniques. There is no question that stress has many negative long-term effects on our bodies (including our brain-chemistry). But it is a serious error to see it as originating in our bodies. Stress in our lives is clearly something we have a lot of control over with the choices that we can make, whether it's in how we respond to situations or in making conscious efforts to change our circumstances.

And the same problem tendency can be seen in many other areas of mental-health, from ADD/ADHD to OCD to PTSD to Bi-polar Disorder to Chronic Fatigue Syndrome and, even, to more extreme forms of mental-health problems, like Autism, Border-line Personality Disorder, Schizophrenia and Dissociative Identity Disorder (multiple personalities). There are certainly people who are afflicted by real brain disorders which require physiological therapies (like medication or surgery). But even people in these situations will usually have a lot of control over their mental health by the choices which they make about their behavior and their thinking.

And the really good news is that many people diagnosed with mental-illness today either have nothing wrong with their brains, or, at least, nothing wrong with their brain-chemistry which can't be corrected by abandoning unhealthy patterns of thinking and behavior and adopting healthy ones. This points toward cognitive behavioral therapy as being preferable to treating people as powerless victims of a physiological malady.

There is no doubt that a lot of people will passionately oppose this approach, calling it overly simplistic and cruel. But you who would make this charge don't know that you are right. You just assume that you are based on biases which come from your worldview. And the charge of cruelty could also be made against those who would falsely deny simple ways in which people can help themselves recover and maintain mental-health.

It is also not surprising that many people today happily embrace the idea that they are victims of their brains, not of bad choices they have made. For a person to view their problems in this way would seem to take away the pressure and guilt that come with the sense that one is responsible (to some extent, at least) for these problems. It is certainly easier for someone to say: "There's something wrong with me. I'm sick." than to say: "I am doing something wrong. I need to change." But, if the former conclusion is incorrect, then the real issue will not be dealt with and any relief that one may experience will only be temporary at best.

There is no question that things have changed dramatically in the mental-health field over the past several decades. And not for the better in most cases. Most of these changes have been driven by Materialism and its view that we are only material beings. So it is believed that all of our problems are physiological problems requiring physiological therapies.

This is the reason why the use of anti-depressants and other mind-altering drugs has skyrocketed in the developed world over the past few decades. And this, in turn, also helps explain why suicide rates have increased alarmingly since 2000.

It is no exagerration to say that the Materialism philosophy actually encourages suicides (though it does not cause them, as should become clear in what follows). First, Materialism drives today's extensive use of medications which are known to produce thoughts of suicide as a side-effect. But, perhaps a bigger reason that Materialism encourages suicidal thinking is that it promotes the idea that we cease to exist when we die. And if this is what people believe, then it is understandable that many who feel overwhelmed by their circumstances may see it as a way out.

By contrast, in the past, when Christianity was the reigning worldview, suicide was seen as a sin and as an act which would deliver a person directly to God for judgment. Some Christians even believe that suicide is a direct ticket to Hell. But, even if it isn't, the spectre of being accountable to one's Creator at the end of our lives made it far less likely that people would ever consider taking their own lives.[51]

Sadly, people who identify as LGBTQ or who secretly struggle with same-sex attractions or confusion regarding their gender also have significantly higher suicide-rates (along with higher rates of depression and, thus, higher usage of anti-depressants and other mind-altering drugs, as well as abuse of such). While the pro-LGBTQ side blames suicides on those who don't support these alternative forms of sexuality, this is unlikely. For, the rate continues to increase despite that fact that there is more support for LGBTQ people in most of the developed world today than ever before. Indeed, those who do not want to support these practices are increasingly punished for this.[52]

Another common tendency today is to blame others for suicides. But this also shows a fundamental misunderstanding of the role of choice in human

---

51 *The disorienting effects of psychotropic medications is probably why even professing Christians sometimes resort to suicide. However, it's likely that many people who kill themselves while under the influence of medications (whether prescribed or not) are not really suicides but cases of accidental self-induced deaths. And it's worth noting that while Christians believe that we will go to Heaven when we die, we believe it would be wrong for us to "punch our own ticket" there, mainly because of how it would devastate those who know and love us.*

52 *Instead of blaming Christians and other traditionalists LGBTQ advocates would do well to consider the possibility that a lot of LGBTQ people, especially many young people, are committing suicide because of despair caused by strong and mixed messages they get both from the world around them and from inside them, in the "world" of their thoughts. Shame and guilt over sexuality and other sinful behavior comes from inside us from our consciences, not just from others.*

It is not hard to see how societal pressure to follow one's same-sex or transgender inclinations, combined with inward sexual desires which are naturally strong can drive people, especially young people, to despair and, even, to suicide when these pressures are in tension with what their consciences are telling them. This is also more likely if one has become convinced that suicide would be a permanent escape from their troubles.

behavior. Indeed, circumstances or medications can sometimes cause people to contemplate suicide. But it is a gross error to say that such things cause suicides. This is because suicide, insofar as it is a deliberate act, is actually the ultimate personal decision that a person can make. (This assumes that the person who does this is not in a state of extreme disorientation either from drugs or from a real brain dysfunction. For, people who kill themselves in these cases are probably cases of accidental self-induced deaths, not suicides.)

In order to see why this is the case, consider this: Even if someone held a loaded gun to the head of a person threatening suicide and demanded that the person pull the trigger (as in a scene from the first "Lethal Weapon" film) it would still always be that person's choice as to whether or not they would do so. Not that I am recommending this for people who are threatening to commit suicide! For doing this would clearly be tempting someone to commit a huge sin, which is a sin in itself.[53]

It is true that others may contribute to circumstances which lead people to kill themselves (and may even be legally culpable for this in some cases). But no one else actually causes someone to commit suicide (or accidentally kill himself or herself) except the person who does it. Suicide is the ultimate personal choice. Indeed, this is one of the reasons expressed by many people who have considered doing this or actually attempted it for why it is appealing to them. This is especially the case with people who have been victims of abuse or who feel that they have no control over their lives for other reasons. But, while suicide is the ultimate personal choice, it is also the choice to end all choices in this world, no matter what you believe about what happens to us when we die.

---

53 *This also shows the dubious nature of so-called "assisted-suicide". It is clearly not equivalent to murder, but is certainly a case of aiding and abetting an act that is questionable at best, even in cases of extreme pain. How does a person in great pain know that they don't need to endure it for their own benefit and/or that of others?*

It is natural and often correct for people to feel guilty that they didn't do enough to help people who end up killing themselves. After all, we could all do more for those around us. But to be considered the cause of someone doing this is just wrong! This is truly a grotesque case of adding insult to the injury which results when someone kills himself or herself. (And insofar as there is legal prosecution for this it adds significant further injury to that caused by the death.)

Furthermore, those who would kill themselves act against our fundamental instinct for self-preservation. This is why some will even say that suicide is therefore a courageous act. But this is a totally perverse twisting of the concept of courage! For, except for cases of disorientation due to the effects of drugs or true cases of physiological mental-illness, intentional suicide is actually the most selfish and cowardly thing that a person can do. Apart from these exceptions, a person who commits suicide essentially says: "I don't want to deal with the world anymore, so I am going to take my ball and go home permanently! I don't care what effect this will have on others."

Suicide is surely the cruelest thing that one could ever do to those who care about the person who does it. And no matter how isolated a person may think they are, there is no one on earth who literally has no one who cares about them. They just haven't given others the opportunity to show that they care. Besides, God always cares.

We badly need a revival of the Christian stigma against suicide. But such will only come with a revival of Christianity itself, as multitudes reject Materialist Humanism and other faulty approaches to life and turn back to their Creator, The One True God (Whom we all know is real) and let Him become their Father, Savior and Lord.[54]

---

54 *The impact of worldviews on suicide is seen in the fact that it has always been considered acceptable in many Asian cultures (for example, with the Hari Kari practice of Japanese tradition) and is even seen as heroic among extreme jihadist Muslims today, with their perverse twist on "martyrdom". Though Christians do commit suicide at times, Christianity has no parallels*

Recent and dramatic changes in perspectives on mental-health and human behavior are also seen in the area of sexuality. Until about 3 decades ago the dominant view of mental-health professionals was that all forms of deviant sexual behavior were psychological/spiritual problems, especially if they became obsessive and "life-dominating". Of course, such a view is vigorously rejected in today's culture, in which homosexuality and many other "alternative" types of sexuality and even desires to change one's gender are now considered normal, healthy and unchangeable. This, too, is consistent with Materialism's disastrous denial of the role of our choices and the false belief that all of our behavior is physiologically-driven.[55]

But the stunningly simple truth about sexuality is that it is always learned behavior, either learned normally (in monogamous heterosexual relationships) or not (in any other way in which sexual pleasure is sought). Once again, this notion will be strongly opposed by most today. But once

---

with these traditions.

Indeed, nothing could be more contrary to suicide than Christian martyrdom. For it is based on the Bible's call to love our neighbors so much that we would be willing to give our lives in order to save them, just as we believe God did for us through His Son Jesus. It was this that led early Christians to be willing to risk their lives, and in some cases sacrifice them to care for victims of plague. But Muslim "martyrs" take their lives not to save others but to kill them.

55 *Of course, some forms of sexuality are still considered wrong, including pedophilia and other types of sexual exploitation. However, the reason for the distinctions are unclear. Clearly pedophilia and some other forms are problematic because there is no mutual consent. But do we really want to say that these are unchangeable?*

And if one says that all acts of mutual consent by adults are legitimate, then prostitution, incest, adultery and dangerous forms of sexual gratification would have to be considered normal, healthy and unchangeable. An example of the latter is that which caused the death of actor David Carradine: seeking sexual pleasure through asphyxiation. This type of "alternative sexuality" was also featured in the 1993 film "Rising Sun".

again this only shows the enormous blinding power of today's reigning, but faulty worldview: Humanism. In this case, allegiance to Humanism keeps millions from seeing what would actually be very easy to see if you are simply willing to stop and think about it. Just a little bit of reflection on your past should reveal that you had to learn how to get sexual satisfaction in whatever way or ways that seemed to work best for you.

It is true that the start of one's pattern of sexuality may not be a choice in many cases (as in cases of sexual-abuse or accidental circumstances). But it is always repeated subsequent choices which establish the pattern (or "tendency", "inclination or "orientation") by which one achieves satisfaction. And, as with other maladies discussed previously, these patterns are changeable if people are just willing to commit to making different choices.

That sexual orientations are changeable is shown by the fact that virtually all men and many women go from masturbation to relations with others as the normal pattern of sexual development. It only takes a little reflection to realize that this is clearly a major change in orientation! And it is one which involves a learning process. Besides, it is also undeniable that many people (including all physically normal women) are able to have relations with both sexes. But many simply _prefer_ doing so with those of their own sex.

Unlike real diseases, which originate in malfunctions of our bodies, all of the problems we have looked at are not determined by our physiology! Of course, people who have a strict Materialist/Physicalist view will claim that they are. This is because they believe that everything is determined by mindless forces of nature acting on matter-energy in space-time.

But the truth is that none of them can actually live as though this is the case. To do so would be impossible. For we all know that we have many real choices to make everyday. And we know that they are meaningful choices, which will either help us or hurt us. But this is only true because Materialism is false.

In the end, it all comes down to our responsibility as human-beings. We all face countless choices in life, many of which are moral choices. With these choices we can either choose rightly or wrongly. But the choices are always <u>our</u> choices. So, to blame what happens to us on others (either people we know or just society in general) or on physiological factors over which we supposedly have no control, as so many do today, is both wrong and self-destructive.

Of course there is always much which is beyond our control. But even with these things we always have the choice in how we will view and react to the things which are out of our control. And The Most Important Choice that all of us have is whether or not we will accept that we have a Creator and Lord. If we accept this then we can know His love and find peace in the knowledge that He is in control of everything. Contrary to what many claim, this is the only way to find complete and permanent peace.

How far will all of these troubling trends of Materialism go? It's telling and quite chilling that religious beliefs and other forms of political dissent came to be viewed as mental illness in the former Soviet Union and they were "treated" with drugs and other extreme measures. George Orwell's fictional account in "1984" reflected what was actually happening behind the "iron-curtain" that divided the Soviet-dominated part of the world from "the free world". (And if you have any doubt that the rest of the world was free compared to those countries dominated by the U.S.S.R. then you need to talk to a few people who escaped from the Soviet empire. And no nation was freer than the United States.)

Today, advocates of the so-called "New Atheism" and other radical secularists openly express Sigmund Freud, Friedrich Nietzche and Karl Marx's belief that religious belief is a mental-illness which needs to be eradicated. It is important to recognize that this is one of many instances in which Humanists ironically and hypocritically seek to delegitimize the beliefs of Christians and others on the basis of their own unprovable beliefs.

But this just reflects the fact that today's "culture war" is precisely a clash of worldviews/philosophies/belief-systems/religions.

How could the views of society have changed so dramatically and quickly? It can be seen that this was a natural outcome of the shift in which the previously-dominant Christian worldview (or Judeo-Christian) had been replaced by Humanism. It was not so much that large numbers of people suddenly changed their view. Rather, what happened was that the Humanist narrative gradually became the dominant one, mainly due to the influence of the educational, media and entertainment establishments. And ever since this happened every subsequent generation has been indoctrinated for Humanism and against other views and, especially, against Christianity. And, after all, as we considered in the first chapter, people naturally tend to believe what they are told day-after-day.

Chapter 6
Humanism's Intellectual Problems

Contrary to those who claim it is a Science versus Religion conflict, the Evolution versus Creation debate is really a Big Picture debate. That is, it is a debate between worldviews: Humanism versus Christianity. And the worldview that one holds will also determine how one looks at climate-change and other aspects of the future of the planet, the solar system and the entire universe. This is not surprising, as these are both areas of historical Science, in which philosophical assumptions make enormous differences, as they also do with the human Sciences (but unlike those Sciences which study how Nature works now).

In the previous chapter we saw how one's worldview dramatically affects how one looks at a variety of issues involving human behavior. But the same is true with regard to the Science of Origins and of the future. Specifically, the question is: Do the origins and future destiny of the human-race, all life, the planet and the universe involve Intelligent influence, as believers in Creation (or Intelligent Design) say, or not, as Evolution-advocates claim?

As with the study of the past, what will happen in the future hinges on whether or not there is an Intelligent influence (or influences) on the cosmic level. In fact, it would not be an exaggeration to say that in the areas of historical and human studies the research is mainly driven by models based on philosophical assumptions. And, today, all research done in mainstream scientific circles is driven by the assumption of anti-theistic Materialism/Naturalism (part of the comprehensive approach of Humanism).

A number of fatal flaws with the philosophy and methods underlying the evolutionary approach will be discussed subsequently. But first, an easy way to see the effect of one's worldview with climate-change is to consider that many climate-change activists fear that humanity may bring about our own extinction due to how we treat the planet. This also shows the connection between climate-change fears and belief in Evolution. We have previously seen how fear of extinction is in tension with the evolutionary claim that extinction is natural and, as such, is neither good nor evil.

But such a fear doesn't exist for those who believe there is a Creator ruling over the universe. This is because we see the destiny both of ourselves and the human race, along with that of the entire universe as being in His hands. (Figuratively speaking, of course!)

And while it would be theoretically possible that an over-ruling Intelligence could allow humanity to disappear, Christians believe that God has revealed that He will never do this. Actually, the Biblical view is that the human race as we now know it WILL eventually disappear, but by way of transformation into one form or another (either glorious or hellish) for everyone who has ever lived. From a Christian perspective it's God Who will determine humanity's ultimate destiny and also when and how the end of the world comes.[56]

It is quite easy to see that cosmic "Big-bang" evolution is built on and driven by the assumption that there is no over-arching Intelligence Who designed and brought the universe into existence. This includes the emergence of life. The evolutionary approach to the origin of life is simply part of the comprehensive anti-Creation/anti-Creator philosophy of Materialism, which, in turn, is part of the Humanism philosophy. In other words, biological evolution is based on cosmic evolution.

Most on the pro-Evolution side vigorously resist that the Evolution versus Creation debate is really a debate over worldviews because they wish to make the issue one of Science over supposedly obsolete religious

---

[56] *The same is true for the Muslim and traditional Jewish perspective, despite the fact that these have a false conception of God in ways which we will consider in chapter 9.*

superstition. But Christianity and Creationism/Intelligent-design has always been entirely compatible with the practice of the scientific method, though not with the philosophical presuppositions of most scientists today. In fact, until the "Darwinian revolution" triumphed in the last century most scientists held Christian or, at least, Theistic or Deistic beliefs.

So the real question here is the same one we began with: Which Philosophy/belief-system/worldview/religion (pick whichever term you prefer) is correct: Christianity or Humanism? Sadly, even many Bible-believing Christians fail to see that this is the real issue.

We have already looked at a number of problems with Materialism and Humanism, which Christianity does not have. Another big one is that the Materialism approach has a subject/object problem. Since Materialism assumes that reality consists only of material objects along with mindless forces in space-time, those who hold to this view must deny that subjects really exist in themselves.

Instead, the Materialist will claim that all subjectivity is reducible to objectivity; that is, to observable phenomena of matter. But, as was previously pointed out, this assumption is itself based on a largely-hidden and logically-false assumption that since Science has proven to be the proper way to study the physical world, then this world must be all that exists.

Aside from being based on a logical fallacy, the attempt by believers in Materialism to reduce all subjectivity to objectivity clearly reduces to absurdity. This can be seen if we look at things from the broadest possible perspective. Materialism has an empty universe problem in that it essentially says that the universe is composed only of observable objects without any observing and knowing subjects. Even though we appear to be distinct from what we observe, it is claimed that the distinction isn't real.

But, amazingly, if this were true, then the priority of many Astronomers and others to try to find life elsewhere in the universe so that we can know that we are not alone in the universe would be a rather pointless task. This is not because of the impossibility of finding out if there is anyone else out there. It is because WE don't even really exist! We are nothing more than fleeting illusions of matter and mindless forces.

And if we look at things on the level of individual experience, to say that consciousness is only "brain-chemistry viewing itself" is pure nonsense! It is a non-explanation which only explains away consciousness, along with everything associated with it (including perception, language, logic, reason, information, knowledge, emotions and memory). In order to see the problem, consider the following.

Neuroscience is the study of brain chemistry. But to say that everything is just brain-chemistry would necessarily include neuroscience. Thus, neuroscience itself would only be brain-chemistry. This is clearly absurd. For, any type of study requires two things: students and that which is studied. Materialists can't answer this simple question: Who is studying the brain-chemistry? (We will return to the problem of consciousness shortly.)

So it is clear that the view which says that reality consists only of physical objects has serious flaws. Moreover, these flaws cannot possibly be overcome. Consciousness and all that it entails is not just a "gap" in our understanding which Science just has not yet filled in (as many claim). Science will never be able to explore this side of reality. This is because Science, by its nature, can only study objects. And the subject side of reality (that is, us and all of our experience) is something that undeniably exists. Indeed, we are often deceived about many things. But no one can reasonably claim that "I don't really exist."

All observation and knowledge requires two types of things: that which is observed and known and observers and knowers of these things. This is the case whether we are talking about the physical world, including our bodies and the world around us or about countless other things that we know which are not found in the physical world.

Even the knowledge that we have of the physical world is not itself a part of the physical world. For example, tables exist in the physical world outside of us. But our knowledge of tables is not outside of us. It is inside of us. This brings us to another major fallacy with the Materialism philosophy: If ultimate reality consists only of mindless forces, then how can the existence of minds, along with perception, logic, reason, information and knowledge be explained?

At this point, it will be helpful to take a very brief look at Philosophy. (I promise it will be very brief and not at all difficult!) It can be said that the history of critical thinking (which is the heart of what Philosophy is about) has been one of an ongoing rivalry between two camps: Materialists and Idealists. Of course, we have already discussed the Materialist approach. Materialists are those who view matter as the starting-point, if not the entire story. Idealists, on the other hand, see the human mind as the starting-point, if not the entire story.

There are two "places" we can begin from in our quest for knowledge. We can begin with what's inside our heads (that is, with how our thinking works). This is the Idealist approach. Or we can begin with what's outside of us (or, as an Idealist might say, what seems to be outside of us), the Materialist starting-point. Rene Descartes' famous statement: "I think, therefore I am." is the classic expression of the Idealist starting-point. A great expression of the Materialist approach is the statement Carl Sagan makes at the beginning of his "Cosmos" mini-series: "The Cosmos is all there is and all there was and all there ever will be." And the Cosmos is understood as being only matter-energy and mindless forces in space-time.

But over the past 200 years or so Idealism has become almost completely vanquished by a dominant Materialist approach, so much so that the Materialist claim that reality is ultimately reducible to matter-energy and mindless forces in space-time is just assumed to be true by most today. But, as Idealists have always asked: How does one explain our minds and all that they do?

One simply can't have a view of reality which says that it is ultimately mindless without either ignoring the existence of our minds, which is obviously wrong, or quietly smuggling them in at some point, thereby contradicting the mindless forces-only restriction. To put the problem another way: How does one go from a mindless reality of objects to the "world" (so to speak) of minds? This is a Big and unsolvable Problem for Materialism.

But both Materialists and Christian Theists will point out that non-theistic Idealists have a Big Problem of their own: namely, in trying to establish beyond reasonable doubt that our thoughts accurately reflect the world around us. In other words, if one starts with what's inside our heads (so to speak), then how does one get outside of this to the outside world? After all, it could be the case that we have all been deceived, either by some higher power (*a la* the film, "The Matrix") or just self-delusion that the world around us is as it appears to be.[57]

---

57 *The Christian perspective is that God designed us so that we would be able to accurately observe and know the world as it is (though not comprehensively, as He can). But ever since our first parents rebelled against God, all of us have been born with a distorted perspective because we all inherit the rebellious nature of our predecessors. This rebelliousness causes us to gravitate to false worldviews (or "matrices", if you will) which actually prevent us from seeing God, ourselves, other people and the world around us properly. But God will help us to throw away these false perspectives if we are willing.*

At the same time, in order to be at all functional and credible, all alternative worldviews must allow a great deal of "the real world" to get through to us. So we cannot be as completely deceived as those who are under the spell of the Matrix from the film of the same name. This is because, whether one wishes to admit it or not, we all must live in the world which the Creator God made. So, alternative worldviews will allow what can reasonably be accepted without the need to acknowledge God, but will distort what tends to lead one in this direction and block whatever clearly points to the Creator.

Indeed, the latter is essentially what most Materialists claim. But, as was pointed out earlier, no one really believes this in practice. In order to function in our daily lives we must assume that our perceptions about the world around us are accurate most of the time. Besides, as was also pointed out previously, there is still the problem of explaining how we can exist as subjects of the supposed illusion.

But Christian Theism has a simple and satisfactory answer to both of these Big and otherwise unsolvable Problems: That with the eternal existence of The Triune Creator God, God's Mind existed before any matter. But God created us as beings who are both material and have minds reflecting God's own Eternal Mind, which are able to understand the rest of God's Creation, including both the material world and other minds, "thinking God's thoughts after Him", as the famous astronomer Johannes Kepler put it.

Returning to the subject of human consciousness, many, if not most neuroscientists today believe the Materialism Big Picture (that matter-energy governed by mindless forces of nature in space-time are all that exists). This, in turn, leads most of them to conclude that our brains and our minds (that is, our consciousness) are one and the same. In other words, "I" am just a product of chemical processes in my brain. If so, then consciousness is merely my brain-chemistry observing itself.

But, again, this is not an explanation. It is just an explaining away of the entire subjective side of reality. So it is that allegiance to a faulty Big Picture causes many of the most intelligent people alive today (even Nobel Prize-winning neuroscientists) to miss what a small child easily and correctly grasps: that "I am not my brain. Rather, I _have_ a body, which includes my brain." Instead, massive amounts of money are devoted to research based on the notion that "you" and "I" are just expressions of brain-chemistry.

The next major problem with the Materialist approach is that it can't explain the two-way causality that we find between brain-chemistry & consciousness.

There has been spirited debate in neuroscientific circles in recent years about the basic nature of consciousness. Some claim that it is just another "emergent" phenomenon or property of matter, part of the physiology of our brains. Others say it is something other than a material phenomenon. But what really can't be disputed is that consciousness can't be only neurochemistry which we can observe in our brains. Why is this?

First, for the reason already cited: that we necessarily speak of these as distinct things. It is often possible to speak of one thing in different ways. But this is clearly not the case with consciousness and brain-chemistry. Thoughts that we have (whatever they are) may be seen to be associated with changes in our brain chemistry, but they are clearly a different type of thing altogether than the chemical changes which we observe.

Secondly, our consciousness and brain chemistry can't be one and the same thing because we observe cause and effect going between them. A cause and effect relationship can't exist unless there are at least two separate things to begin with, or one thing (namely, a cause) which produces something else (an effect).

Some who grant that brain-chemistry actually does produce something else assume that the cause and effect only moves from the brain to consciousness. But this disregards obvious cases where the movement is in the opposite direction. The most obvious example is when one chooses to drink alcohol or use other "mind-altering" drugs. And, as we are increasingly able to map the electrochemical activity of our brains, we are increasingly seeing how we change our brain-chemistry just by deliberately thinking certain things.

Advanced prosthetic work today is successfully retracing the paths of neuron activity going from deliberate thoughts about moving limbs to the actual moving of such limbs. By linking artificial limbs into these pathways we are starting to be able to recreate natural movement with artificial limbs. In other words, one can move an artificial limb directly by our thoughts. Until these recent advances, artificial limbs could only be moved indirectly when people moved the parts of their bodies connected to them.

The point of all of this is that it is showing how we interact with our bodies. I would mention again that this necessarily entails that two different things are in play: us and our bodies. And we recognize in this case also that the direction is from conscious thought to changes in our brains to changes in the rest of our bodies. (As with choosing to drink too much alcohol!)

It has long been recognized that changes in our brain-chemistry produce changes in our consciousness. Though the actual chemistry was not understood until much later, this was actually discovered the first time people realized that they could become inebriated by drinking (or, perhaps, eating) certain things. But, even in this case, is this really a case of brain chemistry determining consciousness? Actually, no. Rather, the process begins with deliberate choices which alter brain-chemistry, which, in turn, alter consciousness.

Another problem for those who claim that our consciousness is merely the result of our brain-chemistry is the fact that our sense of self-identity is continuous over the course of our lives (except, of course, for rare cases of complete amnesia or extreme cases of Dissociative Identity Disorder). But, it is now known that our cells, including our brain cells, are constantly changing, with old ones dying and new ones being formed at such a high rate that our cells are completely changed over the course of about 7 years. So if I am just the product of the chemistry of these cells, then how can I be the same me as I was in the past if my cells are a completely different set of cells than I had previously?[58]

---

58   *This argument is found in Paul Copan's 2005 book "How Do You Know You're Not Wrong?", pp. 108-110.*

There must be something to our identity besides what our cells determine, which provides continuity of our sense of identity. I am not the same person as I was years ago, but I wasn't someone else altogether. I was still me!

Are we merely determined by the chemistry of our brains? Clearly, the answer is: No! We are active in determining the chemistry of our brains in many ways. We do so not only by repeated choices in what we introduce into our bodies, but even in the patterns of our thinking. Neuroscience is increasingly showing that we have a lot of control over the condition of our brains, being able to "wire" or "re-wire" them one way or another, either in destructive ways, as in patterns of addictive behavior or other mental-health pathologies, or in constructive ways, as in examples of successful cognitive behavioral therapy.

All of this is not to say that there aren't many neurological conditions over which we have no control. But we are seeing more and more that we have a great deal of control over our own brains. And also over the minds and brains of others.

A great example of the latter is the increasing body of evidence pointing to the fact that the development of childrens' brains is measurably improved through social interaction. In recent years California has had a public-service campaign called "First Five" in which it encourages parents to talk to, read to and sing to their children from their earliest days of infancy. This is because it has been shown that this is beneficial for brain development, about 80% of which has been found to occur in the first five years of life.

And while a lot of study has been devoted to learning how this works, the question that is rarely asked is this: Why does this work? Clearly, for children to just hear sounds is not sufficient. What they benefit from is speech. But, amazingly, the Materialist view really can't even explain why some sounds convey information (speech) while others (noise or purely instrumental music) don't.

All of this shows the inadequacy of the Materialist conception. We are not our brains. Rather, we have brains, which are the central controllers of the rest of our bodies. It is accurate to say that our brains are computers, which control the rest of our bodies and also control other functions, like perception and memory. But these computers do not have intelligence in themselves. No, both computers which we construct and our brains are vehicles for our intelligence. In the case of actual computers we are also the designers and assemblers of them, as well as the instructors. But information and intelligence aren't observable phenomena in the material world. So, again, there must be more to reality than this.

This brings us to the concept of "artificial intelligence". Computers which we construct will never be anything more than what we make them precisely because they are not what we are: they are only machines. Indeed, we do have machine-like bodies (including our brains). But this is not all that we are.

Unlike us, computers will never be able to become conscious and "think" (or "make up their own minds"). No matter how sophisticated we may be able to make them, they will only be able to respond according to the ways which we have designed and programmed them to respond. This is so no matter how much it might seem otherwise at times with today's extremely sophisticated hardware and programming.

It is accurate to say that computers and other machines have intelligence. But it is only the intelligence which we program into them. Despite all of the scientists and science-fiction novels, films and shows predicting this, no devices which we create will ever have minds of their own. We simply don't have the power to create minds. (Sorry science-fiction fans!)[59]

---

59 *Once again, the correct analogy to computers is not me, myself, it's my physical brain. My brain is indeed a biochemical computer of immense sophistication. But it is a computer which God has given me as a non-physical person, along with the rest of my physical body, so that I can*

The limitations of the machines which we build and program are beginning to be realized with the challenges of self-driving vehicles. It has been shown that such vehicles can function well in a very large number of situations, indeed, probably better than many drivers (as many drivers either have not been well-instructed or just develop bad habits and make many bad decisions). But a machine will never be able to react perfectly to everything that we do on the road. We are just too unpredictable precisely because we have minds of our own and truly can make things up, or create as we go along, either for better or worse. This creativity will allow a human driver to act and react in ways a machine never would.[60]

In general, we as human-beings have the ability to make too many choices to enable us to completely replicate them. This can be seen in the area of facial expressions. While it is true that great progress has been made in creating robots that move like us, not as much progress has been made in replicating our facial expressions. This is because we essentially have limitless options in how we can move our facial muscles. A simulation can only reproduce a limited number of these.[61]

---

interact with the physical world which He has made and also with Him and other minds as a psycho-physical being. So my brain is a tool which, like computers and the other tools that we make, I can use constructively and productively or destructively.

60 *It is commonly assumed today that we can teach machines to think by programming them with so-called "self-learning algorithms". But these are merely specialized instructions allowing machines to react to more possible contingencies and to record these reactions for future replication. No self-reflection and actual decision-making at all is entailed in this. The machine is merely executing its programming. And isn't self-reflection and conscious decision-making the essence of real thinking? Once again we come back to the uniqueness of choice in human experience.*

61 *Attempting to replicate a human-being involves the same challenge faced in reproducing music digitally (but to a far more extreme degree). In digital recording, an analog-to-digital converter functions by "taking pictures" of the electromagnetic waves of sound at various intervals in time. The more frequent these pictures are taken (which is the sampling-rate) and the more*

Not only are computers unlike us because they don't have minds, animals also may just be extremely complex machines. While we often project thought and personality onto them (especially those which have been domesticated or are considered to be more intelligent), it may be that this is just an illusion and that animals are just mindlessly responding to outside circumstances according to their genetic programming. (My apologies to all of you pet-lovers!)[62]

---

detailed each of these pictures are (which is determined by the number of bits that are employed to describe the sound, similar to how a camera which is able to convert an image into more bits will produce a more detailed image), the more accurately the original sound can be captured digitally, so that it can then be converted back to sound-waves by a digital-to-analog converter.

But, as is well known among audiophiles, a digital recording will never be able to capture all of the sound characteristics of a musical performance done by human-beings. There are two reasons for this. First, it is because such performances can only be captured at separate instants in time. No matter how much the sampling-rate is increased, there will always be unsampled intervals between the ones sampled. And, second, because there are actually an endless number of nuances and harmonics in such a performance. No matter how many bits we use to describe the sound, there will always be more details that we haven't described.

So, a musical performance is like a circle, while the digital reproduction of it is like trying to recreate the circle point-by-point. But, in reality, there are an endless number of points in the circle. No matter how many points we capture, there will always be points in between which we haven't captured. This is also the case with countless other aspects of human behavior, as is especially evident in efforts to reproduce the endless nuances of our facial expressions. We are able to reproduce more and more, but we will never be able to capture and replicate all of them.

62 *The incredible sophistication and efficiency of the physiology of both man and beasts is being appreciated more and more across the scientific community. This is driving many scientists and others to at least begin to question that life really could have emerged without a Designer and designs. I am addressing mainly the philosophical problems with Evolution and the*

Some time ago there was a lot of excitement in scientific circles when it was thought that a Lowland Gorilla named Koko had successfully mastered sign-language so that she could now express what she was thinking. But these hopes faded quickly after there was an attempt to have a press conference with Koko. It quickly became clear that Koko could not express any real thinking. The most she could do was to associate certain terms with certain things, as dogs and many other animals can do.

If you think this experiment was a success you should ask yourself why it has never been replicated with other subjects. The scientific method requires that successful experiments be repeated. But this has not occurred with the Koko sign-language experiment because it failed.

Biological Evolution is based on the idea that all of the living things we observe today and find evidence for in the past emerged only from mindless natural forces operating on matter over a sufficiently long period of time (known as Natural Selection). But over the past several decades we have come to understand that even the simplest forms of life are far more complex than we previously thought.[63] This has driven the odds of such things emerging without a Designer and Engineer essentially to zero. Still, those who are adamantly against the idea of a Creator will say: "Anything's possible." But is it?

Materialism on which it is based. These should be seen to be fatal, thereby making it impossible that both are correct. But much good work is also being done by Intelligent Design scientists both in showing the extreme unlikeliness (actually the impossibility) that life could have emerged as the result of undirected forces and also in using design principles to "reverse-engineer" Nature. Some of the work of such scientists can be seen at AnswersinGenesis.org. Another great resource is the video documentary "Evolution's Achilles Heels".

63 *This even applies to single-cell organisms. But it is much more true of more complex forms of life. Consider even a common house fly. We are still very far away from designing an aircraft which can maneuver like it can.*

Believers in Natural Selection claim that if you get enough chimpanzees together and let them pound on keyboards then they will eventually produce novels. But this is not only highly unlikely, it is literally impossible. This is because writing requires understanding of language. This is why we must teach children to do this, but chimpanzees can't be taught this, nor can Lowland Gorillas or any other animal we know.

The fact that music can be randomly-generated leads some to believe that the same thing can be done with language. But the "language" of music does not communicate information in the way that real spoken and written languages do. Indeed, what may initially be considered noise can come to be recognized as music with repetition, as those who learn to play free-form compositions know. This is a matter of recognizing the pattern of the notes because they have been composed in a certain way. So, what appears to be random can be seen as having an order. In other words, it wasn't really random at all. It was composed.

Of course, an orchestra can just play randomly. But in this case it will never produce anything recognizable unless what is played is captured and scored so that it can be reproduced, again requiring deliberate intelligent actions.[64]

---

64 *Similarly, attempts by believers in Evolution to show how "irreducibly complex" systems could be formed without deliberate actions by intelligent agents tend to miss or obscure the role of their own intelligent input. Models which are proposed invariably involve tinkering with conditions so as to make the desired results more likely. But this "fine-tuning" is essentially a rigging of the game which contradicts the supposedly unguided aspect of these models.*

   The necessity of deliberate and intelligent activity in order to create or maintain ordered systems would be obvious to everyone if it weren't for the powerful influence of the Materialism worldview. Both the 2nd Law of Thermodynamics and the reality of Genetic Entropy do pose fundamental challenges to Natural Selection, no matter how much Evolution-defenders will protest otherwise. And protest is all they can do. This is because they can't really refute those who point out that these two principles contradict the faith of Evolution-believers that natural forces alone can create complex

While a musical piece will give listeners impressions, there is no real communication of information in it unless it has words arranged in coherent phrases. For language is not just arranging sounds in certain patterns. Nor is it merely recognizing the association of certain patterns of sounds with certain concepts or objects, as domesticated animals can do, with the aforementioned Koko merely being trained to add physical gestures to the association of words with objects or concepts. Rather, speech is the

---

systems from unorganized matter or maintain such systems.

There is an inescapable fundamental tension between Natural Selection and the other two theories, both of which recognize that in the absence of ordering input systems become less orderly, not more orderly. But one doesn't need to be a Scientist to know this. Anyone who fails to clean their house or apartment regularly can readily see that this is true!

And there are many other examples of this, like dental hygiene, landscape maintenance and maintenance of all sorts of vehicles and machines, which have obviously been designed and built by intelligent human-beings, and all sorts of medical procedures, which can often delay the breakdown of our bodies which eventually leads to death. Orderly environments and systems (whether they are organic or man-made) invariably become less orderly without deliberate efforts to keep this from happening.

It is true that natural forces do sometimes work together to create orderly systems (or, at least, this appears to be the case). The formation of storms and crystalline structures are examples of this. But the problem is that these and all such natural phenomena can't maintain their structure and eventually revert to a less orderly state. Furthermore, that even these phenomena occur due strictly to natural forces cannot be assumed.

It may be that storms, crystallization or other naturally-observed structures are strictly natural occurrences, occurring automatically as the result of the unfolding of natural forces. Many Christians agree with Materialists in this respect, seeing God as the Designer of a self-sustaining physical universe. Nevertheless, God being God, it remains possible that He is more intimately involved even in the realm of natural processes in fine-tuning the circumstances necessary both for the formation and maintenance of complex systems or in order to accomplish other desired outcomes. If not,

deliberate arranging of sounds which make specific connections with other things so as to convey information to others. And the only species we know which can do this is *homo sapiens*.

Despite the fact that these things are not hard to understand, there is no question that there is a great deal of resistance to this type of thinking. But why is this? As mentioned earlier, part of the reason is the simplicity of it in itself, tending to prompt the response: "It can't be that simple!".

But a bigger reason that most resist this kind of thinking is because of a strong fear of where it leads: namely, back to dreaded Christianity. This is the real Phobia which drives Humanism. And it is truly a phobia: a false fear. For, we are drowning in denial (as in the Egyptian river!) and we need to take hold of the Lifesaver which God holds out to us.[65]

Biblical injunctions to pray for rain or physical healing would seem to be superfluous.

Contrary to what many claim, this possibility wouldn't destroy the possibility of Science any more than the possibility of miracles. In either case, the existence of natural processes governed by natural forces and laws which we can understand is still presupposed.

65 *It has become common for defenders of the Materialist approach to try to carve out a place for consciousness as some sort of "emergent property" of matter or quantum mechanics. But, at best, this is an argument from silence which is offered in deliberate disregard of the perfectly-credible Dualism which is part of Christian Theism. (More on this a little later)*

It is not at all clear how such an emergent property could possibly be observed. For the "all objects, but no subjects" problem still comes into play. How could anyone exist to observe such a thing? Contrary to what advocates of the so-called "Non-reductive Materialism" claim, there is no middle-ground between Materialism and Dualism. No matter how you try to explain it, a matter-only universe would be one that ultimately contains only impersonal 3rd-"person" entities (the "it" of objects) without 1st or 2nd or real 3rd-persons. Only a mind and matter Dualism accounts for all perspectives.

Part 2

The strength of the anti-theistic motivation that drives Humanism and its Materialist approach often seems to be underestimated by Christians in their efforts to challenge today's scientists and other intellectuals. As a result, a lot of efforts by Christian academics to challenge mainstream approaches tend to focus mainly on specific problems rather than on the Big Picture.

It is true that many of the problems identified in Christian critiques of

---

It is also clear that many Materialist scientists and other "anti-Higher Intelligence" thinkers look to the unpredictability of "quantum fluctuation" as a way to carve out a place for human freedom and choice and all that this entails without the need to admit the real existence of intelligence and minds as immaterial entities. For many have recognized that a universe governed only by mindless forces and laws of Nature would be one in which everything must unfold according to a strict natural necessity.

Those who recognize the problem in this, namely, that it would make us nothing more than automatons (or robots) with only an illusion of freedom, think that quantum fluctuation offers a way out of this. But this hope is the real illusion. For, it would merely replace a mindless determinism according to natural forces and laws with a universe based only on random fluctuations. To say that all of our choices are matters of random fluctuations fails to explain this just as much as saying that we are governed only by fixed laws of Nature. In either case, it only explains it away.

Ironically, defenders of Evolution have argued that Creationists/Intelligent-design advocates misrepresent the mechanism of Natural Selection as being mere random events, instead pointing to the role of reliable laws of Nature (though they can't explain why these exist or why we can understand them). But by appealing to quantum fluctuation this is exactly what they end up doing. In the end, Heisenberg's Uncertainty Principle devours human choice and all that follows from this just as effectively as the traditional Naturalism, which says that everything is determined only by mindless natural laws.

Evolution and Neuroscience are legitimate and have no conceivable resolution under a Materialist model. But this doesn't stop defenders of the model from searching for answers which will not force them to reconsider their commitment to the model. And, even when they can't come up with any, they will still hold on to hope that such answers will one day be found (though this is the always-weak argument from silence or ignorance). Or, in many cases the problems are just ignored or quickly dismissed.

Pointing out specific failures by "matter-only" scientists in their efforts is not without value, mainly in demonstrating that the challengers have an understanding of the issues and in pointing out the elaborate efforts which are often expended by matter-only researchers in order to preserve their theoretical model. But to stay focussed on the narrow issues rather than the Big Picture is like the proverbial steward who was devoted to re-arranging the deck-chairs on the Titanic after it had struck the ice-berg!

The Humanists' "good ship", Evolution, crafted by mindless forces is not sea-worthy. It's going down, sooner or later. But there's a better ship built by a Master Builder to flee to, which can withstand anything it might encounter, as Noah's ark once did.

Like all people, scientists and other intellectuals often have unlimited stubbornness and determination to take any path possible in order to avoid going down a road that they really don't want to go down; namely, any one leading toward God. An example of this is the wishful thinking by many neuroscientists today that the mystery of consciousness will one day be solved and its material nature understood. This assumption is another part of the false faith in Science discussed earlier, in which it is assumed that because Science is the way to understand the physical world, then this must be all that exists.

Some Christians think that challenging Evolution is a bad strategy because they believe it lays a big stumbling-block in front of unbelievers which will keep many of them from ever taking Christianity seriously. But the real barrier keeping unbelievers from considering Christianity is the blind and false faith which most people today have in Evolution (both on the cosmic level and in the development of life), in Science as the only way to know things, in the Materialism worldview on which these beliefs are based, and in the entire Humanist belief-system, of which Materialism is a fundamental part.

Thus, faith in Evolution is part of the foundation for the entire anti-Christian Humanist worldview. And the best place to attack most structures (whether physical or theoretical) is usually at their foundations.

A person will have no reason to consider other beliefs if you are convinced that the ones you currently hold are adequate. But, if you begin to think carefully and critically about your most fundamental beliefs so that you come to see that they don't hold up, then you will have a good reason to consider the Christian alternative. Once again, you still may not want to do so, but you should.

The quest to understand consciousness as a material phenomenon (which has come to be known as "The Hard Problem") is not a problem which we just haven't solved yet. It's an exercise in futility in which something is sought which is actually incompatible with the "rules" of the Materialism worldview. The same is true of efforts to solve the so-called "problem of other minds". And the same also applies to trying to understand on the basis of Materialism the existence of and communication of information which is necessary for the existence of living things, as well as our ability to understand all of these things and everything else.

All of these are not "hard problems" which, like other past scientific challenges, will eventually be solved. No, they are problems which are impossible to solve because they pertain to entities which are simply not allowed to exist in the Materialist view, but entities which, nevertheless, do undeniably exist.

But from the Christian theistic point-of-view there is no mystery about all of these things. In all of these areas, believers in Materialism make extensive and elaborate attempts to find answers. But, in the end, they can only express a hope that these things will eventually be understood (an argument from ignorance). But Christian Theism has simple explanations for them. As such, the principle of Occam's Razor points to Christianity as the better and correct approach.[66]

Another very simple and basic fallacy of the 21st century, one which, amazingly, is believed by nearly everyone today is this: It is to believe that we can know what happened in the past and what will happen in the future based on what we understand about how Nature works now. Do you believe this? Although no survey has been taken as far as I know, it seems clear that the vast majority of people would say: "Of course!" But there are actually several very simple problems with this assumption which make it untenable.

First, consider this: Just the possibility that some Higher Intelligence exists with power over the universe (something which could never be ruled out) is

---

66 *Even a simple thing like the fact that human beings normally wear clothes exposes a serious problem with evolutionary Materialism and points to the far greater simplicity of the Christian explanation. Of all forms of life we know of, only we wear clothes, even in warm climates where this is not necessary for survival (except for a few isolated primitive tribes and socially-rebellious nudists).*

But how can this be explained from an evolutionary point-of-view? Clearly, human beings need clothing in order to survive in areas with cold weather. But doesn't this point to an inherent genetic weakness which should have caused our extinction or, at least, kept us from living in cold weather regions?

Even most who believe in Naturalism recognize that the act of putting on clothing is not a "natural" act. It's a creative act requiring intelligence and design. On the other hand, Christians find a simple explanation for why we wear clothing in the first book of the Bible, Genesis (chapter 3), an explanation which is at least 3000 years old.

a Huge Unknowable Variable rendering all projection from the present to the past or to the future unreliable. It doesn't matter if this Intelligence is the God of the Bible or just some very advanced life form. Either way, this possibility means that Science alone simply cannot tell us how old the universe, the earth and all life is, or how they came to be or about the future of the universe.

As radical as the preceding may seem, it is just simple logic. To project from the present either to the past or to the future requires that we account for all possible influences. If there is even the possibility of an over-ruling Power (which, again, could never be ruled out), then we can't do this![67]

Now, a common objection to this is that allowing for this possibility would destroy Science altogether. But this just doesn't follow. This is because this possibility doesn't affect the efforts of Science to understand how the physical world works today. Indeed, Science is based on the undeniable fact that Nature works according to absolutely reliable laws which we are capable of discovering and understanding. (Again, though, there is no real explanation for why this is possible if the Materialists' understanding of reality was correct.)

Far from destroying Science, it can be seen that it is the natural order which God built into the universe, combined with our God-given ability to understand this (as rational creatures created to be like Him) which alone

---

[67] *Given the increasingly recognized difficulties in explaining how the very complex precursors of life could have spontaneously emerged from lifeless matter, some advocates of evolution have begun to suggest that life on earth did not emerge from lifeless matter but was "seeded" by some far more advanced species. But this idea doesn't solve the problem at all. It only pushes it back a step. For, it would still have to be explained how this other species emerged. One just can't appeal to an endless chain of such beings as a credible explanation for why we exist. In fact, if this were the case, then one would essentially be saying that the universe contained life from the beginning. (Spoiler alert) An example of the seeding of life idea is found in the film "Mission to Mars".*

makes Science possible. Without The Creator God we simply cannot account for why this order exists (or, for that matter, why anything exists at all). And if God had not made us as rational beings we couldn't explain why it is that we are capable of understanding it.

Unlike historical Science and the historical growth of Science, "hard" laboratory Science does properly rely on the principle of induction, because it can ensure controlled conditions. And these controlled conditions are why Karl Popper's "falsifiability" standard works with this type of research. But, as we will discuss further below, things are quite different with both the so-called "scientific" study of history and the history of Science.

Radiometric dating is considered to be one of the most important keys to understanding how old the universe and earth are, how long life has existed and how all of these came to be as they are today. But all radiometric dating methods used to determine the ages of things in the natural world falsely assume something that is actually unknowable: that the only possible influences on Nature are the natural forces which we understand today acting identically to how we observe them acting today.

This can be seen to be a fallacy on five separate levels, four of which don't even have anything to do with the supernatural. In other words, they are fallacies within the Naturalist/Materialist approach.

First, confidence in radiometric dating falsely assumes that we now know all of the natural forces involved. Second, it falsely assumes that we now understand these forces sufficiently. Third, it falsely assumes that these natural forces always worked exactly as they do today. Fourth, it falsely assumes that we know as much as necessary the conditions under which these forces worked in the past. And, fifth, (as already cited) it falsely assumes that only natural forces can exist.

In effect, most scientists today implicitly assume and proceed as though Science has now reached a sufficient understanding of the forces of nature so that we can understand what happened in the past, as well as predict what will happen in the future. But this is just an arrogant, dogmatic presumption. It is an unwarranted belief that, far from helping advance Science, has actually always tended to block progress in Science in the past!

This is clearly seen in the resistance of scientists whenever a basic point-of-view held by the consensus has been challenged by another point-of-view which eventually proves to be superior. The resistance by advocates of the Ptolemaic geocentric model of the solar system to the heliocentric model advocated by Copernicus and his allies is probably the most famous example of this. But, as Thomas Kuhn (in his landmark book, "The Structure of Scientific Revolutions") and others have pointed out, this is a common reality in the history of Science.

One of the most amazing things in the world today is that, despite being almost universally-accepted, today's so-called "scientific" knowledge about what happened in the beginning of the universe and what will happen in the future is actually a Huge Fraud! It is pure speculation. Moreover it is faulty speculation because it is based on the aforementioned fallacies, any one of which is enough to render such speculations invalid, so as to produce no certain knowledge.

First: Do we really know all of the relevant forces involved in producing what we observe today? This has been a common error throughout the history of Science. But do we really know we are not still guilty of it? The answer is: No. We simply can't know what we don't know!

Second, even if we have come to know all of the natural forces involved, can we really assume we know them well enough to understand all of their effects? Once again, this has proven to be a faulty assumption on many occasions in the history of Science.

Third, can we really assume that the natural forces which we observe today always worked exactly as we observe them today? Indeed, basic operational

Science is dependent on this assumption, so this is clearly valid over the short-term. But isn't it simply a matter of blind faith to assume that the forces of nature could not have worked differently in the past or that they might work differently in the future?[68]

Indeed, can we even speak of the existence of forces of nature in the Singularity which is believed by virtually all evolutionary cosmologists to have existed prior to the supposed "Big Bang"? This brings us to the fourth error: to assume that we adequately understand past conditions. Indeed, just to propose that the known universe began as a Singularity makes this claim ridiculous!

The first four false assumptions themselves reflect a common human tendency to assume that we have now come to a complete knowledge of the laws governing how the universe works. But, again, such hubris, far from protecting Science, has always hindered the progress of Science. Clearly, it was this false confidence that was behind the strong resistance all of the greatest innovators in the history of Science faced (most prominently, Galileo, Copernicus, Kepler, Newton and Einstein).

This brings us to the fifth fallacy, which is the denial of the possibility of

---

68 *Take the speed of light, for example. Since Einstein's theory of General Relativity became accepted in the mid-20th century, it has been assumed that this is a constant. But, how do we know this? Is it not possible that the speed of light was once far greater; perhaps, for all practical purposes, infinite when the universe began? But, since the beginning of the universe it has been slowing, perhaps at an inverse-logarithmic rate so that the change is too small for us to detect today.*

   This possibility was proposed in 1988 by two scientists, Trevor Norman and Barry Setterfield in an article entitled "The Atomic Constants, Light and Time". Such a possibility simply cannot be ruled out. This could be how we can see distant galaxies even if the universe is far younger than most believe it is today. In fact, recent research in mainstream (non-Creationist/Intelligent Design) circles has suggested that the speed of light may not be a constant.

either an over-ruling natural intelligence or an over-ruling God. While I anticipate that many of you will tend to snicker over this one (especially with regard to the idea of an over-ruling God), the important thing to ask is: Why do you dismiss this as impossible and ridiculous?

Does the fact that you have never observed a "miracle" mean that such events are impossible? No, this simply doesn't follow. And does the fact that Science is the proper way to study Nature mean that Nature as we know it is all that can exist? Again, that this is a fallacy should be easy to see.

To dismiss the possibility that supernatural entities exist is both arbitrary and irrational. It is merely the bias which most have been taught since the Darwinian revolution took over the intellectual world, as is the tendency to try to explain away as purely natural events all evidence of the existence of supernatural entities (including that found in our unique nature as human beings), as well as all evidence of supernatural activity.

Furthermore, there is no tension between belief in a natural order and belief in supernatural power. This can be seen when one considers the concept of miracles. Whether one believes in them or not, miracles, by definition, are events which violate the known laws of nature. So, in order for a miracle to be recognized as such there must be enough common knowledge of the natural order so that the miracle may be seen as a unique exception to that order. In other words, far from denying Science, some understanding of the laws of Science must be presupposed, otherwise miracles would be unrecognizable.[69]

---

69 *To assume that miracles can't happen (as well as objections to many other things found in the Bible) can be seen to be a direct consequence of an arbitrary presupposition that the God described in the Bible can't exist. To put it the other way, if this God exists (as Christians say He must), then everything in the Bible is actually credible. (Yes, even talking animals! Indeed, it should be clear that such things are not at all hard for an All-Powerful God.) Not that there are clear explanations for everything. But, in most cases, there are, at least, acceptable possible explanations. And there are never unavoidable contradictions. Obviously, this is a radical challenge*

It is also necessary that the natural order be the norm and miraculous violations of it quite rare. And contrary to a common perception, this is precisely what the Bible portrays (unlike many other sacred scriptures). In most of the Bible's historical accounts miracles are rare. Rather, supernatural activity is concentrated in a few periods: in the initial Creation activity of God, in the separating of Israel as God's People in the Exodus, in the period of the prophets Elijah and Elisha (when Israel was divided), in the time of Jesus' ministry, and in the initial establishment of His Church.

It is a clear historical error to assume that the ancients had no understanding of natural laws. While the world in which Judaism and Christianity emerged certainly lacked the scientific sophistication of today, it was clearly not a world which was hopelessly lost in superstition (like a few remote tribes which have been found in the past century, which stand out precisely because they are exceptions rather than the rule).

Indeed, modern society hails the intellectual and technological achievements of ancient societies, especially the Greeks in the former respect and the Romans in the latter. Furthermore, the reality is that no society can exist without understanding a good deal about the forces of nature, whether consciously or unconsciously. It is not even possible for any individual to survive without this. For example, even truly insane people usually understand basic gravity, among other things, or they would quickly perish. Not being a student of Science does not mean that one is utterly ignorant of the laws of Science.

All of this means that even though the process of induction is one of the foundations of proper Science essential for understanding how the universe works <u>today</u>, one simply cannot use induction in order to understand what happened in the distant past or what will happen in the future. For, strictly speaking, neither is subject to scientific examination.

---

to today's biased thinking and is thus deserving of further discussion later.

The amazing consequence of all of this is that to believe in the speculations of modern cosmologists and, even, to believe in general that we can know the past or future based on the present is essentially a religious position! In other words, it is an act of faith and, indeed, it is actually an act of blind faith by people who arbitrarily and, thus, falsely reject multiple possibilities that make their beliefs impossible to know for certain as true. But, most importantly, such people falsely reject the possible existence of an Almighty Creator God.

The existence of the Almighty Creator God described in the Bible simply cannot be ruled out. And the mere possibility of God's existence means that "all bets are off" concerning both the origins and future of the universe. For, this possibility is a huge unaccountable Variable that makes any analysis which assumes His non-existence invalid.

It is undeniable that anti-theistic Naturalism is at the heart of all secular Science today. So the perspective being presented here is a fundamental challenge to today's scientific community. It is not a surprise, then, that it is treated as a serious threat. Indeed, vocal defenders of Science like Bill Nye and Neil deGrasse Tyson claim that Creation/Intelligent Design is a threat to Science itself. But it is only a threat to that work of Science which depends on the assumption which we have shown to be unwarranted: that Intelligent influence on a cosmic scale is impossible and, therefore, must be ruled out.[70]

---

70 *This is the reason why the peer-review boards of most major scientific journals will flatly refuse even to consider work which is done by scientists who are known to reject or, even, just question the rigid Naturalism which is assumed today, regardless of their scientific credentials or of the demonstrable soundness of their research methods. But this is not proper behavior by scientists. Rather, it is dogmatic allegiance to a philosophical bias which falsely excludes legitimate scientific work. Ironically, it is exactly the same tactic which the Vatican's scientists (and there were many of these) used against Copernicus, Galileo and others who correctly challenged the reigning views of their times. Such exclusiveness is no more appropriate today than it was then. This behavior was famously depicted in Ben Stein's film "Expelled: No Intelligence Allowed".*

It has become common for advocates of Intelligent Design to defend their work as scientific. And rightly so, for this can easily been demonstrated for anyone who is the least bit open to seeing this. For, Intelligent Design (or "ID") research, in order to be accepted as legitimate, must be done under the same criteria and controlled conditions as that done by Evolution-believing scientists.

But, at the same time, it must be recognized that those who arbitrarily reject a Creator are making a religious claim no less than those who presuppose an Intelligent Designer. In other words, this is not a matter of "Science vs. Religion". It is a question of which Religion is the true basis of Science: the Humanism which dominates the academic world today (including its Materialist/Empiricist view of the universe), or Christian Theism.[71]

As we have seen, the Philosophy/Religion assumed by most scientists and intellectuals and, indeed, by most people today absurdly reduces the universe to being composed, ultimately, only of objects without any knowing subjects. So, the rejection of Christian Theism, far from being a positive development in intellectual history, is actually The Largest Intellectual Error (or LIE) in human history.

---

71 *As we observed in chapter 3, one of the silliest claims that atheists and all who reject Theism often make is that they don't have a belief about God. This claim is made in an effort to establish that the burden-of-proof regarding God's existence is only on those who believe that He does.*

But all non-theists do have a belief about God; namely, that the Christian God or other deities don't exist. It doesn't matter if this belief is considered to be true with certainty or not. It's still a belief. Moreover, as was discussed earlier, it's a belief in a negative universal claim, something which could never be known for certain to be true.

Since both Materialism/Empiricism/Humanism and Christianity are comprehensive belief systems they are both under the same epistemological requirements: that they can account for all that we know and experience and that they not fall into self-contradiction or obvious absurdity.

We assert that it is Christian Theism which alone explains why anything exists, why the universe has order, why it is that we can come to understand this order and, even, why we exist as people and can experience or know anything. Without an Intelligent Creator human intelligence, experience and meaning cannot be explained. In short, we only matter because we're not only matter.

This diagram, which was introduced earlier, summarizes the perspective of Christian Theism.

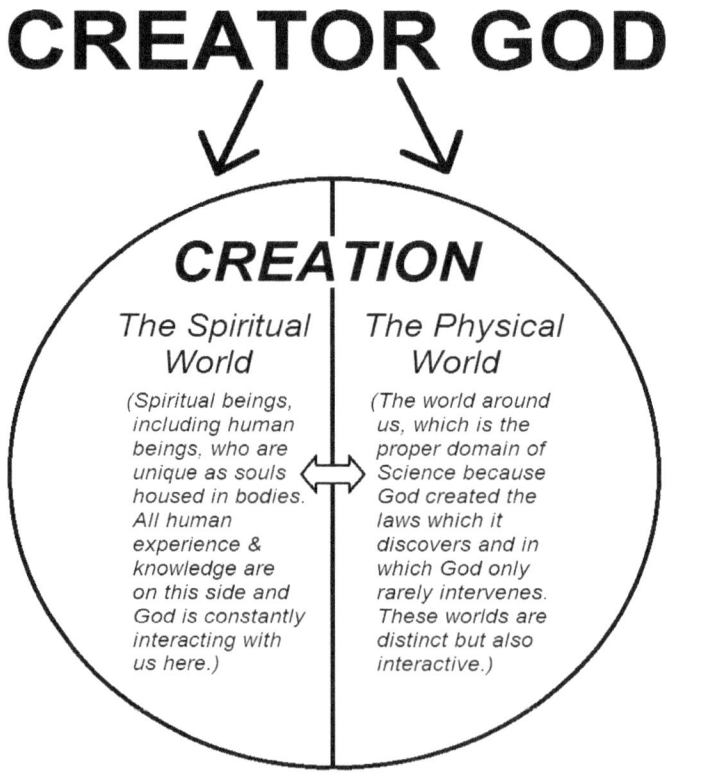

Chapter 7
Humanists' Objections to Christianity are Fallacies.

The number 1 objection that most non-Christians today have to Christianity is probably this one: "Christianity can't be true because all of the evidence says it's false." There is an old saying that "beauty is in the eye of the beholder". But the same is also true of evidence. As we have already discussed, how one looks at everything is always determined by one's basic beliefs, or one's worldview. Because of this Humanists look at everything on the assumption that Humanism is true, Christians on the assumption that Christianity is, Muslims on the assumption that Islam is. Hindus, Buddhists, "New-age" spiritualists and everyone else does the same. This is known as "confirmation bias". And everyone does it.[72]

It is routine today for people who have been educated in Humanism to claim

---

72 *Contrary to what many claim, the fact that everyone has confirmation bias doesn't mean that no one's bias can be correct. This just doesn't follow. In fact, this in itself is just the confirmation bias of those who assume that all truth and knowledge are relative (relativism). But relativism has previously been shown to be a faulty assumption because it is self-defeating: If it is not possible to know the truth of any universal claim, then it isn't possible to know that this claim is universally true. Thus, it is possible that some claims may be universally true.*

There are countless cases where people have prejudices which are later overcome specifically because they are shown to be contrary to the facts, from very mundane preferences (like tastes in food) to very significant ones (like racial biases). It is the claim of this author that The Most Important overcoming of a false confirmation bias is to recognize that The God described in the Bible must exist and that Christianity is true.

there is no evidence that Christianity is true and that all of the evidence says it's false. However, the people making this claim invariably assume that this is the case (which is the fallacy of assuming the conclusion) and view all things accordingly.

So, not only are such people completely closed to any evidence and arguments for the Christian perspective, they are also utterly committed to interpreting everything as material phenomena because it is assumed that this is all that exists. But, we have seen that this is an arbitrary assumption. Furthermore, we have also seen that trying to reduce everything to manifestations of matter-energy and mindless forces in space-time simply won't work.

The faulty bias of anti-Creationists (and even some inconsistent Christian Theists) is even seen in the charge often made against "young earth Creationists" that if the earth is actually much younger than is commonly believed today then God is guilty of deception because the earth and universe have "an appearance of age". But, it must be recognized that there is an appearance of age if and only if radiometric dating and other assumptions made by pro-evolution Materialist/Naturalists are reliable, which requires that they are based on correct assumptions. And we have already seen in the previous chapter that radiometric dating is based on numerous faulty assumptions. In other words, the supposed appearance of age presupposes that Materialism is true and that things came to be as they are by natural forces only.

The problem with evidence is really an interpretation problem. The idea that scientists and other fair-minded people come to conclusions only after surveying and objectively evaluating the evidence is another widely-believed fallacy. For, how one looks at any particular piece of evidence or data, as well as what type of evidence and data one will seek and where one will look are all determined by one's guiding philosophy (or worldview). And this also determines what will "count" as evidence. If there is no materialistic explanation apparent in a particular situation, the committed

Materialist will resort to an argument from ignorance rather than consider that a phenomenon he or she encounters might represent evidence that disproves Materialism and evidence that supports another worldview (especially the Biblical one).

This is because changing one's worldview/philosophy/religion is one of the hardest things a person can do. And this is because we always have a lot of vested interest in our worldview. We have made countless decisions based on it. And it is the lenses through which we view everything. So, to abandon it would change almost everything in unknown ways. And who needs that?! But we who became convinced that we must abandon today's dominant view for Christianity have done so because we have become convinced that it is the true view, while all others are distortions.

One of the most prominent examples in which Materialists argue from ignorance or silence is in the area of consciousness. No Materialist can explain what it is, but many merely express confidence that we will one day be able to do so. But, this will never happen. Why? Because, as we saw previously, it is just not possible to reduce subjectivity to objectivity. Or, to put it another way, "first-person" experience (whether "I" or "we") will never be the same as the "third-person" ("he" or "she", but, especially, "it").

This is one of many things which should be totally obvious but are nevertheless routinely overlooked or, even, denied outright by people trained in Materialist Humanism.[73] So, at the risk of being ridiculously obvious, I believe it's necessary to specify the following. Our consciousness is always in the first-person singular ("I"). What we are conscious of will be either second-person ("you" whether singular or plural) or third ("him", "her" or "them") or first-person plural ("us"). But when we observe our brain function we are observing something which is in the third-person. It isn't really a "person" (that is, "me"), it's just an "it". For all material phenomena

---

73 *Another obvious scientific fact, which was previously accepted by virtually everyone, but is frequently denied today is the fact that one's chromosomes determine which sexual identity one should have, namely, as male or female.*

are third-person "its".

To be fair, Creationists also proceed on the basis of assumptions, but with a different set of assumptions. One key difference, though, is that Creationists, being metaphysical Dualists, don't deny the material in the same way that Materialists deny the immaterial. The truth is that everyone proceeds in the same basic manner. As Philosopher of Science Thomas Kuhn accurately described it in his famous work, "The Structure of Scientific Revolutions", scientists are never neutral in how they view things. And the same is true for all of us.

We all interpret everything we encounter based on our current understanding of what is true and possible. There just isn't any other way to proceed in life. This is not to say that there aren't times when people change their understanding on this level. Indeed, the primary goal of this book is to help people do this and become Christians. But these are not common experiences. Rather, they are rare "revolutionary" moments. Kuhn accurately showed that the history of Science follows this pattern.

Thomas Kuhn's "Structure of Scientific Revolutions" showed that major advances in Science do not occur due to a gradual accumulation of data and other evidence (as many believe). Rather, they occur when, first, a single individual or, perhaps, a small group decide that there are too many problems with a reigning fundamental theory (or paradigm) and, thus, are driven to develop another model. If their assessment of the problems and of the superiority of the alternate model proves to be valid, over time more and more will abandon the previous model and embrace the new one until it eventually supplants the old one.

It is not a matter of an increase in the data (although different models do cause scientists to seek different data). Rather, it is a case of switching to an entirely different way of looking at all of the data. Among other examples, this can be seen in the historic shifts from seeing the earth as the center of the solar system (Ptolemy's geocentrism) to seeing the sun as the center

(Copernicus' heliocentrism) and from Newton's understanding of Physical mechanics to Einstein's Relativity and quantum mechanics.

Consistent with this, Creationists argue that the dominant scientific and intellectual establishment has embraced a false model (that of cosmic Evolution and the anti-theistic Materialism/Empiricism on which it is based) and needs to embrace a different one; in this case, the one which was previously dominant: Creation and dualistic Christian Theism. To return to the jigsaw puzzle analogy, we argue that evolutionists misunderstand the Big Picture. As such, they are often able to identify pieces of the puzzle correctly, but they cannot properly put them together. And in some cases they misinterpret the pieces themselves.

The foregoing lays out the philosophical/religious problems with today's dominant philosophy. But there are also many scientific problems addressed by scientists who have either come over to the side of Creationism or have at least become skeptics of natural selection and evolutionary Materialism. This is what is being done today by over 100 credentialed scientists referenced on the website AnswersinGenesis.org.

As Ben Stein has shown in his video, "No Intelligence Allowed" (and has subsequently been shown by many others), it is sadly common today that the work of many legitimately credentialed scientists done under entirely legitimate scientific conditions and methods is systematically excluded from the peer-review system by most mainstream scientific organizations and journals. And this is simply because these scientists operate on the basis that there is a Creator or Intelligent Designer (as nearly all scientists did prior to Darwin). Furthermore, the same thing is done even if scientists merely seek to show fundamental problems with today's reigning model.

This is entirely unscientific behavior by people who should know better! It only shows the unscientific bias of today's mainstream scientific establishment. Indeed, many will even deny that such exclusion occurs even as they justify it by claiming that anyone who would challenge today's consensus that "Evolution is settled Science" is unscientific by definition. But those who would do this should consider that opponents of virtually every major advance in the history of Science have done the same thing.

An excellent introduction to the real scientific problems with Evolution can also be found in a recent documentary video: "Evolution's Achilles Heels", which features 15 scientists who have changed sides in the debate. A good introduction in book form (which also focusses on the philosophical issues) is Jason Lisle's "The Ultimate Proof of Creation".

Another common objection to Christianity today is this one: "Christianity can't be true because no one knows the truth." This one is much easier to disprove, as it is clearly self-defeating. If no one can know the truth, then the truth that no one can know the truth can't be known. So, it must be possible that the truth can be known.

The "agnosticism" which this claim represents is often presented as an example of humility and modesty. But, in practice, it is actually a stubborn false denial of one's own claims of knowledge, along with a stubborn refusal to consider other claims. We all claim knowledge of many things, both on the mundane level of things, as well as on the grand scale. Even people who don't claim certainty about God and ultimate reality still have working beliefs about such (namely, that God doesn't exist and that the universe is composed only of material entities) and perceive everything and act accordingly. These beliefs are truth claims even if they are not claims made with certainty.

Third, "Christianity is wrong because it's exclusive and it's wrong for any religion to claim that its view is right and every other one is wrong." The fallacy in this objection is that it fails to recognize that all religions and comprehensive philosophies are by nature exclusive. This includes the popular idea that all religions are just different paths to the same destination. If one holds this view he or she automatically considers wrong everyone who believes their religion or philosophy is the only true path! There is no way to avoid exclusivity with one's ultimate beliefs.[74] So, the real issue is which way is true (or ways, if it should turn out that there is more than one, though Christianity says there isn't).

It is just human nature for all of us to embrace what we consider right and reject what we consider wrong. We couldn't survive in life without this. Of course there are many choices in our daily lives in which there is more than one correct answer (like "Which socks should I wear today?"). But there are also many other choices where there is only one right answer (like "Is it right or wrong to kill my neighbor because I don't like him?" or "Does a red traffic-light mean stop or go?").

Many today have been taught that this shouldn't apply to our most important beliefs. But it is actually more important to have confidence that your most basic beliefs are correct compared to other beliefs than it is about many other things we are confident about. This is because these beliefs determine so many other beliefs, as well as our morality and values.

Most serious followers of all of the major religious traditions will usually be willing to admit that they believe their religion is the only correct path or, at

---

74 *In his excellent book "The Reason for God" Tim Keller pointed out the exclusivity of the supposedly all-inclusive approach. People who hold to the idea that there are many paths to the same destination like to cite a famous Buddhist analogy of blind-folded people trying to figure out what an elephant is like. But the analogy doesn't really show that our limited perspectives are all correct, but only in part. Rather, what it illustrates is that there is a comprehensive view (namely, that of the entire elephant) that is correct, while the partial views are insufficient. Indeed, this illustration was originally given to support the claim that the Buddhist perspective is the only true one.*

least, the best path. If they are fair-minded, then, they will not be offended by people of other faiths if they also claim that only their approach is correct or best.

Sometimes the confidence that religious people or non-religious Humanists have is due simply to ignorance of other options. This is why Christians are motivated to share what we believe with others. On the other hand, non-Christian religious people and Humanists may have accurate knowledge of Christianity and other ways but are still confident of their position. In these cases, Christians must respect this.

But in today's world there is actually widespread ignorance of what Christians actually believe and why. Much of what people today think they know about Christianity is actually derogatory false stereotypes promoted by Humanists with an anti-Christian prejudice (Humanism being in itself a reaction mainly against Christianity). For example, if you believe that anyone who is a Bible-believing Christian is just a scientifically-ignorant, self-righteous "Bible-thumper" then you have unfairly embraced a negative stereotype of Christians.[75]

---

75 *Ironically, many of those who hold this negative stereotype of all Christians will also say that stereotypes and even generalizations are wrong. This is clearly hypocritical. Anyone who thinks this way would do well to read what Jesus says about hypocrites in the New Testament Gospels.*

Furthermore, today's antipathy toward stereotypes and generalizations is part of an overall general confusion with post-modern thinking. As conservative commentator Dennis Prager likes to point out, generalizations not only aren't wrong, they are absolutely essential in order to understand countless aspects of reality. For example, if there are dark clouds headed in your direction it is generally true that it will soon be raining and you should grab your umbrella.

Stereotypes are often generally correct and sometimes positive (like the strong emphasis on education and high levels of achievement among Jews and many Asian people) and sometimes negative (like a relative lack of emphasis on education and relatively low levels of achievement among

In order to have honest, respectful and beneficial discussions with others who have different beliefs it is necessary for us to be honest about the fact that we all believe that our beliefs are correct or best. If not, then we wouldn't believe what we do! It really is that simple. Again, this applies also to those who believe it is wrong for anyone to claim exclusivity about one's beliefs. Notice the use of the term "wrong" here. If you believe this then you believe that <u>everyone</u> who doesn't agree with you is wrong! In other words, you are excluding the possibility that these people may be correct. And this includes billions of devout religious people!

So those who make the exclusivity objection need to stop. The fact that Christianity is presented as the only true path is not a valid reason to reject it. The only thing that really matters is: Is it true or not?

Fourth, "Christianity can't be true because its God is morally inferior compared to our understanding of morality today." We have already addressed the main problem with Humanistic morality: it cannot avoid becoming arbitrary. That is, it will always be just a matter of human opinion, whether that opinion is of one person or many people who happen to agree.

And we have also seen how Humanism is also utterly incapable of explaining why we have a moral sense. Beyond this, it can't explain why we exist as conscious beings who experience and know all the things that we do. The only credible explanation for all of this is that it is because God made us

---

African-Americans and Hispanics). And some fundamentalist Christian traditions are overly anti-scientific and hyper-supernatural. But others are not. To deny real tendencies of groups is foolish and counter-productive in many ways. We need to return to the previous understanding that while stereotypes are sometimes accurate, <u>stereotyping</u>, that is, to assume that everyone in a particular group fits the stereotype of that group is always wrong.

this way.

So, those seeking to make a moral case against God are on the shakiest of ground. Actually, they have no foundation at all. They are merely trying to use a sword which God gave them to attack Him. What do you think the odds are that this will succeed? Yeah, right!

However, it is true that some of God's actions and words in the Bible are puzzling even to most, if not all believers. But it is one thing to be puzzled about things in the Bible but believe there are explanations and quite another to assume that the things which one thinks are wrong are actually wrong because the Bible is just a book written by men who lived in a far less advanced culture. Of course, the latter is the Humanist bias. The former is the faith of those who have come to recognize that the God of the Bible must exist and therefore that He both could have and, in fact, has revealed Himself and His ways and will in a Book.

We have already pointed out that God (if He exists, as we say He must) certainly could have done everything the Bible says He did because He is Almighty God! And because He is Good and cannot lie, whatever He has revealed to us must be accurate when properly understood. We simply must assume that God is honest because, if He isn't, then all bets are off. If so we would have a legitimate fear that everything we think we know is an illusion, except for the fact that we exist as the victims of this Grand Illusion.

Of course, if the Bible is truly what it says it is, then how to properly understand it will always be the challenge. But, contrary to today's "conventional wisdom" it is not an impossible challenge. (The second part of this book will focus on Biblical interpretation.)

Many examples of the supposedly inferior morality of the Bible could be cited, but let's go right to The Big One: Hell. There is no question that the Bible's teaching about Hell is one of the biggest stumbling-blocks to believing in the Bible and Christianity. Even many professing Christians in the 21st century reject the idea that a loving God could send anyone to Hell. Now it may seem, at first, that a God Who would just forgive evil-doers would be the most loving God imaginable, kind of a Cosmic Santa Claus. But appearances can often be deceiving.

We have already answered those who say that there is no such thing as evil, so there would be no real evil-doers. Those who say this have a funny way of changing their tune if they become victims of a real act of evil. We simply cannot live without making distinctions between good and evil, even though Humanism has no explanation for why this is.

One may forgive another who does something evil. Indeed, the radical message of Jesus was that Christians must forgive everyone who sins against us. But to forgive someone does not mean that we deny the reality of the evil, otherwise there would be nothing to forgive!

Evil is real and it is something which we all partake of in countless ways and in varying degrees, whether our evils are sins of commission (things which we do that are wrong) or sins of omission (things which we should have done but didn't do). Failing to do good things which we could do is probably the more common form of human evil. None of us can honestly deny that we have done this.

But what if there were no consequences of evil. Wouldn't that destroy the distinction between good and evil? Indeed it would. This is why a good God must also be a God of justice. This combination is evident from the way God is described as introducing Himself to Moses:
> *Then the LORD came down in the cloud and stood there with him and proclaimed His Name, the LORD. And He passed in front of Moses, proclaiming, "The LORD, the LORD, the compassionate and gracious God, slow to anger, abounding in love and faithfulness, maintaining love to thousands, and forgiving wickedness, rebellion and sin. Yet He does not leave the guilty unpunished; He punishes the children*

and their children for the sin of the parents to the third and fourth generation."
(from the 2nd book of the Old Testament, Exodus, chapter 34, verses 5-7)[76]

Would you really want a God who just forgives everyone? You may think you do, but you really don't.

No one really wants a God who would just forgive everyone because it wouldn't be just. If this was really your ideal, then to be consistent with this you could not justify having prisons or, even, any judicial system at all. But no sane person would advocate this and only the most starry-eyed idealist

---

76 *Some will say that the last part of this text contains an injustice: that innocent children are punished for the sins of their parents. But, again, it is a false bias which leads people to assume that this is true and to be unwilling to consider that there may be a way or ways around this. There are usually multiple possibilities when interpreting Biblical passages. A fair-minded interpreter will seek those which avoid contradicting other passages. Scholars routinely do this with other texts. But, sadly, a false bias against the Bible causes many to refuse to do this with the Bible.*

In this case, it is clear elsewhere in the Bible that we are punished for our own sins and that we are all sinners. So, for God to refer to children being punished for the sins of their parents most likely refers to the fact that children typically repeat the sins of their parents and therefore will receive the same punishment. Because we are all sinners we can only hope to receive God's love by way of Him "forgiving (our) wickedness, rebellion and sin"; in other words, as mercy. That God chooses to show mercy to "thousands" but only justice to others only makes Him selectively merciful, not unjust.

And the New Testament makes clear that even His forgiveness is based on an Act which satisfies His perfect justice: namely, the perfect obedience until death of His Eternal Son, Jesus. His obedience is understood as satisfying God's standard of perfect obedience on our behalf, if we trust that this is so, since none of us could live up to it. And His death is also regarded as satisfying God's righteous Judgment on our universal disobedience, if we are willing to accept this.

would say that this could ever be realistic. So this shows the inconsistency of Humanism once again, in which Humanists assume in practice what their worldview denies (namely, that good and evil are real and, therefore, that evil-doers should be held accountable).

It is only because God is moral that He must be just. And it is only because of this that we also have a sense of justice. If there wasn't a Hell then Hitler, suicide-bombers, uncaught murderers and rapists and countless other evil-doers have evaded justice. So it may seem that a God Who hates evil and is wrathful toward evil-doers, in some cases sending them to Hell, is inferior to one who just loves everyone. But this is not really the case.[77]

---

77 *As Francis Schaeffer and others have pointed out, God doesn't actually "send" anyone to Hell. Rather, He offers Heaven to all, but some simply choose Hell instead. And even if it is the case that God foreknows and, even, predetermines (or "predestines") who will accept His offer, and also that He must first work in us before any of us will accept Him and His offer, this still doesn't mean that His offer isn't real. For, as long as we are in this world, none of us (except, perhaps, for the most hardened evil-doers) can possibly know that we are not among those whom God intends to save. So we have no excuse for not seeking His mercy and salvation. And whoever truly seeks this is promised by God that he or she will find it.*

Those who go to Hell don't really go because of any particular sins, but rather because they persist in rejecting God and refuse to repent and accept His offer of forgiveness and transformation. At the same time, the Bible also teaches that there are those whom God hardens so that they will never even consider turning to Him so that they may be saved.

As for Hell lasting forever, it cannot absolutely be ruled out that the Biblical language indicating this is hyperbole intended to emphasize an extremely long duration, but not literally endless. Most of the discussion of what Hell involves (which is actually quite limited in the Bible) is in parts of the Bible which are considered to be in the genre known as "Apocalyptic literature". And it is understood that this genre often features language which is not intended to be taken literally.

Furthermore, if it is in the best spirit of human mercy to hope that even the most hardened evil-doer may be rehabilitated in time, perhaps God works

Fifth, "Christianity can't be true because the Bible has been shown to be filled with errors and things which are impossible to believe." We have already discussed that this objection is based on the faulty assumption that the God described in the Bible doesn't exist. This can't possibly be known. And, indeed, we maintain that every human being who has ever lived has actually known that this God does exist. And if this is the case, then all of the things in the Bible which are regarded as impossible (such a miracles and divine Creation) become possible.

As for the supposed errors, this is another faulty assumption. For, no one has ever proved that anything in the Bible is inevitably wrong. Indeed, many of the so-called errors can be found to have rather simple explanations.[78] Some

---

this way, too. But this cannot be known for certain from the Biblical revelation. So it must be allowed that Hell may indeed be an endless sentence, as most Christians believe.

As with other difficult things in the Bible, the believer trusts that if this is the case, then it must somehow be consistent with God's Perfect Goodness, though we may never fully understand how. Furthermore, this is not because everything that God does is good and just because He does it. For this would actually make God's goodness arbitrary. Nor is God good because He is under a Standard of Goodness which is apart from Him.

It will be discussed later that God's Goodness is a Personal characteristic. Though God could hypothetically do evil, since He is a free Moral Being, He never does because He is a perfectly Good Person. So we trust Him as such, much as we trust other people whom we have come to regard as good.

78 *A clear example of a false charge of a Bible contradiction (due to prejudice against the Bible's veracity) is Proverbs 26:4-5 - "Do not answer a fool according to his folly, or you yourself will be just like him. Answer a fool according to his folly, or he will be wise in his own eyes." It has been claimed by some that these two sentences contradict each other, as if the compiler of the book somehow missed the contradiction or didn't understand it. But this is a silly assumption which fails to consider an*

have multiple possible ways in which they can be understood as being true. And even in cases where no one has come up with a possible resolution, this doesn't prove that there isn't one in the Mind of God.

Much of the confusion in this area, even among Christians, is due to the fact that the Bible contains various literary genres, some of which are meant to be read literally, including the historical books of the Old Testament and the New Testament Gospels and the Book of Acts, and also specific Old Testament instructions and case-laws. But other parts of the Bible should be read more figuratively, like poetic and apocalyptic sections. And other parts, like general commands, wisdom literature, and the Epistles of the New Testament, must be interpreted more situationally.[79]

Sixth, "Christianity can't be true because of all the evil things done by people claiming to be Christians." This is known as the *ad hominem* fallacy. It is also a false equivocation in which it is assumed that whatever is true

---

obvious explanation which harmonizes the two verses: that answering a fool is a matter of discretion. Sometimes it's wise not to do it and sometimes it's wise to do it.

79 *Genesis 1 is a case where it is unclear if it is meant to be read as poetry, since it clearly has a highly-stylized structure, or as history. But there are no inevitable contradictions if one reads it as a linear historical account, albeit with some allowances for language used loosely (not meant to be understood literally) in order to make it understandable to the original readers. It could be that God is both poetically and accurately describing His work of Creation.*

For example, it would not be a problem for God to create light before He created the sun and stars. Indeed, His Presence to the Israelites later on is in the form of a glorious radiance. And supposed contradictions between Genesis 1 and chapter 2 can be answered by recognizing that chapter 1 is an overview of the Creation period of divine supernatural activity, while chapter 2 is a tightly-focused view of the creation of humanity and the beginning of the post-Creation era governed by natural processes and laws.

must be good.

No matter how badly some Christians (or would-be Christians) act, it simply doesn't follow that this must mean that Christianity can't be true. Even if all Christians acted badly this wouldn't prove that Christianity is false or, even, bad. It could just be that it is true and good, but impossible to live up to. (Indeed, it will subsequently be pointed out that this is precisely what Christians believe.) And it could also be theoretically possible that Christianity is true but not good. (But, thankfully, Christians are able to trust that this is not actually the case.)

Of course, people who use this as an excuse inevitably ignore all of the undeniably good things done by professing Christians. And this argument can also be used just as well against Atheism, Islam or any other religion, since bad actors can always be found in all human circles. Lastly, as we have already shown, the concept of evil itself would be arbitrary and meaningless if the Humanist understanding of ultimate reality was correct.

Related to this objection is the common practice of rejecting The God of the Bible because one doesn't like what the Bible describes Him saying and doing. But the fact that one doesn't like what God says or does has no bearing whatsoever on the question of His existence. To reject God on this basis is actually the logical equivalent of a small child closing his eyes and covering his ears and pretending that his parents don't exist when he doesn't want to accept what they are saying to him.

You can decide that you don't like God because you don't like what the Bible says He has said and done (which is a different problem and is clearly a Big One if He does actually exist). But you can't decide that He doesn't exist on account of this. That is simply irrational.

Seventh, "Christianity can't be true because of all of the progress we have made since it was rejected as the guiding viewpoint of society." This objection is invalid because it is based on the unknowable assumption that the shift from Christian Theism to Humanism has produced more progress than we would have seen otherwise.

It must be recognized that the rise of the modern Age of Science, as well as the discovery of many of the foundations of modernity (including electricity, artificial propulsion, and advances in medicine) actually occurred prior to this shift. So it could just as well be argued that the shift actually hindered the forward movement of Science and society.

And, while it is undeniable that there has been much progress since the shift occurred, it can be argued that this is merely the product of momentum which had been come from the strength of the previous approach; momentum which will eventually run out if society continues to reject its true Foundation. We just can't know that things would have been worse had Christianity remained the dominant viewpoint of the developed world. This is merely assumed as part of today's anti-Christian Humanist bias.

A good question to ask is this: Why is the developed world more developed than the developing world? Ever since the Humanist point-of-view took over the standard answer has been that what used to be called "the third world" was poor and undeveloped because it had been exploited by European colonists. But there are a few problems with this. First, most of Asia (including China and Japan) and the entire Western Hemisphere prior to the 17th century was never dominated by Europe. Yet, it is clear that these parts of the world still lagged behind Europe, especially in Science and technology during the time that Europe was experiencing its Renaissance.

Another question that is rarely asked by Humanists is this: Why were the European powers able to take over the regions which they colonized? The answer that used to be given was this: because European culture was more advanced and powerful. It's a testimony to the power of the Humanist indoctrination that many of you will quickly say: "That's racist!" And you will simply dismiss this as a possible explanation.

But this explains what happened in a way that Humanist "cultural relativism" can't. Cultural relativism says that all human cultures are equally valid. But, if so, then why is it that history is replete with examples of cultures conquering and ruling other cultures?

And the same thing could be said about the developing world that was just said about the colonized portions of the developed world: it is impossible to know if these cultures would have been better off or worse had they not been colonized. We'll never know, just as we'll never know if the developed world wouldn't have been better off had the Christian worldview continued to rule Europe and America instead of being supplanted by Humanism.

There is certainly room to doubt today's reigning assumption that the rise of Humanism was a beneficial development overall. For, it can certainly be debated that the 20th century was all that "progressive". While there was progress in many ways, the 20th century also saw the most massive and widespread destruction, loss of life and oppression in human history.

Indeed, the widespread optimism which prevailed in the early part of the century that humanity would eventually succeed in creating heaven on earth was dealt a crushing blow by World War I and would be blown up altogether in World War II. So, while one can still find optimism today in some circles, virtually no one talks in universal utopian terms anymore. Indeed, apocalyptic visions of the future of human existence abound instead.

If the triumph of Humanism during the 20th century was such a positive development, then why is it that Humanists tend to have fewer children than Bible-believing Christians or other religious people? This is something which is commonly recognized. Indeed, environmentally-conscious Humanists (who fear over-population and catastrophic climate-change) often criticize Christians and others for having too many children.

But, aside from the questionable assumption that it would contribute to over-population, it can be seen that there are two other primary reasons for why progressive Humanists have fewer kids than religious folks. And both of them reflect poorly on Humanism as a desirable worldview.

The first is just selfishness. Many Humanists tend to regard children as a significant hindrance to their own self-fulfillment. This is actually quite understandable. There is no question that having children will throw a serious "monkey-wrench" into the career plans and dreams of many young people (especially women). And there is also no question that the more children that people have, the greater is the pressure to give them the care that they need, usually at the expense of pursuing other things.

If getting married is a big anti-dote to our basic selfishness (among other things, as will be argued in Chapter 9), then having kids should permanently eradicate our natural tendency to seek our own interests first. This is the way people who understand what love is will view things.[80]

The second major reason why Humanists tend to have fewer children than Christians or other religious people is because they tend to have a general pessimism about the future. This pessimism is reflected in the Pew Forum's 2015 Religious Landscape Study cited in chapter 5.

In this survey 3966 people who reported that religion is "not at all important to them" were asked: "How often do you get a feeling of peace and well-being?" 39% answered "seldom or never". On the other hand, of 18,725 people who said that religion is "very important to them" only 6% answered "seldom or never". And 76% of the latter group reported feeling peace and well-being "at least once-a-week", while only 36% of those who said

---

80 *We will deal with the question of what love really is and where it came from in Chapter 9. For now, we will introduce the simple definition that love is caring about and for others more than one's self.*

religion is not all important to them reported this.[81]

Once again, this pessimism is quite understandable in the light of all of the undeniable problems and dangers in the world. It is certainly true that Humanists and Christians will differ over some of these problems, as well as their priority and, most certainly, over the solutions to the problems. But that the world today has serious problems is one thing which Humanists and Christians and others can certainly agree upon. But it does not reflect well on Humanism that pessimism about the future clearly has a much greater influence on the decision of Humanists to have children than it does for Christians and others.

Even if Humanists' fears of a dark future and, even, the possibility that the human-race will go extinct are correct (and Bible-believing Christians can agree on the possibility of the first, but we should not with the second), then shouldn't you at least be hopeful that the superiority of Humanism will help us to overcome the challenges that we face so that we may be able to pass a better world on to our children? If not, then what good is this perspective?

And, while Humanists may say that they remain optimistic, it remains the case that many don't want to bring kids into the world, or, at least not many kids.[82] A worldview that tends to discourage its own propagation by means of reproduction and that tends to be more influenced by selfishness and pessimism than Christianity and other views is questionable at best.

---

81 *http://www.pewforum.org/religious-landscape-study/importance-of-religion-in-ones-life/#frequency-of-feeling-spiritual-peace-and-wellbeing*
82 *If we are worried about over-population then lowering the birth-rate in some areas may make sense. But we have clearly done that already in most of Europe, North America and China. Indeed, the birth-rate among Humanists in Europe and North America is so low that the non-immigrant population is shrinking, and very quickly in some places.*

Eighth, "Christianity can't be true because I don't like what it says." The absurdity of this objection is so obvious that it shouldn't even require rebuttal. Again, it's like the child closing his eyes and covering his ears so as not to hear what his parents are saying to him. Nevertheless, it is the real objection behind all other objections to Christianity. The root of this error, along with all of the other errors of Humanism is the false assumption that we (whether individually or corporately) are the ultimate determiners of what is true and good, not our Maker. But this assumption is inescapably circular and, thus, invalid.

The circularity of Humanist "reasoning" is well-summarized as follows: "I know my reasoning is valid because I checked the validity of my reasoning using my reasoning. Therefore, I know that my reasoning is valid." (From www.godorabsurdity.com)

While all of these fallacies and the other problems outlined in the previous chapters don't prove that Christianity is true, they do show that Humanism cannot be established as certainly true and that Christianity may be true after all. This leads us to Part 2.

Part 2

Chapter 8
Why Christianity Is True And Approaches Which Do Not Begin With One God Fail.

All philosophies or religions which do not begin by recognizing the existence of The Creator God fail for the following reasons. First, the God described in the Bible is "the God Who is there" (as Francis Schaeffer put it). He is always present in our minds and everywhere in His creation, regardless of whether or not this is recognized.

Up until now we have looked at various problems with Humanism, which show that it is not credible when examined carefully. This should cause people who have embraced this view (whether consciously or subconsciously) to reconsider their position and, ideally, decide to look at other options, as the writer did almost 40 years ago.

Of course, the hope is that those who are willing to think carefully and critically will turn to its predecessor as the reigning worldview of the developed world: Christianity. This is because of our confidence that it is able to withstand critical scrutiny (when done fairly) in a way that no other worldview can.

The same reason that Humanism must be rejected can also be seen to apply to all other anti-theistic philosophies or religions. And it also applies to any religion that claims the existence of deities which are not The Supreme Being described in the Bible and also presented as speaking to us there. For, every human-being who has ever lived has inevitably known not just that some God exists, but that the Biblical God exists, whether or not he or she has ever heard of the Bible.

God not only created us and everything that exists, He also sustains every one of us moment-by-moment, along with the entire universe. Everyone actually knows this, but most will do almost anything not to admit it. But this is the ultimate tragic mistake because God made us so that we can be His beloved children, if we are willing. Far from God needing to prove His existence and goodness to us, those who deny God have to make a constant effort to use the minds and breath that He gives them to deny Him.

Fortunately for us, God is also very patient. But there will be a time for each of us when His patience will run out, either when our individual lifespans in this world come to an end, or when God brings about the end of this world and the full establishment of His Kingdom. Of course, most today simply dismiss this as impossible and ridiculous. But that this isn't true is both logically impossible to know and in conflict with what we actually know in our hearts. Once again, just because you don't like something doesn't mean it isn't true.

And as Francis Schaeffer also put it, God doesn't send anyone to Hell. Rather, He offers Heaven to all of us. Those who end up in Hell do so because they insist until their final breath on rejecting God's free offer of forgiveness and endless, immeasurable blessing. In other words, in the ultimate expression of foolish pride, they actually choose Hell over Heaven.[83]

---

83 *Schaeffer asserted that all of us constantly condition ourselves throughout our lives either for Heaven or Hell by the choices we make in what to think, say and do. However, Christians thank God that many of us who were headed for Hell (at least from our point-of-view) turned around and got on the path leading to Heaven by embracing God's gift of salvation on account of the Atonement accomplished by His Son, Jesus Christ and applied to us by His Holy Spirit. And so we hope to encourage others to do the same.*

   It seems correct to say that those who are generally decent people have the opportunity to ask for and receive the salvation that God offers until the end

Second, God must be presupposed in order to be opposed. To claim that God doesn't exist is the ultimate case of Denial in the psychological sense of the term – that is, pretending that what you know to be true isn't true because you aren't ready to accept that it is true. In fact, it can be said that this is the root of all sin and error.

One of Humanism's fundamental beliefs is that we ultimately determine what is true and good. But why do Humanists assume this? Some will say that it is because we haven't found any more advanced species that knows this better than we do. But even if we did, would that guarantee that they know truth and goodness without error? No it wouldn't. For there could always be an even higher species that knows it better. And so on.

And as we have already seen, the reality is that moral certainty will always be impossible unless there is some Absolute Standard of Truth and Goodness to compare both our conceptions and any others' against. Indeed, it has previously been pointed out that truth and goodness would only be meaningless words (actually, they would just be sounds) if reality was merely matter-energy and mindless forces in space-time.

---

of their lives. Nevertheless, procrastinating on this is quite perilous. For it is clearly true that none of us knows when our lives will end and it can also come very suddenly. Besides, the more we resist, the more likely it is that God will just leave us in our rebellion against Him because those who have devoted their lives to sin are just given over to this eventually by God so that they will never repent and be saved.

It is rarely the case that we can know for sure when God has hardened someone so that they cannot be saved. So the Gospel offer should be given to everyone. However, it would be safe to say that people like Adolf Hitler and terrorists who give their lives in order to kill civilians would fit into this category. For to believe it possible that Hitler and the hijackers who committed the attacks on America on 9/11/2001 might have repented in their last moments so that they were saved would beg the question: Who then is in Hell if they aren't?

All discussions about truth and goodness actually assume that there is absolute truth and goodness. This is because if one was to say that all such discussions are just differences of opinion it would effectively end the discussions. But the only reason that there is absolute truth and goodness is because there is a final Authority Who defines what is true and good.

It is true that those of the "post-modern" persuasion will try to opt out of this by claiming that truth and goodness are actually arbitrary concepts. But such people can never make any claims at all without contradicting themselves on this. It has been pointed out that even the claim: "There is no such thing as absolute truth." itself implies that something must be absolutely true, namely the claim itself. So it is a self-contradictory claim.

Truth claims (as well as moral claims) are unavoidable. And they are only meaningful because there is an Absolute Standard and Source of truth and goodness against which all claims of truth and morality can be measured.

This Absolute can be none other than The Creator God described in the Bible. This is something which we all inevitably know by instinct. We know this because our Creator made us to know Him from our first moments of awareness. This has been called the *sensus divinitatis* (or "sense of the Divine"). And this is not a general sense that some God must exist. Rather, it is an actual sense of His Presence.

And all of us also know God's existence through our experiences. For, our Creator makes Himself known to every human being who has ever lived, in our minds (by having the idea of Him and also through our consciences) and also in the world around us (in His handiwork, both in the physical world and in the "world" of human experience). No amount of denying this and pursuing alternatives can eradicate this knowledge.

We will subsequently see that it is surprisingly easy to distinguish The True God from all other would-be rivals. And all of these show that they presuppose the existence of The True God by the very fact that they selectively borrow attributes and qualities from Him. In the same way Humanism borrows truth and morality from God because it cannot explain why these exist within its own view of reality (in which everything is merely governed by mindless forces).

Of course, most people resist all of this fiercely. This is because, while we are born to know our Creator, we are also born with a natural tendency to rebel against Him. We do so by constantly suppressing our knowledge of Him so that we can deny that He is there, and by seeking to get along without Him in any way that we can. We do this naturally and also because, in most cases throughout history and, especially, today, we have been taught by most of those around us to do so. For it is not surprising that people who are rebels by nature against God will also teach the same rebellious thinking and living to their children.

Our rebellious nature in itself points to the fact that there is Someone against Whom we are rebelling. So, no matter how much we may resist and suppress this we always know that God is there and that we're wrong to pretend that He isn't and to try to live as though He isn't there. Once again, it is truly the original case of the psychological problem of Denial. And it is a universal malady of humanity unless God Himself helps us to overcome it.

Again, most people will reject all of this out-of-hand. But isn't this exactly how denial always works? We know this because we all have been in denial of various things in our lives at one time or another. And all those whom God has cured of The Big Denial know that all of this was true of us before He cured us.[84]

---

84 *Christians have long debated over the state of unbelievers' knowledge of God. But it is clear from the 2nd half of the 1st chapter of Paul's Letter to the Romans that all people who have ever lived truly know our Creator and that it is our knowledge of Him which leaves us without excuse for not living for Him. Indeed, we normally suppress this knowledge and, furthermore, we will do so continually unless God overcomes this in us. But to suppress something implies that what is suppressed is always there...*

But if only God Himself can cure our Denial, then are we really to blame for remaining in this state? It may seem that we aren't. But this is not really the case. For, every human being who has ever lived has known what we should do: to call out to our Creator to cure us. And, as far as we know, all of us are capable of asking our Creator to do this. And all we have to do is to ask and He will surely cure us. But if we never ask then we have no one to blame but ourselves. That is just how it works because it is how God made us.

> *So, contrary to many "evidentialists", there is never the need to bring an unbeliever into knowledge of God. This is because he or she always knows God. And contrary to some "presuppositionalists", the suppression by unbelievers of their knowledge of God (part of the "noetic effect of sin") is never able to completely obliterate their knowledge of Him so that they must be brought back into this knowledge. So, while learning more and more <u>about</u> God is something that all of us always need, no one ever really needs to be taught Who God is. This is because, even though God is invisible, He is always present. And, as such, His Presence must be inescapable. After all, even our presence is normally inescapable wherever we are! So how much more must this be the case with God?*
>
> *The problem is always one of a lack of awareness of Him rather than a lack of knowledge, even for those who have never had any exposure to the Gospel and regardless of how devoted people may be to false beliefs. As stated previously, the True God is always "the elephant in the room" Whom everyone knows is there, but most just don't want to acknowledge. What we need to do is to show people that what they are doing is an act of Denial, that all of their efforts are based on a false pretense that God isn't there and that this is the height of foolishness. If we succeed, then they will usually abandon their false gods/idols/belief-systems for Him.*
>
> *This universal knowledge of the True God is also why there is no real danger that helping people to get in touch with their knowledge of God in extra-biblical ways will lead some to believe in false gods instead of The True God. Indeed, people follow false gods all the time. But they follow these as rebels against The True God, Whom they still know. And they can get in touch with Him at any moment.*
>
> *Moreover, distinguishing The True God from idols is often very simple and doesn't require sophisticated arguments or appeals to the Bible. Indeed, just*

Third, the various so-called "proofs" of God's existence are actually only arguments and evidence that confirm what everyone already knows, mainly showing why it is reasonable to accept that the God described in the Bible exists but not reasonable to deny this.

<u>It is simply not necessary to prove the existence of someone whom one already knows</u>. And such is the case with our Creator for every human-being who has ever lived. But various arguments for God's existence are valid and remind us of Who He is and of His Glory. These are helpful precisely because we are naturally predisposed to suppress and deny that we know Him and to seek to get along without Him (foolishly).

---

pointing out the points of agreement (which are borrowed attributes and qualities of The True God) and disagreement (falsely rejected or distorted attributes and qualities of The True God) between peoples' idols and The True God may be all that is needed. Of course, the more knowledge believers have of the Bible and its God, the more we will be able to recognize and point out the similarities and differences.

All of this means that we are placing an unnecessary and impassable barrier in front of many unbelievers if our initial goal is always to try to get people to presuppose that the Bible is true. For, what we really need to do is to get them to realize that they already presuppose the existence of The God of the Bible, whether they are aware of this or not. For, if we succeed in helping them to see this, then this will lead them to accept that the Bible is what it says it is: the very Word of The One True God.

Finally, we should recognize that coming to faith is often a process which occurs over varying lengths of time. Consequently, there will be people who are "on the way" to becoming believers but are not yet fully there. So, it is wrong to assume that every unbeliever we meet is absolutely committed to rejecting God and the Gospel until they fully embrace Him and it. From God's point-of-view, He knows who the elect are and He works in those who are elect differently than in those who are not elect, even prior to bringing them to the point of conscious faith. But we don't know who is elect among those with whom we are sharing the Gospel. But we should focus on those who show promising signs that they are.

Some arguments for God's existence are flawed and can be logically countered. For example, some Christians and others try to argue from claims of supernatural healings that God must exist. But such claims can always be countered by pointing to the possibility that such healings are actually natural processes, even if we don't yet understand exactly how.

But other arguments for God's existence can't be refuted, only resisted. Among these is the cosmological argument, which asserts that the existence of contingent beings requires the prior existence of a Necessary Being. Contingent beings are things which only exist because they were caused by beings that existed before they did. Each of us is a contingent being because we only exist because our parents existed first. But they only exist because their parents existed first, and so on, going all the way back to the first human-beings. But they didn't bring themselves into existence either.

It is a matter of common experience that every cause and effect sequence must start with some sort of initial cause. But what is true with respect to things which we cause must also be true for the entire universe. In order for the cause and effect chain which we observe in the universe to exist, there must be a First Cause, which is un-caused, as its Source. Scientists commonly agree that matter-energy can't be this and they also can't explain why a Singularity which was believed to exist prior to the Big Bang would spontaneously explode and produce the universe that we observe. And it's not as if they may someday discover why. For, how could this Singularity be studied? And how could a Singularity contain all of the laws of nature which we have discovered?[85]

---

85 *What is thought to have existed prior to the Big Bang is usually referred to as a Singularity. Some believe it was actually a massive black-hole. But a black-hole is really just a void. To say that it was a massive black-hole would be incorrect because a black-hole would have no mass or energy (at least insofar as anything would be coming out of it). So it is Big Bang cosmology and not the Christian account of Creation that really does require belief in Magic: namely, that everything somehow came from a Void; in other words, from nothing. . .*

Furthermore, it is simply the nature of the case that Science will never be able to answer the question: Why does something exist rather than nothing? The only rational answer is that it is because there was an un-created Creator before anything else existed, which is exactly how the Bible describes God.

The transcendental argument also can't be refuted, only resisted. This is the claim that logic, mathematics, Science, all knowledge and, even, all information only exist because God exists as the Original Mind and made us rational beings capable of understanding the world around us which He has made, "thinking His thoughts after Him".

The absolute reliability of logic and mathematics and the general reliability of our senses and memories in order to provide us with information are all things which are accepted by all sane people. But none of these things can be found in the physical world. Rather, these things must exist in us in order for us to be able to understand the world around us and, also, ourselves, other people and the past and the future (to the extent in which we are capable of understanding these).

But if one simply replaces the Singularity with the God described in the Bible then there is an entirely reasonable explanation for how everything else came to exist. "In the Beginning, God created the heavens and the earth." This 1st verse of the 1st book of the Bible (Genesis) implies what is specified elsewhere in the Bible: that God existed (as the Eternal Mind in 3 Persons) before He created the universe. The 2nd verse says this: "The earth was without form and void, and darkness was over the face of the deep. And the Spirit of God was hovering over the surface of the waters." While the 2nd verse of Genesis is in words which were intended to be understood by common people, it can be understood to be consistent with all that we know today. What it refers to is unformed matter and energy, with "the face of the deep" and "waters" being non-technical metaphorical language suitable for all readers: the primal material for the entire universe. From this God created the physical universe, the reliable laws of nature, living things, and human-beings with rational and moral minds/souls/spirits.

This includes understanding our brain-chemistry. So, our brain-chemistry can't be the source of this. In short, the irrefutable existence of our minds and the information which they discover points to the existence of Another Mind, Who could only be God, our Creator.

The argument from morality is another which can't be refuted. Though many try to deny it, especially in 21st century "post-modern" circles, it is simply not possible to live without knowing that certain things are absolutely wrong. But this can only be the case if there is a Supreme Authority for morality. As we already observed, if this was just a more advanced Intelligence than humanity, it would not be sufficient. For it could still be imagined that there is a higher one than this which could prove it wrong. And so on.

The only way that right and wrong exist is because there is an Original Moral Being Who is also The Absolute Moral Authority. Once again, this points to The Creator God described in the Bible and described as speaking to us there. Without God right and wrong can only be arbitrary. And the same would also be true of human-rights.[86]

And one more argument which can only be resisted is the one which was presented in Chapter 1 (which I call the presuppositional argument):
God made us to know Him ---> We know Him ---> God exists

The premises of this argument and its conclusion (which must follow from this soundly-constructed argument) can certainly be denied. But they cannot be refuted. The flow-chart introduced in chapter 2 shows the rational path to

---

[86] *There is no question that different human cultures have different conceptions of human-rights. For example, those held by Americans are clearly different than those of the Muslim world and China (as well as those of the past, like the view of Nazi Germany). How can these differences be resolved? They can only be resolved if there is an Absolute Source and Standard for right and wrong. And, again, that is none other than The God Who reveals Himself in the Bible. We also know this God in our minds and as the Creator and The One Who sustains the entire universe.*

knowing God.

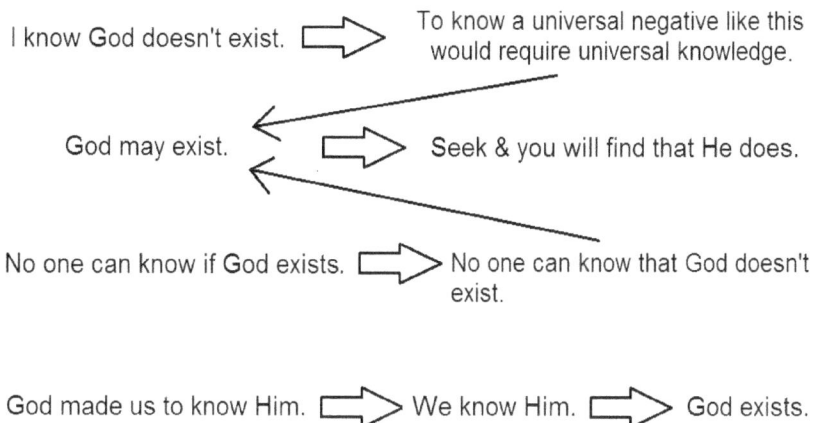

Part 2

We have already examined the Humanist worldview and shown its shortcomings. But what about other views? As was noted in Chapter 1, there are 4 primary worldviews in the world today: Humanism, Christianity, Islam and Hinduism/Buddhism. This is not to deny the fact that there are hundreds, if not thousands of differing sects within these basic categories. But the variations within these groups do not change the fact that they have fundamental points of agreement and fundamental disagreements with those in the other groups.

For example, Hindus and Buddhists (like Humanists) reject the Creator God as He is described in the Bible. And Muslims (like believing Jews) reject the Christian view that God is a Trinity of equally-divine Persons and that God came into this world as the man, Jesus Christ in order to save us. And although there are many variants, the vast majority of people can be found to fall within one of these general categories. These 4 are represented in the chart on the following page.

The Four Leading Worldviews Today & Yesterday

Which one do you believe?

Worldview	View of Reality	Ethical Authority	World War 2 Parallel
Humanism	Materialism: Nothing exists other than matter-energy & mindless forces of Nature in space-time. Both the universe & all life developed through evolution.	Us: Human-beings can determine for ourselves what is true & good and what we need to do in order for our species to survive & prosper.	The Soviet Union: Like today's Humanists, the Soviets sought to establish a worldwide community of economic equality (Socialism) based on anti-religious Materialism.
Christianity (Judeo-Christian)	Theistic Dualism: An Eternal God made both a material universe & a "world" of minds (or souls or spirits), in which human-beings are unique as minds housed in bodies.	The God of the Bible: Human-beings are made in God's image as rational, moral beings for the purpose of being His children. God is the Source & Ground of truth & goodness.	America & our non-Communist Allies: Mostly Christian nations opposed to the religious & general oppression of the Nazi's & Soviet Union, but allied with the 2nd vs. the 1st
Islam	Theistic Dualism: An Eternal God made both a material universe & a "world" of minds (or souls or spirits), in which human-beings are unique as minds housed in bodies.	The God of the Quran: Human-beings are made to be obedient subjects of the Almighty King of the Universe as stipulated in the Quran.	Nazi Germany: Like today's Muslims, the Nazi's sought to conquer the world and establish a worldwide totalitarian empire based on a claim of divine authority.
Hinduism/Buddhism	Spiritualism: Emphasis on our spiritual lives over our material existence, even to the extreme of denying that the latter exists.	Karma: Ethical principles which are part of how the universe works.	None: This tradition tends to be introspective & passive. So most serious followers tended to be neutral.

First, some likely objections to the World War 2 associations in this chart should be addressed. It is to be expected that many of you will object to Humanism being linked to the former Soviet Union, with Christianity being linked with the United States of America. But, it will be especially objectionable for some that Islam is linked with Nazism. So we will begin by addressing this.

It simply cannot be stressed enough that showing a linkage between Islam and Nazism does not at all mean that all Muslims are the moral equivalent of Nazi's! Nothing could be further from the truth. There are many Muslims who are good people. However, their religion clearly has problems.

Just as bad people sometimes have true and good beliefs, good people can have bad beliefs (or, at least, support people with bad beliefs). Such is the case within Islam. For Islam is in need of reform in several major ways. Most significantly, both Humanists and Christians (and others) should agree that Islam needs to abandon its ideal of worldwide conquest (as Christians long ago did, except for a very few marginalized extremists). And Islam needs to learn how to separate religion and politics (again, as Christians have learned to do, except for a few marginalized extremists, although this took centuries to occur).

These two problems may be seen to be the root of many other problems found in "the Muslim world". These include frequent attempts to spread Islamic rule by force, and the lack of religious freedom and other types of freedom in Muslim lands, especially for women and LGBTQ people. Indeed, that there even is such a thing as "the Muslim world" points to the problem. By contrast, what was once known as "Christendom" is now seen as an antiquated thing (which was not ideal and, thus, is not desirable to re-establish looking forward) among nearly all Christians.

It cannot be reasonably denied that the Muslim world's problems parallel what arose in Germany prior to World War 2. This even includes hatred of Jews which, sadly, is seen in most places with significant Muslim populations.

And it has always been the case that when the Muslim population reaches a certain point in a society, civil unrest begins to grow within the Muslim population, with the desire to establish self-governing enclaves. This is because secular or other non-Muslim rule is not accepted by most Muslims. And if self-governing enclaves are established, then conflicts between these enclaves and the areas surrounding them will inevitably arise. We have already begun to see this in many European and Asian countries, though this has not yet occurred in America as of the writing of this book.

It does the world no good to pretend that these problems aren't real. In fact, it hurts Muslims even more than non-Muslims, as they are far more often the victims of Muslim violence and oppression than non-Muslims.

As Germans in the 1920's & 30's needed to challenge the Nazi's and their evil views, so it is that peace-loving Muslims today need to challenge those in their religion who practice evil in the name of God (even as the Nazi's did). They also need to reject the ways in which Islam's teachings encourage oppression and war.

Second, many will strongly object to Humanism being linked with the former Soviet Union in the preceding chart. But the philosophical connections between the ideology of the U.S.S.R. and the Humanism which dominates the intellectual establishment in America and the rest of the developed world today are actually quite simple.

Both are "secularist" approaches which seek to exclude religious influence on society in favor of a so-called "scientific" worldview (known as Materialism). And both view Socialism, not Capitalism, as the best economic system. But the "egalitarian" ideal of Socialism demands an ever-increasing role of government. And where the role of government increases, freedom will inevitably decrease. (More on this in chapter 12.)[87]

The main reason most people don't see these connections is because the Humanist perspective which dominates today simply dismisses the possibility that these are true connections. And most of us have also been taught the Humanist belief that a return to Christianity as the dominant view will inevitably take us back to the "dark ages" of Medieval Europe, to rampant superstition and to theocratic rule. But, those of us who have turned to Christianity have come to see that this is not true.

---

87 *As civics classes used to teach, the American Vision was one in which the people were to have as much freedom as possible under a strictly-limited democratic government "of, by and for the People". The government was to be limited because it was understood that all people have a God-given right to "life, liberty and the pursuit of happiness" and that the role of the government should be to protect these rights, not to limit them. It should be noted that the theistic foundation of freedom was explicitly expressed and was considered necessary and indispensable.*

This government was never intended to regulate all areas of life, as so many today seem to assume and as is the case in all socialistic societies, whether these are established by public consent and gradually (as in the "creeping socialism" of Western European nations, which is favored by those on the political Left in America today), or by revolution and, thus, very quickly, as in the former Soviet Union and other Marxist states. Rather, the role of the government was to be only for the protection of the nation against foreign threats and to protect the peoples' freedoms and property from being threatened or taken away by those who would abuse their liberties to oppress others.

The ideal of America's founders was that the people should be under "the rule of (a Higher) Law", not under the rule either of the majority, or a few, or one ruling dictator. The Constitution was intended to outline the principles and limits of this rule. The ideal that we should be a republic rather than a pure democracy also was intended to protect against "mob rule". Unfortunately, though, to eliminate the "God-given" aspect of the vision (or, at the least, to deny the idea that there is a Higher Law than human opinions) is to undermine it at its foundation. For, if there is no Higher Law than man, then human rights can only be arbitrary and fleeting, whether these are defined by a majority, a few or one.

On the contrary, it was during the time in which Christianity was the prevailing point-of-view (which was the case until the early 20th century) that the "American Experiment" in Democracy was launched and advanced, as was the modern age of Science. And although the turning-point in the shift from Christianity to Humanism as the guiding philosophy of America had already occurred by the time World War 2 broke out, the effects of this shift were not yet widespread across the land. So it could still be said that America was a predominantly Christian nation.

Part 3

Next, we will look at the fact that, unlike Humanism, Christianity accounts for all that we experience and know, including consciousness, perception, rationality, intelligence, morality, guilt and all knowledge, including that of the physical world, history, other people, ideas and of God.

In the previous chapters we have focused extensively on Humanism's failure to account for the existence of and to explain the nature of consciousness, perception, rationality, intelligence, morality, guilt and all knowledge, including that of the physical world, history, other people, ideas and of God. All of these things clearly exist and must therefore be accounted for and understood for what they are in themselves. But Humanism, insofar as it is slave to Materialism, can only claim that everything on the side of consciousness and human subjective experience is either some other material phenomenon which we can't currently describe or just an illusion of brain-chemistry.

But if it just another physical phemonenon, it would still require an observer in order for it to be observed and known. To say that it observes itself (as some say about our brains) is a non-explanation. In other words, it can't explain what these observations are, nor can it explain our existence as observers.

And to say that it is all illusion is also a non-explanation which no one really believes, not even people who are clinically insane. It's just impossible to live on the basis of this view. So there is no choice except to go back to recognizing that reality is dualistic, including both objects (material things or bodies) and observers, who are more than material entities. So it is that human-beings must be seen as immaterial minds/souls/spirits joined to physical bodies. And this is precisely the view of Christianity.

So Christianity provides the simple explanation for why we exist and why we can experience and know the world around us. Indeed, it is so simple that it doesn't even really require any explanation beyond saying that we exist and experience and know what we do simply because God made us and made us so that we can experience and know all that we do.

In fact, this is why atheists often accuse Christians of using the "God did it" explanation as a cop-out for people who are too intellectually lazy to understand their world. But it is atheists who expend extraordinary and entirely unnecessary intellectual energy pursuing an exercise in futility: trying to understand us and everything else God created without Him.

Ironically, while atheists will often accuse the Christian view of being overly simplistic, they will also often claim that the principle of "Occam's Razor" favors their view. Occam's Razor is a principle attributed to a Medieval philosopher known as William of Ockham. The principle is that, all things being equal, the simplest explanation for something is usually the correct one. But atheist critics of Christianity can't have it both ways. If the Christian explanation is the simpler one (which we will agree is the case), then Occam's Razor cuts against the elaborate atheist and anti-theistic Humanist explanations, not the Christian approach.

And the Christian worldview is the simple explanation that works (if only a person is willing to be open to this), while Humanism's elaborate alternatives just don't. It's simply foolish to ignore an explanation which has been proven to work and to try to fabricate an entirely different one.

Next we will look at the Hindu/Buddhism group as the other of the 4 primary groups that, like Humanism, rejects the basic Theism of both Christianity and Islam. Despite major differences (which will be the focus of the next chapter), both Christians and Muslims agree that there is an Almighty, Omniscient, Omnipresent God, Who is radically-distinct both from what He has created and also from every human-being or other being whom He has created as The Supreme Being.

But, while the Asian traditions share Humanism's rejection of One True God, they have a basic difference with Humanism in this. Humanism denies the reality of the spiritual, while Hinduism and Buddhism affirm this side of reality. But, unlike Christianity, the Asian traditions tend either to elevate the spiritual over the physical or to deny the physical altogether. But the Christian approach says that both sides are equally-real and important.

Furthermore, the Asian traditions also deny that human-beings and other beings have been created by a Creator so that each one of us would have a person-to-Person relationship with our Creator (or, more accurately, a person-to-Persons relationship; but we will focus on the necessity of the latter plural in the next chapter). But Christianity not only accounts for the real existence of both the physical and spiritual realms, it also accounts for why we exist as distinct personalities, distinct from the universe around us, distinct from other individuals and distinct from our Creator.

It is not a mere coincidence that many Westerners educated in Humanism are often attracted to the Asian traditions, whether in their traditional forms or in what have been called "New Age" expressions. This is because the Asian approaches, like Humanism, are fundamentally anti-theistic. Some strands of Hinduism do have many deities, but none of them is equal to The Almighty God of the Bible. So it is anti-theistic with regard to the God of the Bible, Who is The Supreme Being. Meanwhile Buddhism, like Humanism, is completely anti-theistic.

Those who believe in multiple deities always attribute some attributes of the God of the Bible to their "gods" so as to distinguish them as superior to us (such as immortality and supernatural power). But they always deny other attributes of the Biblical God. And, in some cases human characteristics are attributed to these deities which are clearly in conflict with what the Bible says about God. In other words, it is sometimes quite clear that they are just sinful human-beings "writ large". So, in these ways these supposed deities are "lesser gods" in comparison to the Biblical God.

For those who are "polytheists" the list of denied attributes naturally includes God's One-ness. And it usually includes other attributes which theologians have called "incommunicable attributes" (that is, attributes which are inconceivable for us to have), like omnipresence, omnipotence and omniscience. That polytheists inevitably reject certain attributes of the Biblical God should be obvious for the simple reason that if they accepted all of the attributes of God described in the Bible (including God's One-ness) then they would have no conflict with those who believe in the God of the Bible.

Furthermore, approaches which say that there is a scale of being which we can ascend (as in Hinduism and Mormonism) also reject the Supremacy of God.[88] They also reject the absolute "Other-ness" of God in relation to us. This is because of the fact that if we either are or can become equal to "God" in any real sense, then there would be no absolute distinction between God and us.

---

88 *I anticipate that some readers will object to my reference to Mormonism here. But a study of traditional Mormon doctrine will show that this is one of the tenets of the Latter Day Saints movement, one of many which have distinguished it from all other Christian denominations. It is true that many Mormons today would either downplay or, even, reject this, as well as other doctrines which the church has held in the past that conflict with the basic theology shared by all historic Christian denominations (as is reflected in the Apostles' Creed).*

It seems that the LDS Church in general is wanting to be perceived as just another Christian denomination today, rather than as the only true Church (though there are, no doubt, still some who would claim the latter). I would add that this also seems to be occurring with the Jehovah's Witnesses. In both cases this is seen as a good development. Insofar as the LDS Church and Jehovah's Witnesses do this they contribute to the unity of Christianity rather than being separatist cults. What categorizes a cult is not so much differences in theology (which are manifold and often quite extreme among the many denominations of Christianity) as it is the claim that, because of differences in theology, "only our Church is The True Church".

All of these are clear efforts to craft gods or a god in our likeness, a rejection and reversal of the reality that God made us in His likeness so that we can know Him. This is why the Bible constantly condemns all such thinking as idolatry. In short, the answer to all non-theistic and all polytheistic worldviews is the same: There is a God and He is definitely not me or you or any other being in the universe!

In addition to polytheism, Pantheism (all is God) or Pan-en-theism (God is in all) also fail because they deny the Otherness of God. But they also fail because seeing everything as God or God as everything or seeing God as equally in everything ultimately eliminates the meaningfulness of the concept. In this case "God" just becomes a label for everything.

This is evident in the "evolution" of physicist Stephen Hawkings' use of the term God. While he originally used the term in his best-seller: "A Brief History of Time", it was clear that he merely used "God" as a label for all that exists or as a synonym for the "theory of everything" which he was seeking to find. So it was not surprising that he would abandon speaking of "God" in his later writings.

Religious thinking based on the Asian traditions differs in how it views the universe as a whole, with some seeing it as "divine" in either a Pantheist or Pan-en-theist way (in many Hindu traditions) and some seeing it as completely impersonal (in many Buddhist circles). But what is agreed upon is that there is no God Who is distinct from us and the universe. In this respect the Asian traditions are radically at odds with Christianity, but in agreement with modern Humanism. This is why many Westerners trained in Humanism often have an affinity for these approaches (as this writer once had).

Only the monotheistic traditions maintain that God is wholly Other. To use the pronouns of old English: God is "Thou" and we are "thee". The Bible-connected traditions all teach that there is a "Creator-creature distinction"; or, more broadly, a "Creator-Creation distinction". (This includes Judaism,

Christianity and Islam, since Muhammad was clearly inspired in part by the other two. But, as will be discussed in the next chapter, those who reject the Christian Trinity also have a demonstrably inferior understanding of The Supremacy and Self-sufficiency of God.)

But if the universe is either Divine and Personal as a whole or just impersonal, our individuality as persons cannot be explained. Indeed, in many cases Buddhists will directly assert that individuality is an illusion, as will some of the more extreme Materialistic Humanists. (We would say that such Materialists are actually consistent with what they profess to believe. But as such they show the bankruptcy of this.) And whether it is thought that we will all eventually be absorbed into a Universal Soul or just impersonal matter seems to be a distinction without a significant difference. In either case, you and I would cease to exist.

But the question remains: Why do we exist now as individuals? Again, the answer: "We don't really exist." simply won't work. For we all know that we exist as individuals even if we doubt everything else. In the film, "The Matrix" all of the people plugged into the Matrix were completely deceived about their lives. But it is not possible that they could have been deceived about their existence. If so, the entire plot of the film would fall apart. Denial of one's individual existence is the ultimate example of a self-defeating claim. And even if it was the case that each of us is just part of a Universal Soul, it is still undeniable that, for now at least, we are still real individual parts of this.[89]

---

89 *Insofar as Buddhists and Materialists claim that the universe is ultimately impersonal they both fail to account for the existence of morality. For morality is inherently a personal quality. This was also an error of the ancient Greek Idealists and those who followed them. To claim that personal qualities can somehow exist in the abstract rather than as qualities of people or God or gods makes no sense at all.*

People and God or gods can be right or wrong. One may even wish to argue that animals can be right or wrong. But clearly a rock can't be! So Buddhists and Secularists who see the universe as ultimately impersonal

It is not hard to see that anti-individuality thinking will tend to lead to the idea that focusing on individuals and individual rights is wrong; or, at best, it is not of ultimate importance. If individuality is considered to be either an illusion or temporary, then what is considered real and lasting (whether it's a human collective or Nature) will naturally be given priority. But history has always shown that wherever this type of thinking prevails, freedom disappears and tyranny reigns. For this is one of the hallmarks of totalitarian regimes, in contrast with free societies.

Totalitarian regimes have come in many forms throughout history. But one thing that they always have in common is that they always claim to seek "the good of the many" and require that the freedom of individuals must be sacrificed for this. This is the case when these tyrannical regimes are in the form of secular Marxist states, like the former Soviet Union. It is also the case with totalitarian religious societies, like "the Muslim world" of theocratic states, and, yes, intolerant, comformity-demanding Christian

---

can be seen to take the moral sense which only God could have given them and project it onto a God-less universe.

On the other hand, Hindus and others who argue for the existence of some sort of "Universal Soul" can account for the universality of morality. But they ultimately deny individuality also. Also, they seemingly can't avoid attributing both good and evil to the Universal Soul. So their view tends toward an unsatisfying moral Dualism. And whereas a metaphysical (mind & body or body & soul) Dualism has been advocated here as necessary, a moral Dualism is to be rejected.

The "Star Wars" view of morality is a good example of the problem with such a Dualism. Based on how the Force is described, there is really no explanation for why good should be considered superior to evil ("the Dark Side"), nor is there any explanation for why it should be expected that good will eventually triumph over evil. But the Star Wars saga would be very unappealing indeed if both of these weren't assumed. So, even though the Star Wars universe is of course fictional, it nonetheless illustrates how elements of Christian morality are often smuggled into a non-Christian worldview.

theocracies of the past. And it is also the case with nationalist tyrannical states, like the Nazi regime or Imperial Japan from the middle of the last century. The chart on the next page illustrates the real continuum of human governments.

The Continuum of Governments

by Christopher Angrus
December 5, 2017

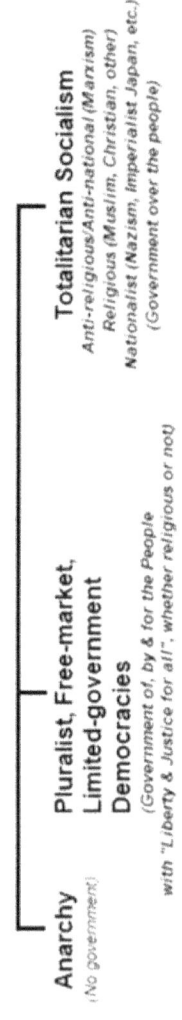

Anarchy	Pluralist, Free-market, Limited-government Democracies	Totalitarian Socialism
(No government)	(Government of, by & for the People with "Liberty & Justice for all", whether religious or not)	Anti-religious/Anti-national (Marxism) Religious (Muslim, Christian, other) Nationalist (Nazism, Imperialist Japan, etc.) (Government over the people)

Contrary to the conventional Left versus Right distinction, the real difference in societies is in how much government control exists versus how much freedom individuals and groups have. Socialist societies hold that it is the Government that ultimately determines both the rights of individuals and, even, what is right and wrong. This is the case whether such societies emerge quickly through revolutions (as with Bolshevik revolution in Russia) or through a gradual growth of the size and power of government (which has been known as "Fabian creeping Socialism" and has been the trend in the United States of America for almost 100 years).

Historically, most societies have embraced some form of Socialism because people will normally be willing to sacrifice freedom in the hope of having more security. But the United States of America was unique in being founded on the idea that both human rights and right and wrong are higher than any government, group or individual as part of the order of the universe as created by God. This Higher Law was understood to be conveyed both through Nature through the consciences and experience of humanity (Natural Law) and through God's revelation in the Bible. The only way to avoid both anarchy and the tyranny of human governments is to have a society in which most people are able to police themselves because they recognize and follow the Higher Law. Without this, societies will always move toward police states.

Since totalitarian regimes emphasize the collective over the individual they will always tend to see individuality as a threat. So they will discourage or, if necessary, punish individual expression.

It is sadly true that a lot of the history of Christianity has been bloodstained by tyranny. But this is actually in spite of what the Christian worldview (rightly understood) says. But the oppression of individuals and individuality is actually consistent with all other worldviews.[90]

Most importantly, love would a meaningless illusion without our existence as real individuals, along with the existence of other individuals for us to love. As they say, "it takes two to tango". And it would also be an illusion unless it came from God as a characteristic of His multi-Personal nature from all eternity, which He also decided to share with beings He would create, so that they could love both each other and Him. (More on this, too, in the next chapter.)

So, our individuality not only implies the existence of other human-beings who are distinct from us, it also implies the existence of a God Who is also distinct from us. And, once again, we all know, at least on a sub-conscious level, that this God exists.

The diagram to follow shows the contrast between the Christian view and

---

90 *An example of this is seen in how those who believe in Karma and reincarnation often view right and wrong in this world. It is not surprising that people who believe in Karma tend to be more indifferent to and tolerant of evil in this world in many cases, even to the point of refusing to take up arms to fight extreme and violent examples of it, as many Hindus and Buddhists did during World War 2. This is because those who hold to the concept of Karma have the tendency to see the suffering of people as being "karmic backlash" for evils done by them in prior lives. This even includes situations in which people are clearly oppressed and suffer through no fault of their own. For instance, a child who is the victim of sexual abuse may be considered to be paying the price for having done the same thing to others in a past life! (The writer credits radio commentator Dennis Prager for furnishing this point and example.)*

that of Humanism and the Asian faiths. As with the earlier circle diagram (found at the end of Chapter 6), the Creator/Creation distinction is seen with the circle on the left. Non-theistic systems deny this. And they not only deny the existence of a Creator distinct from what "He" creates, these systems cannot really explain our existence as beings distinct from the world around us (and from our Creator), nor can they explain why anything exists at all.

And it should also be recognized there cannot be more than one Creator, Who is The Original and, thus, The Supreme Being. This alone shows that polytheism can't be true. However, it is possible for there to be Co-creators, Who are perfectly equal as The Supreme Being and eternal (that is, as existing prior to creating anything and anyone). And this is exactly how the Bible describes God, even from its beginning in Genesis 1 (in using plural pronouns to refer to God).

And, as has already been discussed, it is necessary for there to be a Plurality of Beings in order for God to have any personal attributes, including goodness, justice and love. Without this, such attributes would be meaningless.

CHRISTIAN THEISM

God the Father
⇦ ⇨   ⇦ ⇨

⇧ ⇩   **God the Spirit**
⇧ ⇩

God the Son

(The box above signifies that
The Eternal Son has become
permanently embodied as God
in the body of the man Jesus.)

ALL NON-THEISTIC SYSTEMS

(Includes Humanism/Hinduism/Buddhism/"New Age")

Nothing exists other than the Universe

(The broken borders on the personal circles signify that there is no real distinction between us and the universe, just the illusion of such. But both God and we are real beings distinct from the world around us.)

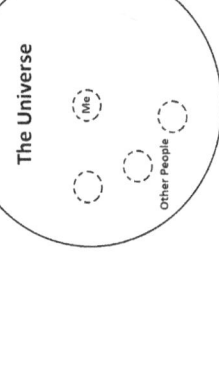

The Asian traditions at least recognize the necessary existence of the "world" of minds and the meaningfulness and morality which are included in this. But they can't explain why they exist any more than Humanism can. But Christianity does. They exist because God is The Original Mind and Moral Being and because He made us as finite reflections of Him.

Whereas Humanism tends to deny the spiritual (or mental) side of reality, Buddhism is based on the idea that the physical is not real. But this makes no more sense than the Humanist belief that the mental (or spiritual) side of existence is merely a material phenomenon. Either way, one will founder on the rocks of reality, either by denying that there actually is a world around us and that we have real physical bodies or by denying that our experiences are real and are not just reducible to material phenomena. No one really believes either one of these things, no matter what they claim.

So in rejecting the God of the Bible the Asian traditions have the same problem as Humanism. They have no explanation for where our existence as individual personal beings came from. From the Humanist, Hindu or Buddhist perspective our existence as individuals is either temporary or just an illusion. But Christianity, Judaism and Islam (despite crucial differences between them) all say that God made us individuals for eternity.

And, like Humanism, the Asian traditions can't provide a coherent explanation for why good and evil exist. This is because good and evil are inevitably personal characteristics. To say that they reflect impersonal laws of the universe (which is what Karma represents) simply won't cut it. It really makes no more sense to attribute goodness or evil to supposed moral forces which are impersonal than to attribute goodness or evil to impersonal physical forces.[91]

---

91 *Once again, there are some who believe that we are just members of a universal Being (or Soul) with moral characteristics. But if this were so, then seeing ourselves as individuals would just be a malady of the universal Being needing to be cured. So, as already indicated, this is an anti-individual perspective, which can only lead to the oppression of individuals*

This brings us to a more general problem. A religion or worldview can't be true if one can't live according to its claims. And no one has ever been able to live according to the claims of Humanism, Hinduism or Buddhism. This is because, in one way or another these approaches deny essential aspects of human existence, especially that we are real rational moral personal beings living in a real physical world.

---

in the name of the supposed "common good".

And if the entire universe is One Soul or Mind then what is known as "the Euthyphro problem" comes into play. That is, how can good and evil avoid being arbitrary, with whatever this Single Being does being good by definition? In this case good and evil could not be meaningfully distinguished. This problem also affects all absolute "monist" theologies (that is, those which deny the "One God in 3 Persons" of the Christian Trinity). But it will subsequently be shown that the Christian conception of God, properly understood, avoids this problem.

Chapter 9
Why Christianity Is True And Other Approaches Which Begin With One God Fail.

Christian Triune Monotheism is superior to Muslim and Jewish theology and, thus, describes The True Supreme Being, the Only One Worthy of The Name and our devotion.

By now it should be clear that if there is a Supreme Being, then saying there isn't one or, at least, doubting this is a Big Problem. In reality, it's The Biggest Problem. This is the peril of Humanists and Buddhists. And it should also be clear that saying that there is more than one god (as some Hindus and others do) is also a denial of God as The Supreme Being, as is the view which says that god is somehow identified with the universe (the belief of some Hindus and others). And to hold that there is one true god but then deny that this god has certain attributes is also a failure to recognize God properly. In this chapter we will see how non-Christian monotheist (one-god) theologies fail to present The One True God in His full Glory.

The first element of Christianity's unique monotheism which we will look at is the Trinity. Over the years it has been common for Muslims and others to accuse Christians of being tri-theists (that is, worshippers of 3 gods). But the short answer to this accusation is this: "With all due respect, who are you to tell us Whom we worship? We know that we worship One God! But this God manifests Himself as 3 Equal Persons. It's you who needs to understand how this works."[92]

---

92 *In some cases Muslims falsely understand the Christian Trinity as God the Father, Jesus the Son and Mary the Mother. This shows the level of*

The Christian understanding of One God in 3 Persons is entirely different than worshipping 3 different gods with different personalities and characteristics. It's not hard to see the difference (once again, if you are willing to see it). Ancient Greek mythology featured tales of the struggles between various deities, who were distinguished from each other by having different personalities, powers and domains. And it was common for people to worship more than one of these. But such worshipers self-consciously

---

ignorance about Christianity which has traditionally existed in Muslim circles. But it also reflects the fact that Mary has been unduly exalted in Roman Catholic circles for over 1000 years and even up to the present day in some areas.

Another thing that reflects ignorance of Christianity is the tendency of many contemporary critics in the developed world to think that Christians consider God to be male. This usually comes from Humanists, although some of these claim to be Christians. Such people are often found in the so-called "mainline" Christian denominations or other non-traditional sects. But should be understood that whenever Christians use the male pronoun, "He" it is just a linguistic convention which is used because of the lack of a suitable pronoun in the English language which would depict Who God really Is: The Creator of both maleness and femaleness.

In other words, God is "Supra-gender". (Not "Transgender"!) It is ridiculous for critics to call Christians' use of the male pronoun "sexist". We do so because calling Him "It" just doesn't cut it. It's too impersonal. Indeed, the fact that God is the Creator of both the male and female genders (which, contrary to today's transgender insanity, is synonymous with "sex") means that both men and women equally bear the image of God, as is clearly stated in the first chapter of the Bible (Genesis 1, verse 27).

A key consequence of this is that the supreme reflection of God which is possible for us is the spiritual union of a man and woman in marriage. (This was was memorably pointed out in a sermon heard by this writer years ago. Thank-you, Marty Scales!) This is one of the reasons why it is desirable for most people to marry someone of the opposite sex. And the fact that the last part of the last sentence didn't even have to be mentioned anywhere in the world until about 30 years ago shows how radical the developed world has become. . .

worshiped multiple gods. Never was it claimed that they were really worshiping only one god in different forms, as Christians assert that we do.

And, as was cited in the last chapter, never did any of the worshipers of the Greek gods really worship The God Whom Christians worshiped. Some may have initially claimed that the Christian God was just Zeus rebranded. But in rejecting what early Christians testified both about Jesus and God in general they, in effect, chose Zeus over the Biblical God. For, if they had been willing to accept Jesus as Lord (that is, as God coming to earth as a man), then there would have been no reason not to abandon their previous manner of worship and join the Church.

Indeed, the Gospel preached by the Christians of the first few centuries to their polytheistic neighbors was that they should abandon their false gods for The One True Lord, Jesus Christ, not three new Gods. This is clear both from the Biblical literature and from other literature of the time. It also seems clear that controversy over the Trinity which emerged in the first 3 centuries was really an internal Church issue and that it was actually driven mainly by a concern for the need to preserve the Oneness of God (among most, at least). The question was: What was the proper way to describe God, Jesus and the Holy Spirit so as not to lose the Oneness of God? For, the latter was regarded as sacrosanct.

So, it was always the "Tri" part of the Trinity which was in danger of being denied for the sake of preserving the Unity, usually either by making Jesus and the Holy Spirit not truly equal to God the Father or only temporary manifestations of the Father. Though there was considerable controversy and struggle to get there, it was eventually concluded that both the Unity and

---

Past cultures have been quite tolerant of homosexuality (including the Greco-Roman world in which Christianity and the New Testament emerged). But no other known culture in human history has ever sought to normalize "LGBTQ" in the way the dominant culture of the developed world today does. And seeking to do so with the "T" ("Transgender") was not even thinkable until the latter half of the 20th century.

Plurality of God must be asserted without compromise, as difficult as it may be to explain how God can be "Three-in-One" or "One-in-Three".

Contrary to a common charge, there is no inherent contradiction in the Trinity. Indeed, it is not at all hard to conceive of 3 beings who are entirely identical in nature yet distinct persons. Isn't this what triplets are? The Christian conception of God's rule is like a land which has three identical triplets as Kings or Queens.

Of course, due to variations in development human triplets are not absolutely identical. But the advent of cloning has given us a better analogy for the Trinity. God the Father, God the Son and God the Holy Spirit are like perfectly-identical clones, although they manifest Themselves in distinct ways, most amazingly in the 2nd Person having become a real human-being.

Furthermore, it is only because God is a Plurality of Persons that He can be Self-sufficient as a relational Being. This is because, if this was not the case, then God would need to create other beings to relate to. In other words, if God was only One Person (as Islam, Judaism and other anti-trinitarian theologies teach), He would be forever lonely unless He created someone else.

It is commonly recognized that human beings cannot be fulfilled without relationships with other people, as is reflected in the old saying: "No man is an island.". But what is true of us as people made in the image of a Tri-Personal God is also true for God, the Archetype of us as people. This is not a deficiency in God because, unlike the God of Islam and Judaism, The Christian God has the fulfillment of His Personality within His multiplicity of Persons.

And as with us, many of the qualities which make God a Person would be either meaningless or hollow without relationships. In order to see this consider the "fruit of the Spirit" described in Paul's Letter to the Galatians (chapter 5, verses 22-23): *"love, joy, peace, patience, kindness, goodness, faithfulness, gentleness and self-control"*. All of these are clearly relational qualities, except perhaps for joy. However, joy would be hollow if one was not able to share it with others, as would all of the other qualities.

While Christians typically focus on the fruit of the Spirit as qualities which should be seen in us, it is important to recognize that these are actually divine qualities, which are conveyed by God, the Holy Spirit. The Spirit can convey these because they are qualities which "He Himself" possessed from eternity in equal measure with God the Father and God the Son.

Most importantly, consider love. How could a single-Person God have love in Himself? Although it is common today for people to say that we must love ourselves, this was not really a way in which this word was used until quite recently (only within the past 50 years or so). And love of one's self can't really be considered a virtue. For if we "love" ourselves more than we love others, that is just selfishness!

The 2nd "Great Commandment" (after "love the LORD your God with all of your heart, mind, soul and strength") is to "love your neighbor as yourself". That the commandment is stated in this way can be seen to be a concession to human selfishness. In giving the commandment God understood that fallen humanity was invariably selfish, naturally seeking what is best for us. In other words, we all "love" ourselves without trying! The genius of the commandment, then, is that it calls us to seek what is best for others instead of just seeking what is best for us.

Human nature is at its best when we care about others more than we do about ourselves. And isn't this the essence of love? As the title character of the film "Forrest Gump" told his beloved Jenny: "I'm not a smart man. But I know what love is!" Even the mentally-limited Forrest knew that his devotion to Jenny, in which he cared about her more than he cared about himself or anything else, was real love.[93]

---

93 *It is true that caring about and for others more than one's self can sometimes go too far and lead to destructive "co-dependency" . . .*

And when the Bible says that *God is love* it means that God is always outwardly-oriented, not inwardly-oriented. Before God created the universe this applied to each Person of the Trinity loving the other 2 Persons. But, most amazingly, God also created us to be the objects of His love, <u>if we are willing</u>. And we are called to love and worship God not because He needs this. Rather, it's because <u>we</u> need this in order to be fulfilled as human-beings!

---

relationships. But such relationships are easily distinguished from healthy relationships in that they are one-sided, whereas in a healthy love relationship the attitude of caring about and for the other person more than one's self goes both ways.

It is also worth adding that Jesus took the 2nd great Commandment (to love your neighbor as yourself) even further in commanding his followers to love even our enemies and to do good to and pray for those who hate and persecute us. This is found in 2 parallel passages in the Gospels of Matthew (chapter 5, verses 43-48) and Luke (chapter 6, verses 27-36).

But, contrary to what many today seem to think, love does not mean that we must permit others to do whatever they wish. To love someone else doesn't mean that we may not oppose what they do, say or think, even very strongly at times. We see this most clearly in relationships with people with addictions or other clearly destructive behavior patterns. And while political opponents in a civil society often will oppose each other fiercely, this does not mean that they must hate those on the other side. Rather, it is still possible to love them and do good to them. This was widely-accepted and pursued as recently as the late 20th century. We desperately need to go back to this dynamic in America today.

An extreme case of this dynamic exists occurs in times of war, in which one is required to kill the enemy. But even in this situation it doesn't mean that we must hate them personally. In a famous episode during World War 1 enemy combatants agreed to a cease-fire so that they could get together to celebrate Christmas. In doing so they showed that the conflict was not really personal. This is also why prisoners-of-war should be treated humanely. And from the Christian point-of-view it is not contradictory in war to seek to kill the enemies but also pray that they might be saved.

So it's only because God is not just a Unity that He is a fully-realized Personal God, including being a Lover of others. And it is only in relation to Him that we can be fully-realized people. To reject that there is Another Who loves us and Who calls us to love Him is to be selfish in the end. This is the problem for Humanists, Hindus, Buddhists, New-age spiritualists and anyone else who worships someone or something other than the Triune God. And any monotheists who reject the Trinity, including Muslims, Jews and those in anti-trinitarian Christian sects, either reject the True God and worship a non-existent and inferior substitute or fail to know God fully, according to how He has revealed Himself to us.[94]

This is not to say that non-Christians can't be loving toward others. In fact, to the shame of us Christians, many non-Christians often do much better than many of us in loving their neighbors as themselves. But this is only because God first loved them and created them with this ability (which some theologians call "common grace"). So, there is no excuse for anyone not to love God, especially by embracing His loving offer of forgiveness, transformation and Salvation which He has provided in the sending of His Eternal Son, Jesus Christ.

Furthermore, men should certainly love other men and women other women. But this means caring about the other person more than you care about yourself, not being sexually-attracted to them. Sexual attraction isn't love! Even the use of the term "make love" for sex was unknown until the latter half of the 20th century. As common as this is today, people just didn't speak this way until the 1960's. Until then, sexual activity other than that which occurs in the marriage relationship between a man and a woman (or any other way of seeking sexual gratification) was called something else: fornication (or perversion) or sin.[95]

---

94 *The term "reject" is "crucial" here (pun intended). People who have never had the Trinity explained to them will either be willing to accept it or not. If they reject it, then they have rejected Whom God has revealed Himself to be. And there is no logical or moral reason to reject this.*

A late 20th century song by the group Roxy Music called "Love is a Drug" points to the intoxicating effect of what is today called "love", but is really sexual obsession (whether it is for someone of the opposite sex or for someone of the same sex or for something else). Either from the evolutionary or Christian perspective, it is clear that the drive for sexual pleasure is one of the strongest desires that most people have.

And like introducing intoxicants into our bodies, sexual thinking and activity

---

95 *Today's confusion between love and sexuality is also seen in the expression "public displays of affection" (or PDA's). Today these are understood as moments in which couples show sexual desire for each other; in other words, as sexual fore-play. But in the past this was not how the word "affection" was understood. Affection was just when people show that they care for one another (that is, that they love each other in the traditional sense) in a visible way by hugging, holding hands, rubbing noses together (among the Aleutian people) or with some other form of contact, or, even, just an affectionate tone of voice or look. There is no sexuality in this whatsoever! Sadly, today's obsession with sexual expression and "freedom" has tended to discourage people from showing affection to others, especially to those of the same sex, and even more especially between men and between adults (especially men) and children.*

Another example of today's confusion is found in the 2016 Academy Award-winning film "Moonlight". (Spoiler alert) The film follows a young African-American boy through three periods of his life: as a 10 year-old, a 17 year-old and a few years later. As the child of a drug-addicted mom and mostly-absent dad, "Chiron" was a very withdrawn boy and was frequently the object of bullying. (But not because he was actually a homosexual, unless we are to believe that all shy and timid boys must be gay! Rather, Chiron was bullied because he was timid and wouldn't fight back.) However, Chiron was befriended by one other boy, "Kevin".

When we meet Chiron again in high school he is still very isolated, although his friendship with Kevin had continued. But one night the two have a sexual encounter. The next day, a classmate who had long bullied Chiron ("Terrel") goaded Kevin into punching his friend repeatedly until he went down and was then kicked numerous times by others. The following day Chiron finally fights back by breaking a chair over Terrel in a classroom. But for this he is expelled and subsequently moves from Miami to Atlanta. In

has been shown to release dopamine in our brains. So, sex is indeed like a drug. But to be primarily focussed on getting this pleasure or, even, to be overly concerned with giving someone else this pleasure is not really love anymore than taking drugs and giving them to others in order to get high.

Even in the context of monogamous heterosexuality in marriage, obsession with sexual pleasure can turn what is supposed to be the ultimate physical expression of love between a man and a woman into a destructive impulse akin to an addiction. When this happens, the focus will inevitably shift from what is good for the other person (which is what love is about) to what is good for me.

If you really want to know what love really is (as the rock band "Foreigner"

---

the final stage of the film Chiron goes to meet Kevin (whom he hasn't seen for years). In the final scene Chiron reveals that the one sexual encounter he had with Kevin had been his only sexual experience.

LGBTQ advocates hailed the film for its portrayal of a gay black man. But how can a person who has had only one sexual encounter know that this is what he is? Indeed, Kevin had gone on to have a girlfriend and a child without any indication of continuing homosexual activity. Chiron's relationship with Kevin had been one of friendly affection until the one episode of sexual experimentation. The episode clearly left Chiron confused. And it is apparent that neither of the two had made any effort to stay in touch after Chiron had been expelled.

In the intervening years, Chiron simply hadn't developed sexually, either with men or women, although he had taken on a tough-guy persona to cover-up his insecurity and isolation. In the end, the film seems to leave the audience in doubt as to whether Chiron's reunion with Kevin would lead to a homosexual relationship between them. But to assume that this would happen and that an isolated incident between friends necessarily changes a friendship into a sexual relationship is a reach, at best. And it is surely a "bridge-too-far" to conclude that one sexual experience defines one's sexuality for life. Instead, a person like Chiron would be wise to develop some relationships with women, not assume that he must be a homosexual.

sang in the 1970's), the apostle Paul lists its characteristics in his first Letter to the Corinthians, chapter 13:

> *"Love is patient, love is kind. It does not envy, it does not boast, it is not proud. It does not dishonor others, it is not self-seeking, it is not easily angered, it keeps no record of wrongs. Love does not delight in evil but rejoices with the truth. It always protects, always trusts, always hopes, always perseveres." (New International Version, verses 4-7)*

That these words are often a part of wedding ceremonies is quite appropriate. But what is most amazing is that these words describe both the love that God always had and always will have within His inter-trinitarian relationships and also the love the True God offers His created children! Unfortunately, both these words and the actual wedding vow are often forgotten by many of us. But this is to neglect the meaning of the vow, which, in effect, is the signing of a solemn lifetime contract with only very limited "escape clauses".[96]

---

96 *A common excuse for ending marriages is "I don't love him (or her) anymore." But this also distorts the true meaning of love. Those who speak this way also confuse love with sexual attraction, as well as with romantic feelings. Nevertheless, what is called "falling in love" or "being in love" (in other words, romance) is certainly a wonderful aspect of human experience, which is most to be desired in a marriage relationship between a man and a woman.*

God is love. And God also invented and endorses romance. This is most obvious in the Old Testament Song of Solomon. Even if the Song of Solomon (or Song of Songs) is meant to be understood as an allegory of God's love for His people (as many believe), to describe this love in the way that this love poem does surely must mean that the sentiments described are good ones for men and women to have. And, amazingly, if the Song of Solomon is describing God's love for His people, then this means that He has romantic love for us. Of course, this does not involve sex, but it still means that the love between a man and a woman in marriage is meant to be a reflection of God's love for His children. The use of marriage and romantic language to describe God's relationship with people is also found in the 2nd half of the

In another letter, the same inspired writer helps us to see what this solemn vow is supposed to mean. In Paul's Letter to the Ephesians (in chapter 5, verses 22-33) he says that a wife's love means being willing to sacrifice your own desires and to submit to your husband whenever this is necessary for the sake of the union. And a husband's love means being willing to sacrifice your own desires and, even, your own life if this is necessary in order to care for and protect your wife.

The simple fact is that we must go back to the previous view of things, both in sexuality and elsewhere. But one must become a Christian first before he or she can live the Christian life. This is always the First Priority and the main purpose of this book. Sexual purity can't save anyone, nor can any form of obedience. It is only if Jesus Christ has saved you that you can be saved. (More on this in the following section)

Of course, sexual activity outside of heterosexual marriage often feels good. But far from being good for us and our partners, it is actually detrimental both to us and them in the long run. And we are all capable of finding a spouse of the opposite sex, even if some can't consummate this relationship physically due to physical limitations.[97] There are a few of us who don't

---

2nd chapter of the Old Testament book of Hosea and in the New Testament book of Revelation (chapter 19, verses 7-9).

But, for us, having romantic feelings is only appropriate in a real loving relationship between a man and a woman. No matter how strong such feelings may be, they are entirely inappropriate in other contexts (including adulterous heterosexual relationships as well as homosexual ones).

97 *It is unfortunately the case that some Christians today have bought into a common false notion that one's same-sex impulses (or other dysfunctional impulses) can't be replaced by sexual attraction to someone of the opposite sex. Romans 1:26 points to what is wrong about homosexuality: that it is the rejection of the heterosexuality that we are made for. Consequently, a person who has a history of homosexual practice should not assume that his or her only option is to be sexually abstinent. God will help many to realize the true purpose for which God invented sexuality: not just for reproduction, but*

need this. The apostle Paul expressed this about himself in the 7th chapter of his 1st letter to the Corinthians. But most of us need this, both for sexual fulfillment and, especially, for our personal development.

God made us sexual beings so that the sexual union would be the ultimate physical expression of the intimate personal union between a man and a woman in marriage. Of course, it also happens to be the means of human reproduction. But, contrary to the traditional Roman Catholic understanding, the first purpose is more important.[98] And no other relationship in this world

---

as the most intimate and (hopefully) enjoyable physical way to express the devotion of a husband and a wife. So if a person has any significant ongoing desires for sexual gratification (even if this is currently focused on people of the same sex, or on other things, like fetishes, or, even, on children), then this is an indicator that he or she should seek a spouse of the opposite sex.

98 *This can be seen as the real reason why the apostle Paul urges in his 1st Letter to the Corinthians (chapter 7) that husbands and wives not abstain from having sexual relations, except for limited periods of time due to specific vows. This chapter of the Bible is one of many that will likely surprise people who have never read it. While Paul's injunctions are not quite as simple and absolute as direct commands from God (as in the 10 Commandments), they nevertheless show the will of God. In this case, God desires that husbands and wives should not often withhold themselves sexually from their partners. In other words, He wants you to enjoy each other in this way!*

Sadly, this writer has seen evidence at various points that Christian women have bought into a false feminist notion that even husbands don't have the right to expect their wives to fulfill their sexual urges, except when she is "in the mood". Sometimes this can work the opposite way, too. But it seems clear that this is much less common than wives withholding sex from husbands. That wives will decline the requests of their husbands for sex is certainly understandable and acceptable on occasion. But it should be the exception, not the norm.

Even worse is a tendency for some women to refuse to help their husbands work their way out of involvement in pornography or, even, sexual temptations which they profess to have had but did not act on, by refusing to forgive them and also by punishing them by not making themselves available to them sexually. Granted, it is very hurtful to a wife to learn that

is equal to the marriage of a man and a woman.

Though the film "Vanilla Sky" is by no means a classic, there is a great line in it in which the character played by Cameron Diaz asks the character played by Tom Cruise this: "Don't you know that when you sleep with someone your body makes a promise whether you do or not?" That promise is supposed to be the marriage vow. And only a man and woman can unite both physically and spiritually and become one in marriage. Anatomy and Biology alone should make the physical aspect of this obvious! And experience will prove this about the spiritual aspect.

---

her husband has been unfaithful to her in this way, even if it was only in their imaginations. But entertaining lustful thoughts or even using pornography is not as bad as actual adultery. Wives simply must forgive their husbands of this, especially when they are repentant (that is, seeking to stop doing it), as they are obligated to be. And wives are obligated to help their husbands in this area, especially by improving their sexual relationships. (Again, the same would apply in reverse.)

Furthermore, it should be understood that even actual marital unfaithfulness is not necessarily a "deal-breaker" for a marriage. That one is unfaithful in this way doesn't mean that he or she can't truly become repentant and willing to restore the marriage relationship. And, if this occurs, the offended party should make every effort to forgive his or her partner and preserve the marriage. Indeed, the requirement of forgiveness is there even if there isn't repentance.

In addition to the influence of Feminism, a common hesitancy of many Christians both to accept these things and to discuss them can also be seen to be a hold-over from what was really an un-Biblical Victorian view of sexuality which was common in the developed world in the late 19th and early 20th centuries. This widely-recognized Victorian prudishness about sex can be seen to have been part of an approach to the Christian life which had become overly moralistic in general, too often focusing on "do's and don'ts" (many of which had dubious or no Biblical support) and not on the Christian's liberty from man-made restrictions, being under the Lordship of God alone, and, as such, being under the benefits of God's patience, mercy, forgiveness and grace.

However there is one relationship which is always more important than marriage between a man and a woman. That is the relationship which we are all called to have with God (whether we have human spouses or not), which is also described as a marriage in the Bible. (See footnote 96) So in a real sense human marriage in this world exists primarily for the purpose of helping each of us in our eternal union with God.

The more-important marriage between God and us grows in this life but is only made perfect in Heaven, after God's children go to be with Him at the time when we die (the end of life from the world's perspective, though not from the perspective of the one who dies), or when Christ returns, whichever comes first. So the marriage between a man and a woman is meant to be a "love triangle" between a man, a woman and God. But two men or two women simply can't have this relationship.

Furthermore, while the marriage relationship is a unique "three-way" relationship, it is also the case that all of our other relationships are only fulfilled insofar as they are connected to our relationship with God. In other words, they are also triangular relationships between two individuals and God. If two people each have a relationship with God then this will empower them to have the proper relationship with each other. In this case, each person will help the other to grow closer to God. And, as they do, they also grow closer to each other. But, without the "vertical relationship" with God, there is no sure basis for mutually-fulfilling human-to-human relationships.[99]

---

99 *This is why no Christian should marry someone if they are not confident that he or she is a fellow believer. The author owes the "triperspectival" understanding of human relationships expressed here to the work of a former professor, John Frame. Frame's basic idea is both obvious and simple enough for a small child to understand, yet also endless in its ramifications: that every human-being who has ever lived was born with 3 different perspectives: an inward perspective (including our thought life and self-knowledge), a perspective on the world around us (including relationships with other people), and a perspective on God (whether it is in the form of a living relationship or one of denial on our part).*

Anyone who lacks the vertical relationship with God lacks the most important relationship of all, which is the main purpose for which God made us. And that those who read this book would establish this relationship is the main reason that it has been written. It has been said that without knowing God one is like an orphan: Fatherless. But when one comes to know God he or she becomes a beloved son or daughter of God. This understanding of the Divine-human relationship is unique to Christianity.[100]

Marriage is such an important relationship that it can be said that a single person will always be alone in the world compared to someone married to a spouse of the opposite sex. This will even be true of someone who considers himself or herself to be married to someone of the same sex. It will also be true of people who are in sexual relationships without the marriage bond or of people who have the most intimate friendships imaginable. If you don't want to be lonely in this world, then there is only one way to go.

But, a person without God as his or her Father will always be alone in a more profound way, even if you are in a proper marriage bond. On the other hand, a person who knows God as Father will never be alone, regardless of your other relationships (or lack of these). This is due to the fact that only a Divine-human relationship cannot be ended by the death of the other party (from our point-of-view). But it is also due to the fact that the Divine-human relationship is with Someone Who knows us perfectly and, therefore, can have a completely intimate relationship with us. And this is exactly what He seeks with us (though not in a sexual way, of course).

There is nothing more amazing than this: even though God knows all of our

---

[100] *The idea that becoming a Christian is a matter of going from being an orphan to being a beloved child of God was wonderfully developed in a 1970's curriculum called "Sonship" written by C. John (Jack) Miller. But this idea was also expressed over 1500 years earlier in one of the most famous lines from Augustine's "Confessions": "Thou hast made us for Thyself, O Lord, and our heart is restless until it finds its rest in Thee."*

flaws and dark secrets, He is still committed to loving us forever. Again, no human religion or philosophy compares to this.

Countless Christian hymns and songs of praise have been written about this love. And many non-Christian love-songs can be also be seen to reflect the love between God and us (less any sexual aspects, of course, or other elements that are either sinful or reflect failure or futility in the love relationship). We can sing these songs to God. But, more amazingly, we can actually realize that He sings them to us! Pick a favorite love-song and try it! "Your Still the One" by Shania Twain, "The First Time Ever I Saw Your Face" by Roberta Flack, "I'll Stand By You" by the Pretenders, "Can't Help Falling in Love with You" by Elvis Presley and "All the Way" by Frank Sinatra are a few of my favorites.

The love triangle which God intends for us is seen in the diagram below.

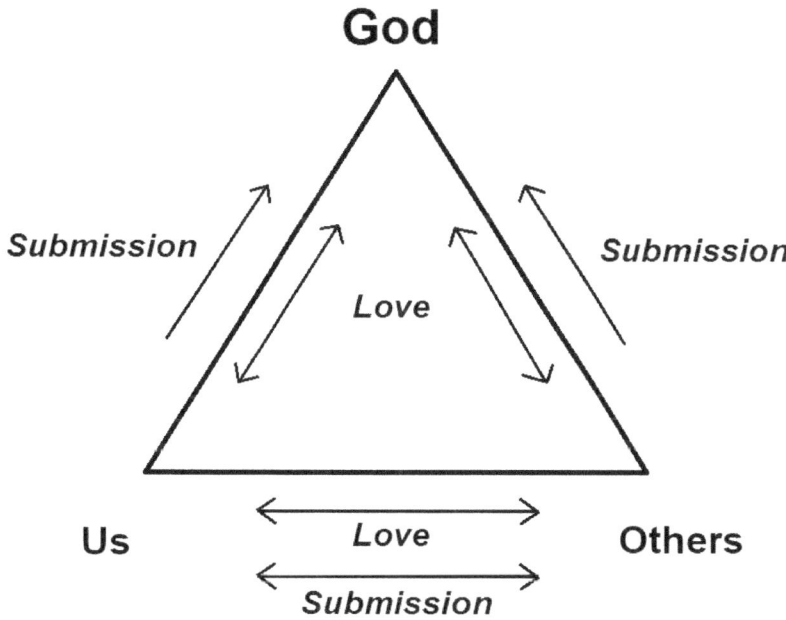

But if God loves all of us it is fair to ask: Why doesn't God save all of us? The answer is that real relationships of love must always be two-way voluntary relationships. Someone can love someone else, but not be loved by that person. In such cases, the second person will not be willing to receive the love of the first or return this love. But when this is the case, it is not a real "love match". Rather, it is unrequited love from the perspective of the one who loves. And in such cases the relationship won't last. This is just the reality of such relationships. And it applies just as much to a relationship between God and each of us because our relationships are analogous to God's relationships, both those which He has within the Trinity and with others.

So, in order to have a relationship with God you must be open to His love. To put it another way, if you want to be one of God's <u>beloved</u>, you must be willing to <u>be loved</u>. And, if you are, then you will receive God's love and also start on the path of loving Him. Without this, there is no relationship, even though God would love you. So, in a sense, even God can't make someone love Him. Again, a true love relationship must be voluntary on both sides. It can't be compulsory.

The second distinctive element that is unique to the Christian monotheism is the Incarnation; that is, that God Personally came into this world about 2000 years ago and became the man known as Jesus of Nazareth. In their objection to the Trinity Muslims and others commonly claim that God could not become a man without somehow compromising or corrupting His Deity. But the simple answer to this is: "Why not?" There is no inherent immorality or contradiction in this. This is merely a man-made limitation on what God can or cannot do. Such thinking can be seen to have been widespread in the centuries before Muhammad came on the scene.[101]

---

101 *It seems likely that Muhammad was influenced against the Incarnation (the belief that God had become a man in the person of Jesus of Nazareth) by Jewish theology and perhaps also by Christian groups living on the edge of Christianity's expansion who held to anti-Incarnation "Docetic" theology, though most of the Christian world had embraced the Incarnation. . .*

Once again, because He is Almighty God, He can do anything. The only exceptions are things which are logical impossible, because logic is the pattern in which His Mind works. And He cannot do what is evil, because He is Perfectly-Good as a Person; actually 3 completely-equal Persons. ("Persons" seems better than "People" because the latter may falsely suggest the types of personal differences which we have.)

The Incarnation (the theological term for God becoming a man) is one of the

---

Docetism, or the belief that God did not really take on human flesh, He only appeared to have done so, had been ruled to be outside of the pale of orthodox Christian theology at the first great Council of the Church at Nicaea in 325 AD. But that this view was defeated at that time didn't mean that it went away.

It seems clear that Docetism was influenced by a Greco-Roman tendency to view the material world as being intrinsically corrupt, unlike the spiritual realm and, thus, inferior to the latter. Such thinking traced its roots back to the classic era of Greek philosophy with the writings of Plato, Aristotle and others. In the 3rd century AD such thinking saw a revival in popularity as a result of the writings of the philosopher Plotinus, who is regarded as the principal source for the rise of what came to be known as Neo-Platonism.

The same belief that "the material world is evil, but the spiritual world is good" was one of the basic principles of the well-documented Gnostic movement which flourished in the 3rd and 4th centuries. Related to Gnosticism was the Manichean philosophy which Augustine of Hippo had been partial to prior to his conversion to Christianity in 386. This philosophy and Augustine's conversion was described in his famous "Confessions".

The Neo-Platonic/Gnostic/Manichean Dualism can be seen to be a corruption of the Biblical Dualism, in which both the spiritual and physical worlds were described as being part of God's good Creation in Genesis 1 and only became corrupted (on both sides) after the rebellion of Adam and Eve. Clearly, this type of dualistic thinking survived the condemnation by the Council of Nicaea in North Africa, where Augustine lived. So, it would not be surprising that it could also have persisted on the remote Arabian peninsula until Muhammad's time in the early 7th century.

common stumbling-blocks non-Christians and even professing Christians have always had. But, the Incarnation of "God, the Son" is neither a logical contradiction nor an immoral act. On the contrary, it may be seen to be the most amazing Act of Love one could possibly imagine. ("God, the Son" also seems to better represent the Equality of the Trinity than "the Son of God".)

While Jesus' death and resurrection, which are the focus of the Easter celebration are rightly considered to be the central events of the Gospel, these events were dependent on the Christmas Event of the Incarnation. If Jesus had been merely a man his death would have been just an ordinary event. At best, he would have been just another failed would-be reformer crushed by the wheels of the establishment. But it is an entirely different story (indeed, The Greatest Story of All History) if He was The Creator God Himself, the Eternal Son, Who became a man for the specific purpose of dying so that we could be saved.

When Joan Osborne asked "What if God was one of us?" in her 1995 hit song "One of Us" she was seemingly unaware of Christianity's central teaching that God did become one of us! And He was no "slob on a bus, trying to make his way home" (as the song says). Instead, the Christian Gospel says that God, the Son had deliberately left His home in Heaven in order to become one of us as an ordinary Jewish carpenter, Who would eventually become an itinerant minister and was ultimately willing to give Himself over to be executed.[102]

---

102 *The common charges that the Jesus described in the New Testament Gospels either never existed at all, or that His resurrection along with His miraculous acts were fabricated, or that His resurrection was misunderstood as being a real return from death have been been extensively and amply answered by many Christian apologists. Such answers are readily available to anyone who is interested in them. But the Bible itself sufficiently answers these charges.*

However, the unique prejudice against the Bible and Christianity is seen in the fact that the Biblical writings are simply dismissed by many despite the fact that they are by far the most extensively documented ancient writings

So Islam and Judaism and every other anti-trinitarian monotheism all fall short of Christian monotheism in two crucial ways. First, in denying the Fullness of God as a Plurality of Persons. Second, in rejecting that God could and, in fact, did become a man while remaining God.

And unlike Islam and the other approaches, Christianity points to our Biggest Problem: being alienated from our Creator. But, in the next chapter we will focus on how Christianity also presents God's Solution: the reconciling work of God's Eternal Son, Jesus Christ. Through Him we are forgiven of our rebellion and sin and restored to the relationship with God which He created us for: as beloved sons and daughters of The King of Kings. And it also reveals the renovating work of God's Eternal Holy Spirit, in which "He" comes to live inside us for the purpose of transforming us into beings who are worthy of Heaven.

---

and that virtually all Biblical scholars agree that most of them were written well before the end of the 1st century. On the other hand, many of those who summarily dismiss the Biblical texts readily accept the legitimacy of other texts from the same period or earlier which have far less documentation.

Once again, the key is whether or not one is really interested in the answers given in the Bible and by Christians. If so, it will be quite easy to recognize that Christianity could have never spread as it did in the first few decades after the time in which Jesus was claimed to have ministered and died if it didn't happen as His disciples testified and as was recorded in the Biblical Gospels. After all, there were still plenty of people living who had been around during the time in which He was said to be around who could have discredited the disciples' testimonies. And, contrary to the assumption of many today, claims that Jesus had done miraculous healings and miraculous acts and that He rose from the dead were as extraordinary for most in the Roman Empire at the time as they would be today. Indeed, the Biblical accounts themselves reflect this.

Chapter 10
More Ways in which Christianity Shows Its Superiority Over Other Approaches

We have seen how other religions/philosophies/worldviews cannot account for many aspects of experience and knowledge. But Christianity can account for these things. In this chapter we will explore how Christianity (properly understood) differs from how the other approaches work and also shows what is wrong with them. This is especially important with regard to the various ideas that people have about the ultimate goal of human existence and about how to get there (regardless of whether the ultimate goal is called "salvation" or something else).

Almost everyone and every major religious or philosophical tradition has some sort of understanding of what constitutes a good life and also believes that living such a life will lead to some sort of a reward.[103] A good way to see the differences is to consider that there are four ways which these three are believed to relate: faith, good works and salvation. They are as follows:

1) *"Faith"* → *Salvation* (Good Works are unnecessary.)

2) *"Good Works"* → *"Salvation"* (No particular kind of Faith is necessary.)

3) *"Faith"* + *"Good Works"* → *Salvation*

---

[103] *It is true that some Humanists and, even, some religious people and groups advocate "universalism" and thereby believe that neither what we believe nor what we do matter in the end. The same fate will befall us all no matter what. But, to truly believe this would undermine all real motivation for goodness, as well as making morality itself meaningless. So, no decent person can really believe this.*

4) Salvation (Accomplished by Christ) → Faith → Good Works → Heaven

"Faith" → Salvation (Good Works are unnecessary.)

The first of these is what many believe the Protestant Christian Gospel teaches. But it is a misunderstanding of what Christianity is about. However, it is regrettably true that some churches do sometimes fall into this error. This misunderstanding of how one is saved is known as Antinomianism. It has also been called "cheap grace". But it is really a denial of grace.

For, even though the credo of the Reformation was that we are saved by faith alone, it has always been understood that true faith will always lead to the doing of good works as opportunities present themselves. This is in keeping with the words of the New Testament book of James (chapter 2, verse 26): *"For just as the body without the spirit is dead, so also faith without works is dead."* Another way of putting it is that "we are saved by faith alone, but not by faith that is alone."

Consequently, a person claiming to have faith who doesn't show this faith by doing good deeds, as opportunities come, is rightly regarded as being either a liar or self-deceived.[104] This is why "Faith" has been placed in quotes above. Any understanding of faith which does not hold good works to be a necessary result of faith is a false view of faith. To put it another way, those who believe that their faith saves them without the necessity of subsequent obedience don't have saving faith. They have nothing at all to stand on. This

---

104 *The thief who was crucified next to Jesus, who asked Jesus to have mercy on him, was showing faith in Jesus in making this request and was assured of salvation by Jesus. Obviously, this man had no opportunity to show his faith by a life of good works. However, in rebuking the other man who had been crucified with them and pointing out that Jesus, unlike them, had been innocent, this man did do a good work before he died. And that Jesus told the man: "Today you will be with Me in Paradise." seems to indicate that believers proceed immediately from this world to Heaven upon our deaths. Amazingly, this means that we will not really die from our point-of-view. (More on this in what follows)*

is also reflected in the New Testament book of 1 John (chapter 3, verses 17-19):

> *"But whoever has the world's goods, and sees his brother in need and closes his heart against him, how does the love of God abide in him? Little children, let us not love with word or with tongue, but in deed and truth. We will know by this that we are of the truth, and will assure our heart before Him."*

This perspective can also be found among Buddhists who claim that only what we believe, or how we view things really matters in the end, not what we do. In chapter 6 we discussed the problems with Buddhism. Most importantly, it denies the existence of The God Whom we all know to exist and to Whom we all know that we are accountable.

"Good Works" → ***"Salvation"*** (No particular kind of Faith is necessary.)

The second perspective is known as Moralism. It is the view held by most people who identify themselves as non-religious (that is, secular Humanists). It is also the common view of nominally-religious people. The nominally-religious are those who claim to belong to a particular religion but do not really hold to the teachings of that religion. So they are Christians, Muslims or part of another tradition in name only. It is also a view common among Hindus and other religious groups who believe that what we believe doesn't really matter in the end, only what we do. Usually, the "salvation" in view for most of these people (aside from the Hindus) is a sense of well-being in this world, rather than in a future world. This is why "salvation" is in quotes.

Unfortunately, this is also a way that does not work. This is because, from the Christian point-of-view no matter how many "good works" one does, these could not wash away the sin that separates us from God. Our sins include what we should not do and do, in deeds, words and, even, our thoughts ("sins of commission"). And they include what we should do and don't in deeds, words and thoughts ("sins of omission"). No reasonable person can deny that we are guilty in these areas, especially in the second.

And underlying our specific sins is the real root of mankind's universal sinfulness – our inescapable tendency to deny and resist God. So it is that even when we do good, if we are still in Denial of Him, then even our good works are not really purely good. They will inevitably be tainted by selfish motives. This is why Christians should never claim that our works contribute to our salvation. And this is also why "Good Works" is in quotes.

If you think you can earn either an eternal Reward or, at least, peace of conscience in this world by trying your best to be good, you will never succeed. There are two reasons for this. First, only complete and perfect goodness, which none of us could ever achieve in this world, can merit God's blessing or bring complete peace. There will always be areas where we fall short or could do more. And, second, this obedience would have had to exist from start-to-finish. So, not only do our future slip-ups doom us, our past ones already did.

"Faith" + "Good Works" → Salvation

Despite differences in terminology (especially with regard to the goal), the third conception is the most common one for serious practitioners of all of the major religions of the world. Devout Muslims, Jews, Roman Catholics, Eastern Orthodox, and, even (in practice, at least) Protestant Christians usually believe that one must have both right beliefs and right practices. As for the non-theistic faiths, many Hindus and Buddhists also hold this view, but there are also many Hindus who hold the previous view, while many Buddhists hold the first view presented here.

However, in spite of the popularity of this view and regardless of the sincerity with which it is pursued, this too is a false way! This is the error of Legalism, which makes Salvation dependent on what we do: namely, to have the right kind of "Faith" and the right "Good Works". But, we are unable to have either on our own.[105]

We have already considered the problem on the works side. The problem with basing one's standing on having a particular kind of faith is that it could always be the wrong type of faith. Or, even if it is the right kind of faith, how can one know that he or she will be able to continue in this faith? We simply can't know this. This is why the only way we can have a firm confidence that we will be OK in the end is if it depends only on what God

---

[105] *Related to this is a view which considers Faith and Good Works to be two sides of the same coin. Thus:*
Faith/Works → Salvation; or, in other words, "The Obedience of Faith" or Faithfulness → Salvation
This view has become popular in some Christian circles influenced by what has become known as "the New Perspective on Paul". But while this view is somewhat of an improvement on the first two ways, in pointing to the inseparability of Faith and Good Works, it too fails to capture the true nature of God's Saving Grace, as expressed in the 4th perspective. It also fails to recognize that Faith and Works, while inseparable, are nonetheless also distinct entities, with the former being passive and the latter active.

Sadly, this view effectively abandons the Reformation's seminal rediscovery – that our salvation comes exclusively through God's sovereign activity both on our behalf and within us. E.P. Sanders and those who agree with his "New Perspective" on the apostle Paul's view of why Christianity is superior to and supersedes Judaism are correct that God's Covenant with Israel in the Old Testament was not a purely legalistic Covenant. That is, it was not simply a Covenant promising blessing for obedience and cursing for disobedience. Indeed, the Old Covenant was based on a foundation of faith in both the Person and Words of God in many ways. So it can accurately be called a "Covenantal Nomism", in which there was the need both for faith in God and the Covenant which He had established with Israel and also for obedience to the Law embodied in the Covenant.

But the highly-destructive error of those who advocate this view is their failure to see that the True Way of Salvation described in the New Testament is the complete antithesis both of a purely legalistic approach and of a Covenantal Nomist one! This is because both of these futilely seek to move from our level <u>upward</u> and fail to see that salvation can only originate in God's activity and move from His level <u>downward</u> to us. . .

does, not at all on what we may or may not do.

We are not saved <u>by</u> our faith. Rather, we are saved by God. And we merely experience this salvation <u>through</u> our faith. Faith is not something which we do. Rather, it is a passive receiving of God's free Gift of Salvation and all that this includes. To put it another way, faith is merely the means or channel by which we receive the salvation which God provides. Our placing of faith in Christ is not the cause of our salvation. This why Paul says: *"For it is by grace you have been saved, <u>through</u> faith – <u>and this not from yourselves, it is the gift of God – not by works, so that no one can boast</u>."* (Ephesians 2:8-9)

Even our faith is not something which we would have unless God gave it to us as a gift of His grace. Contrary to what many Christians believe, regeneration, or being "born-again" leads to faith, not the other way around.[106] Nevertheless, all of us are culpable insofar as we reject His offer to save us or, at least, refuse to accept that we need His mercy. This is

---

> *Both advocates of the New Perspective and many Evangelicals fail to understand that Israel's Covenant, while given to them by God, was never intended to bring about their salvation. On the contrary, its goal was to prove that the Israelites, despite the fact that they were "God's chosen People", couldn't achieve the righteousness necessary for salvation through obedience to the Law of God. For, like the nations around them, they were also under the power of sin, as all humanity had been since Adam and Eve violated God's commandment in the Garden. So, like them, they were equally in need of a Messiah. And the ceremonial aspects of Israel's Law prefigured the atoning sacrifice which that Messiah, Jesus Christ would accomplish.*

106 *There are many good resources available for those who doubt this. But the simple reason why we cannot even contribute the faith which we need to be saved is because the New Testament declares in Ephesians 2:1 that all of us were "dead in our sins" so that God had to revive us (verse 5). Though we are not physically dead, we are all spiritually dead until God saves us. And those who are spiritually dead can't do anything spiritual (which exercising faith certainly is) any more than those who are physically dead can do anything physical. So it is fitting that Salvation is called "New Life" and "passing from death to life".*

because every human-being who has ever lived has known that our Creator exists and that we are guilty before Him and, therefore, in need of His mercy and grace. This brings us to the final conception, the only one that can possibly work and, thankfully, actually does work.

Salvation (Accomplished by Christ) → Faith → Good Works → Heaven

This is the true understanding because it is the only one which can possibly succeed. This is because every human being who has ever lived is born as a rebel against our Creator and we cannot overcome this on our own, even though we are culpable for this and also if we resist God's offer of rescue.

We all begin as truly lost sinners. And the definition of being lost is that you can't find your way out. So it is necessary that God must rescue us, just as park rangers must rescue lost hikers or else they will die! This is precisely what God did in sending His Eternal Son, Jesus Christ into the world to become the Savior of those who would believe in Him.

This is what Jesus referred to as *"the narrow path which leads to life"* (in contrast with the other ways, which make up *"the broad way which leads to destruction"*). For, the true Christian Gospel declares that Salvation is dependent only on what God does (in the past, the present and the future), both what He has done <u>for</u> us, in the saving work of His Eternal Son, Jesus Christ and what He does <u>in</u> us, in giving us true Faith and the gift of His Holy Spirit to dwell inside us in order to transform us gradually into new creatures with a new natural inclination not to sin but to do true Good Works. In this way, the Salvation which was perfectly accomplished by Christ is applied to believers in Him more and more until they are brought to Full Salvation in eternity.

The application of the Salvation accomplished by the Lord Jesus Christ comes through the working of the Holy Spirit, Who takes up residence in the heart of God's true Children as a true Divine Presence and Counselor. In this we see the necessity of the Third Person of the Trinity, the Holy Spirit, as well as the Second, the Son of God, Jesus Christ, in order for Salvation to be possible.

The uniqueness of the true Christian Gospel (or "Good News"), then, is the glorious truth that <u>we have already been saved by Christ, although we have not yet reached the full experience of our salvation</u>. This means that, if Christ died for us, our salvation is certain because it has already been fully accomplished. But it is not yet complete from our point-of-view. And it won't be until our days in this world or complete or, if we are still alive at this time, until this present world comes to an end in "the Day of the Lord" and is replaced by the Kingdom of God in its glorious fullness, which was the goal of God's Creation from the beginning.

The only thing that matters, then, is this: Is Jesus Christ truly your Savior and Lord? Do you truly believe that God came into the world in the Person of The Eternal Son and that He accomplished the obedience that none of us could ever accomplish and also received the penalty for our disobedience in dying on a cross? (That is, the death-penalty which God had actually promised from the beginning, as described in His warning about *"the tree of the knowledge of good and evil"* in Genesis 3.) Do you believe that Jesus was raised from the dead, thereby vindicating that He is our Savior and Lord? And do you believe that He has sent the Holy Spirit to dwell within you, which joins you to Him and Him to you? If these things are true for you, then all of the blessings of Heaven are guaranteed to you, but all of the glory belongs to God.

Part 2

Mankind's universal need to create alternative religions or comprehensive philosophies is driven by the fact that abandoning our Maker creates what has been called "a God-shaped void" in our souls. As discussed earlier, we all must have a worldview consisting of a set of beliefs which we assume to be true and through which we view everything else. Whether we are aware of our worldview or not, it is simply impossible to proceed in life without having some sort of belief-system, which seeks to give us direction and purpose in life. But the big question about one's belief-system will always be this: Is it correct? A correct worldview will be both coherent (that is, free of self-contradictions or other clear absurdities) and consistently able to account for who we are and all that we know and experience.

Atheists like to claim that the vast number of religions humanity has come up with proves that none of them is true. But this is another fallacy. While it could hypothetically be true that there is no true religion (although, of course, we say that there is), this is not proven by the fact that there are so many religions in the world. This is because there is another possible explanation for why all of these religions exist. That is the Bible's explanation: that people who reject their Maker need to find a different way to view themselves and the world around them. These ways are actually unique for every rebel against God. But there are also many similarities. These similarities are the reason that like-minded people gather together into religious or philosophical groups.

So, atheists are right about all other gods and religions: they are cases of humanity making gods in our image, crafting gods or other ultimate authorities according to our desires. But Christians say that we only do this after we have rejected The One in Whose image we have been created.

One thing which Christians, Humanists and others agree about is that there are many people who claim to serve The True God but are either lying or are just deceived that this is the case. Violent Muslim jihadists are probably the most obvious case today. But all Christians should be willing to admit that there have also been all too many examples of professing Christians doing this. Hitler and his subordinates are an obvious case of this.[107]

Yet, as was discussed in chapter 6, it is a fallacy to claim that this proves that the God of the Bible doesn't exist. On the contrary, we assert not only that this God does exist, but that everyone also knows it, although most suppress this knowledge in favor of substitute religions or philosophies.

This act of substitution also includes people who claim to serve The One True God but really don't. And like those who explicitly reject God, such people also must know on some level that they are wrong because they, too, know The True God. But in their case they reject Him for a counterfeit which they seek to pass off as the True God. This is the case with Muslims, Jews and also with many who claim to be Christians but nonetheless construct an idea of God to their own liking. All who do so have, in effect, rejected both God and the Bible as God's authoritative Word, His unique written revelation of Himself and His ways.

That all unbelievers suppress the fact that they know God exists (and, even, that they know a great deal about Him)) is the basis for their culpability before Him. But it can also be seen as the basis for their hope. This is because, if one must constantly suppress his or her knowledge of God, then it is always possible that one can stop suppressing this and accept that He is real.[108]

---

107 *Atheists commonly try to argue that anyone who professes to be a Christian should be considered a Christian. But to do so would effectively destroy any meaningful sense of the term, as professing Christians have been known to hold contradictory positions in many situations. It's telling that this is not done with any other group.*

108 *That is, for most people, at least. The Bible does say that God hardens some so that they will never turn to Him. But it is not possible for most people to know that they are one of these unless they stubbornly persist in resisting His call until they end up in Hell. After all, how can you know that God*

All approaches other than Christianity must borrow much that is true because God made it that way, but deny the God who made it all.

In the end, every approach other than Christianity is wrong because they all reject The One True God as He has revealed Himself to us in our minds, in the world around us and in the Bible. And all other philosophies and religions are only correct insofar as they agree with what God has revealed in our minds, in the world around us and in the Bible.

All other philosophies and religions must borrow much from God's general and special revelation in order to have any success at all in the world God has made and, thus, to have any credibility. But to accept things which are true only because God has made them true but to reject Him is akin to taking pieces of the puzzle which reveals God and trying to assemble them into a different puzzle (as was discussed in chapter 4).

And, once again, to reject this perspective because it is exclusive is invalid. This is because all religions and comprehensive philosophies are by nature exclusive. When it comes to one's basic beliefs everyone thinks that what he or she believes is correct and all other views which disagree with this are wrong. This is just an inevitable and universal reality of human thought. And while we may agree on many things, to disagree about God and Christianity is far more important than any agreements we may have. This is because this basic disagreement will lead to many other disagreements. But it is especially because it will determine whether or not we will have a relationship with our Creator.

What ultimately matters is that we truly have God as our Father, Jesus as our Lord and Savior and the Holy Spirit as our "live-in" Counselor. And as

---

won't transform you into a believing and obeying child of God in the next moment? This is why God calls all of us to seek Him and to ask Him to transform us. And He also promises that whoever truly seeks will find, and whoever asks will receive.

valuable as it is to have as good an understanding of this as possible, what we absolutely must understand about this in order to be saved is actually quite limited.

In the New Testament Gospel of Luke, chapter 18 verses 9-14, Jesus tells a parable in which two people come before God: a tax-collector and a Pharisee. The tax-collector simply beats his breast and cries out: *"God have mercy on me, a sinner."* But the Pharisee presents his good deeds and his moral superiority to the tax-collector and others as his claim for God's blessing. Now, the tax-collector would have been considered among the most despised people to Jesus' audience, while a Pharisee was considered to be one of the religious elites. But Jesus no doubt shocked His hearers by declaring that the tax-collector rather than the Pharisee went home justified before God.[109]

With this parable Jesus not only pointed to the futility of trying to be saved by virtue of one's good works (as discussed in the previous section), He also pointed (in effect) to the minimum requirement to be saved. First, it is to admit that The One True God exists, which all of us already know by nature. Second, it is to admit that "I am a sinner before God, who needs God's mercy." This mercy includes forgiveness, cleansing and renewal. Third, it is to accept God offer of all of this.

Anyone who truly seeks God's mercy will surely receive it, along with all of the blessings of Salvation. This includes:

---

109 *That Jesus pronounced that this man went home justified even though He had not yet accomplished His work of Atonement shows that justifying faith need not be in Jesus Christ specifically. All believers before Christ accomplished the obedience necessary for our salvation lacked the ability to know their Savior as we can. But all true believers know that we need a Savior. Not knowing Who this Savior is, or having a quite faulty understanding of Him and His work, does not make it impossible to be saved. However, you cannot be saved if you either reject your need for a Savior or reject the simple Gospel that God has provided that Savior in the Person of Jesus Christ when that Gospel is presented to you.*

1) Permanent adoption into God's Family

2) Permanent justification: This means being permanently in good-standing before God, so that believers are always in "the state of grace" and in God's favor (as the old saying goes, "just as if I never sinned").[110]

3) Progressive sanctification. This occurs as the Holy Spirit gradually transforms us to be more and more like Jesus, working uniquely in each of us according to God's personalized plan so that we will all be equally perfected in the end, yet distinct as people. (This growth in holiness, while it must be evident in all true believers, is nevertheless accompanied by much remaining sinfulness until God makes us perfect in Heaven, which we will go to when we die, unless we are in the generation in which Jesus Christ returns. In this case Heaven will come to us.)

4) Perfect glorification. This will occur when we pass from this world to the next or when Jesus returns bringing His Heavenly Kingdom on the Day of the Lord (or "Judgment Day"), whichever comes first.

Though not all Christians agree on this, it may be that those who come into a saving relationship with God will never die from our point-of-view. Of course, we do die from the point-of-view of others (that is, unless we happen to be part of the last generation and are alive when "Judgment Day" comes). But when Jesus assured the thief on the cross that *"Today you will be with Me in Paradise"* it suggests that when our time in this world ends we will immediately proceed to eternity.

---

110 *This is so in spite of our past sins and, even, in spite of any future sins we will be guilty of (which will also be forgiven on the basis of the completed work of Jesus Christ). The chief initiator of the Protestant Reformation, Martin Luther (not to be confused with Martin Luther King!) described Christians as "justified sinners". By contrast, though, Luther's opponents in the Roman Catholic Church had taught that we are only justified if we are without sin. But none of us will ever be in this state as long as we are in this world.*

Actually, this is so for all people, whether we go to Glory or eternal damnation. This fact alone should have an enormous impact on our relationship with God and, in turn, on how we live. However, it is quite amazing that most people rarely consider this, including many Christians. If you think about it, <u>there is no reason for you to fear your death if you have accepted God's loving offer of forgiveness and everlasting life</u>. This is why the apostle Paul says that *"death has lost its sting"* for those who have been saved through the atoning work of Jesus Christ, the Eternal Son.[111]

This is so amazing, yet so rarely thought about even by people who believe it, that it deserves repeating. While we observe the deaths of others, we won't actually experience our own deaths as such. We may experience the process of dying (if we don't die suddenly). But at the end of our lives in this world we simply pass on to the next stage of life.

Of course, it is the nature of the case that this must be taken on faith, as it must be experienced personally. But today's prevailing view that this is impossible and that we simply pass out of existence when we die is also just a belief which reflects today's dominant worldview. It is not possible to know that this is the case either. Besides, we have looked at numerous reasons why the Materialism worldview is not tenable.[112]

---

111 *Clearly, many people do fear death greatly. Some will do <u>anything</u> to try to forestall it. But the question is: "Why?" The apostle gives us the answer: "the sting of death is sin". Whereas it appears that some are able to suppress their knowledge of their Creator so much that they falsely believe that death will be an escape from their accountability to Him, others are not able to eradicate the sense that they have a Judge before Whom they are inescapably guilty. But their Judge offers them pardon and blessings beyond imagination if only they will accept the offer.*

112 *Some people think they can find comfort in the belief that they will pass out of existence when they die. Indeed, it was suggested earlier that this may be a factor in higher rates of suicide in today's Humanist-dominated developed world. But if one really thinks about it, this notion is actually quite dubious as a source of comfort.*

Aside from the fact that we believe it is dreadfully mistaken, even if it we did

There is another amazing reality if God's children do proceed immediately from here to Heaven at the end of our time in this world. People often comfort themselves with the idea that their loved ones who die are still with them. But, if the foregoing is true, then it may be the case that when believers die, we immediately join our loved ones in Heaven. And if this is so, then it may be more accurate to say that, when beloved believers die, they are with us in Heaven!

This is not only a more amazing idea, it is far more comforting for those grieving lost loved ones because it not only points to their liberation, but also to the certainty of the future liberation of believers whom they left behind here. So, in stark contrast to how most people today view death, Christians can say of our deceased, believing loved ones that: "They're not dead. They just went ahead!"

It has been said that Christians can have so much confidence in our future in Heaven that it is as if we are already there. But, it seems more accurate to say that we ARE actually already there, just not from our current point-of-view! This seems to be suggested in the Apostle Paul's comment in his letter to the Colossians (chapter 3, verse 3) where he says that believers' lives *"are now hidden with Christ in God"*.

---

cease to exist when we die, it would be a matter of losing everything that you have at the time of your death, along with all of your recollections on your life (including many good things, even for those of us who have had very hard lives) and gaining nothing. This is clearly a hollow sort of comfort.

And this is so not just with respect to the end of our own days in this world, but also with how we view the deaths of others whom we have loved. Memorial services for Christians can be and actually should always be celebrations of the salvation of the departed. But the departure of loved ones can never be such for those who see death as the end.

Another consequence of how we are saved is that having a thorough understanding of salvation is not necessary in order to be saved. All that is needed is actual faith in Christ's saving work. Nonetheless, that faith must be more than just a knowledge of the Gospel Way of Salvation and more than just an assent that God did actually send His Son to be the Savior of the world. Rather, it is must be a firm trust that God actually did this for me.

And, once a person has become saved he or she will have an openness and desire to learn more and more about what God reveals in His written Revelation: the Bible. The Spirit will help us to do this. And so will other believers, both those from the past (whom we "meet" through their writings, including the historic creeds of the Church) and those we meet today.[113]

---

113 *While it is always desirable to understand as accurately as possible the theology of how salvation works, one's salvation is not really dependent on how well one understands this. We are saved if and only if we are among those whom Jesus came to save (the "elect"), which will be shown by putting our trust in what God has done.*

It is somewhat ironic that Reformed Christians tend to put more of an emphasis on having the correct theology than other Christians. After all, Reformed Christians believe that whether or not we are saved is solely determined by whether or not we've been predestined for salvation from eternity. So, other than having a basic trust in Jesus as our Savior, what else we believe doesn't matter for our salvation, nor does it matter which church we are in. Nonetheless, we should all be in a church because we all need the help of other believers in order to mature as Christians. We should therefore find a church which facilitates this adequately.

Differences in theology are only "crucial" (Pun intended again!) if they cause a person to deny the basic Gospel message. We are judged by God only if we reject what He has done in order to save us. The membership vows often used by Reformed churches are good summaries of the basic Gospel message. These include belief that we are lost sinners with no hope of saving ourselves and that God has sent His Son, Jesus Christ in order to save us. Therefore, we will trust in Him and Him alone as our Savior and Lord. The person who truly believes this will be saved, regardless of what else he or she believes in addition to this, so long as it doesn't contradict this.

The more we understand the Salvation which God accomplishes through Jesus Christ and all that it entails, the better. This is why it is essential to be a part of a body of other believers whenever this is possible. But everything else we do really only matters insofar as it supports and does not undermine what God has done <u>for</u> us in the work of His Eternal Son, Jesus and what He is doing <u>in</u> us by His Holy Spirit. And it is up to each individual to determine when this is happening and when it isn't.[114]

So it is that true believers can be found in churches with widely differing theologies. In fact, it is even possible to be a believer in non-Christian contexts so long as one doesn't embrace teaching which conflicts with the basic Gospel and/or prevents us from living in accord with this Gospel. In such cases believers will in effect be missionaries, that is, messengers of the true Gospel among unbelievers.

Next, we may see that the so-called "Euthyphro problem" is a false dilemma due to a failure to understand the Personality of God. The Euthyphro problem has been a long-standing problem in the history of thought. It says that God can't be the Ultimate Source and Standard of Goodness without making everything God does good by definition and, thus, arbitrary. But God is Good not because what He does is good by definition (which would be arbitrary), nor because He Himself is under a Higher Standard of Goodness (which would deny that He is Lord over all). Rather, God is Good because His Goodness is a quality of His Personality, in which His 3 Persons are equal.

---

114 *It is not unusual for God to use what is incorrect for the benefit of His children. For example, a preacher or teacher may wrongly interpret or apply things from the Bible and yet, because they are true nonetheless, God will use these things for the benefit of the hearers. Indeed, He even uses things which are in themselves wrong or evil. This is why the most prized verse for many Christians is Romans 8:28, which says: "God works in all things for the good of those who love Him, who have been called according to His purpose."*

So, while God, as a free Moral Being, could theoretically do evil, He just never does.[115] This includes never lying to us or misleading us. As discussed earlier, it is this alone that gives us confidence that we cannot be utterly deceived about who we are and about our experience and knowledge in this world. Of course, this requires faith on our part. But without this faith, all bets are off.

In a similar manner as God's perfect Goodness, logic and rationality are also part of God's essential Nature, as the way His Mind works. So, they are not abstract principles which He is under, nor do they arbitrarily come from Him. And God's Omnipotence is not abstract, but is in conjunction with His Perfect Goodness and Perfect Logical Mind. This is why He cannot lie or do anything else evil, nor do what is logically-contradictory (for example, the Almighty God creating a stone too heavy for Him to lift).

Finally, the plurality of Persons in the Christian Trinity solves the perennial paradoxes of Philosophy. First, it answers "the Problem of the One and the Many" in that it shows that both the unity and diversity that are basic aspects of human experience are grounded in God's Nature in that He is both One and Many.[116]

---

115 *Contrary to some, evil is not just the absence of good. Rather, it has always been the contrary of good, even within God's eternal existence. Since morality is inevitably a characteristic of inter-personal relationships, it was actually theoretically possible that One of the Divine Persons could have done evil to the Others prior to the existence of the universe. But this would have been contrary to the working of love, in which the Other is always valued and cared for more than One's Self. So the fact that "God is love" (equally in all 3 Persons) meant that this would never happen.*

But when God created other beings with real freedom, but not perfected in love (including us and angelic beings), then evil became not only possible, it actually occurred (both in humanity and among angels). However, God has promised to make those of us who ask perfect in love like Him. When He does, then we, too, will never choose to sin. But this is a promise which will only be fulfilled in Heaven.

Second, the existence of both objectivity and subjectivity in human experience can be seen to be a reflection of the fact that The One True God of the Bible is both the Ultimate Object and Subject.[117] (Objectivity in with respect to God is not in the physical sense, but relationally, since the Persons of God are both Subjects and Objects in their eternal inter-Personal relationships.) And, finally, the Triune God is also the original case of the existence of "other minds". Although God's 3 Persons are perfectly in harmony with One Another, so that God could be said to be "of One Mind", they are actually the 3 distinct Persons with distinct, yet identical Minds.

---

116 *"The Problem of the One and the Many" concerns how it is that we are aware both of distinctions and similarities between different things... Specifically, if everything is ultimately reducible to consisting of the same thing or things (as the so-called "scientific perspective" claims), then why can we recognize distinctions between things? On the other hand, if reality is ultimately composed of countless different things, then how is it that we can find relationships between them?*

117 *The failure of Humanism to account for our existence as observing and knowing subjects was discussed in chapter 6.*

Chapter 11
Christianity Both Defines and Promotes Freedom.

Christianity, unlike all other approaches, explains how we are both free and also bound in some respects.

A common objection which atheists and other Humanists have about Christianity is that it supposedly takes away one's freedom. But is any human-being ever really free? If the Materialism on which Humanism is based was correct then there would be no such thing as freedom. What we do, say and think would only be what our brains determine that we will do, say and think.

Even if one appeals to uncertainties based on Quantum Physics this still would not change the fact that we would merely be slaves to mindless Physics. Absolute determinism simply can't be avoided with this view. Indeed, many scientists and other intellectuals today don't deny this and actually assert that we human-beings are nothing other than biochemical machines governed only by immutable laws of Nature. So, any claims that we have freedom actually must assume that it comes from something else.

Unlike Humanism, Christianity can explain why there is a meaningful idea of freedom. (And, for that matter, why there are any meaningful ideas at all!) It's because God made us to be free rational and moral beings like Him, albeit finite and corruptible. That we actually rebelled against our Creator and became corrupted is only because we were created with real freedom of choice.

The real freedom which we have is in spite of the fact that God knew what Adam and Eve would choose and, even, knows everything that we will choose. Moreover, He not only foreknows everything that happens, He actually foreordains it all. This is not only taught in the Bible, it is also logically entailed by God's Nature. He simply wouldn't be God if He wasn't the Creator and Ruler of all, even down to the smallest detail. Hence, Jesus told His disciples that *not even a single sparrow falls to the ground without God's care and that even the hairs on their heads were numbered.* (Matthew 10:29-30) And David declared that *all of his days were ordained by God before one of them came to be.* (Psalms 139:16)[118]

---

118 *It has been pointed out by some that the Bible describes God as changing His mind, regretting things and even repenting at times. But this language should not be understood in the same sense as it is for us. For God to change His mind or repent should be understood to express when God makes a change-of-course from our point-of-view. But from God's point-of-view it is all according to His Plan. And for God to regret things merely reflects the natural aversion that a perfectly Good and Loving Being will have to evil.*

As discussed previously, evil was conceivable even within God's Triune Being. ("Triune" being just another way to say "Trinity") But that it is contrary to God's own Good Nature is the only reason none of God's 3 Persons ever does it, although They would always be free to do so. God regrets evil. But it was His Wisdom (which is also understood to be perfect) to create free beings which were not perfected in love. This made the advent of evil possible, but also regrettable. So, once evil came to pass, God would always regret it.

This is why God is said to desire that all be saved. But this cannot be at the expense of the freedom that He gave to us (as well as to angelic beings). So God's offer to save us from evil and perfect us in goodness is subject to the possibility that we can either accept it or reject it from our point-of-view.

And it is only our point-of-view that really matters here. That God does not intend to save any one of us can never be known by us (except perhaps for some extreme examples of hardened sinners) unless we have rejected His offer until the moment of death. It does seem clear that those who devote their lives to evil eventually become hardened by God so that they will never

Is it not clear that in order for God to be God He must have the final say in everything that happens? For if anything that we or anyone or anything else can do can frustrate His plans then He is not truly Almighty and, thus, not as powerful as can be imagined. And whether one accepts His existence or not, it should be agreed that in order to be "The Most High God" He must be The One of Whom it is true that no one greater can be imagined. But God also creates us with real freedom.

It is also true that all of us know that human beings are free, at least in some ways. Morality and responsibility, which no one can completely deny, depend on this being true. This is so even if we can't fully understand how we can be free either from the Humanist or Christian or any other perspective. (And it must be admitted that there is ultimately mystery in the Christian position.) But neither Humanism nor any other worldview besides Christianity can explain at all where our sense of freedom comes from.

In order to understand the uniqueness of the Christian point-of-view it is perhaps helpful to compare our freedom in a universe which is completely controlled by the Creator God to the freedom and responsibility which characters of a novel have within the context of the novel, even though everything they do is determined by what the author has written. No reasonable person would blame the author of a novel for evil done by a character in the novel he has created. So it is that God could create a story (and we say that history is His-story) with evil characters in it, but nevertheless not be responsible for the evil these created characters do.

Of course, we are real characters with real freedom. But it is still possible to consider that God somehow exists in a "meta-reality" (a reality which is above our own, kind of like another dimension) which allows both His complete control and real freedom for us without making Him responsible

---

seek His forgiveness (even if they may claim that they do). But, except for the exceptionally evil, we should all believe that God will save us if we ask Him to. And there is absolutely no good reason not to ask!

for our disobedience. That we can't reconcile the two realities doesn't necessarily mean that they are irreconcilable.

God has the most freedom conceivable, although even His freedom is in the context of His other characteristics as a Real Person (actually, 3 Co-equal Persons). So He cannot do what is logically impossible because logic is the way His Mind works and He never does what is evil because He is perfectly Good as a Personal God, even though He is not otherwise prevented from doing evil (something that even many Christians will probably find surprising).

In the case of an absolute human ruler he or she could do good or evil. A good ruler will always try to do good, but never fully successfully because we are all flawed. But the God described in the Bible can successfully do only good things (as hard as it often is for us to see this from our point-of-view) because He is not flawed.

God originally created humanity with a true ability to choose either to obey or disobey Him. But, having taken option B (unfortunately), we lost the freedom to choose to obey Him purely and wholeheartedly. Yet, we still retained freedom to make countless real choices. Indeed, it is only because we are free that God can rightly hold us culpable for our choices, including the original choice to disobey Him, which all of us continue to do by nature. Once more, both choice and responsibility only exist because Humanism and all other views are false and Christianity true.

Like God, our freedom is in the context of our nature as free rational moral beings. But in our case we are beings who have become corrupted both by the disobedience of our ancestors as well as by our own disobedience. So none of us is completely free.

In the New Testament Letter to the Romans, chapter 6, the writer, the Apostle Paul says that all sinners are actually slaves to our sins (as Jesus is also recorded as saying in the Gospel of John, chapter 8). And the Bible makes clear that all of us are sinners. But, we will subsequently look at the glorious Good News that he also declares in Romans, chapter 6: that those whom God saves become slaves to righteousness, who not only recover the ability to obey God with a pure heart but actually are bound to do so increasingly.

So, while you may believe you are totally free, this is not really the case. In the early 1980's singer Bob Dylan had a brief Christian phase. Being the gifted song-writer that he is, he expressed the situation of all humanity with this apt phrase: "You've got to serve somebody. It may be the devil or it may be the Lord." In actuality, there are three major types of masters which sinners will have. These have traditionally been called "the world, the flesh and the Devil" (based mainly on Paul's Letter to the Ephesians, chapter 2 verses 2-3).

The first ("the world") includes anything in the world which can gain our allegiance (whether it's a material or immaterial thing). This is especially seen in people who are driven by the desire for wealth, material possessions, worldly fame or power. If any of these is what you seek most in life, then this, in effect, is your lord.

The second one, "the flesh" has often been identified with sexuality. But it includes far more than this. Those who live for the flesh are driven by desires for personal pleasure, comfort or well-being, regardless of how their pursuit of these things may hurt them or others. But, again, if this is what is most important for you, then this is your lord. This is what you serve and are are slave to.

The third, those whose lord is "the Devil" may literally be under the power of Satan or demons (though this is usually impossible to know for sure). But in practice this may be seen to describe those who are slave to evil ideologies. This is most obvious in cases like Nazism, but also applies to any ideology or religion insofar as it opposes the authentic Gospel of Christianity presented in the Bible, including Humanism and false "Christian" gospels.

But, within the context of our slavery we still have freedom in many ways. That this is not contradictory can be seen in the fact that real human slaves always retain freedom in many ways with respect to other relationships and many details of their lives and, even, in the freedom to try to escape from or kill their masters.

In short, then, we are all free, but not completely free. <u>And the most freedom that we can possibly have is to be only under God's rule, not under the rule of someone or something else</u>. This is what happens if, and only if God sets us free. If God is truly our Lord we are truly free of the rule of anyone or anything else. And contrary to what many atheists and others think, this even includes religious leaders and government authorities.

All of us are under various authorities in many ways (like employers or teachers and political leaders) and some of us have placed ourselves under the authority of church leaders. But Christians are not bound to obey any of these if they either command us to do what our consciences say not to do or forbid us from doing what our consciences say we must do. This is the ultimate significance of what Martin Luther did and of the Protestant Reformation which followed.

While there are many people today who are overly rebellious, there are also many who have false attitudes of servitude. This includes many Christians and often leads to a false allegiance to church authorities. It is true that joining a church does entail being willing to submit to the leadership, priorities and agenda of the church (just as would be the case when one joins any voluntary association). So it is wrong to join a voluntary organization with the goal of transforming it so that it matches your priorities and agenda. If a particular organization doesn't already match these (for the most part, at least), then you should find another organization that more closely matches them or, perhaps, start such an organization.

But submission to any organization or authority should never trump our universal obligation "to obey God rather than men", as Peter expressed it to the Jewish religious authorities of his day when they demanded that he and the other disciples stop preaching about Jesus. So if any authorities call us to believe, say or do anything that violates our consciences, then we are free to disobey them. Indeed, in such cases, we are actually obligated to do so.

This is precisely what Martin Luther did when the Roman Catholic Church demanded that he recant of what Church authorities considered heresy. But, sadly, it is what many professing Christians failed to do when Nazi authorities ordered them to do evil things to Jews and others. To be a Christian means to be free of all human rule when it conflicts with what God calls us to do because only God is our Lord.

Religion & ritual versus relationship

It has been said that Christianity is a relationship rather than a religion.[119] All other religions and philosophies call for ritual and/or knowledge in order to get one into a supposedly-ideal state-of-mind. In other words, they seek to move from humanity upward. But Christianity is unique in working not from humanity upward. Rather, its direction is from God downward. This was the direction with Creation and it is also the direction of Salvation (or Redemption).

This is also why unbelief, regardless of what form it takes, is not really unbelief. Rather, it is disbelief in, or Denial of the relationship which God

---

119 *This is not to agree with the belief of many in today's dominant secular culture that "religion" is always a bad thing, which needs to eradicated or, at least, restricted to private expression. Indeed, it has previously been asserted here that all of us are religious in one way or another for all practical purposes, even Humanists who deny the existence of any supernatural entities. If you consider yourself non-religious it's only because you have not yet realized that your ultimate beliefs are essentially religious – ideas which you cannot prove to be true but nevertheless assume to be true and don't even question in most cases. These ultimate beliefs, in turn, determine how you view everything else. That is how religions work.*

created us for and continuously calls us to. So, while sin is usually seen as the failure to obey God, beneath this, it is really a relationship problem. And this is so both between us and other people (with our "horizontal" relationships) and between us and God (with our "vertical" relationship). With the latter, the problem for non-Christians is not really a problem of what you think, say and do. Rather, the problem is a lack of a relationship with God. And with Christians our primary problem isn't our thoughts, words or actions either. Rather, when we go wrong with any of these it is because we have allowed a temporary break in our relationship with God to occur.

That relationship is what it is all about can be seen in the Proverb which says that *"The fear of the Lord is the beginning of wisdom"* (Proverbs 9:10). As Christians, we understand this fear to be in the sense of reverence for *"our Father in Heaven"* rather than a fear of destruction from God as our Judge. This is because Jesus Christ has taken away the possibility of our destruction by receiving in our place the death-penalty which our rebellion incurred. So we obey God because of our reverent relationship with Him, knowing that He will always love us.

In order to see better the difference between human religions and the relationship between us and God it is helpful to consider how different traditions understand prayer. Many people don't realize what Muslims mean by prayer. Prayer ("Salah" in Arabic) for Muslims is a formalized ritual which is believed to be required by Allah five times a day. That it is a ritual rather than a personal expression is seen in the fact that the recitation is in Arabic, which the majority of Muslims don't speak.

Many today also don't realize that until the 1960's the Roman Catholic Mass was entirely in Latin, although the vast majority of Catholics have never been competent in Latin. But reciting established phrases in a language which one doesn't speak (even if one believes and has a personal identification with the words) is completely different from how people who see themselves in a vibrant relationship with God understand prayer. The purpose of prayer for such people is to speak to our God from our hearts, ideally in our own words.

This is not to say that repeating previously-composed prayers is wrong. Such prayers, including the Lord's Prayer, the Serenity Prayer, the Prayer of Saint Francis of Assisi and many other "common prayers" used in worship or prayers taught to Children are often useful.[120] These prayers can certainly be valid expressions to God if the person praying them truly means what he or she is praying and is truly speaking to God as one would speak to another person. In other words, they should not be just a "recitation" but a heartfelt speaking to God. True prayer is based on the one praying and God having a "speaking relationship". Without this, "prayer" is merely an act of ritual.[121]

Jesus gave what has become known as the Lord's Prayer as His answer to His disciples asking Him how they should pray. So it is clear that Jesus meant this to be a model for prayer, but certainly not the only prayer that we should ever pray. If this or some other prayer (like the Muslim Salah or the "Hail Mary") is the only prayer that you ever pray, then you need to learn how to pray to God in a personal way.[122]

---

120 *A personal favorite of this writer is the "Day-by-Day" prayer attributed to St. Richard of Chichester and popularized in the otherwise highly-irreverent musical "Godspell": "Day-by-day, oh dear Lord three things I pray: To see You more clearly; Love You more dearly; Follow You more nearly, day-by-day." The same that is true of prayer is also true of singing in worship. We ought to think about and agree with the words as much as possible.*

121 *The same is true for when one is being led in prayer by another person who is praying out loud in their own words, as is common in Evangelical churches. In this case we should affirm what is being prayed in our minds as much as we are able.*

122 *Non-Catholic Christians don't use the "Hail Mary" because they don't believe that Mary, the mother of Jesus should be prayed to, since she is not God. The same is also true of prayers which are offered to "saints". Indeed, the whole concept of sainthood is a major difference between Roman Catholics and Protestant Evangelicals. (The term "Evangelical" describes those individuals and churches which hold to historic Christian beliefs, including that Jesus is truly God and that He became man, worked miracles,*

And meditation which is not directed to God is not equivalent to real prayer, regardless of what benefits you may feel that you get from this. The Asian faiths have traditions of meditation specifically because these traditions reject that there is a God to pray to, although many sects have developed traditions of praying to forerunners who have been deemed to be exceptionally advanced or, even, to have reached the ultimate goal (like Buddha, the Dalai Lama or Krishna).

---

rose from the dead and is the only Savior of humanity and that the Bible, properly understood, is God's Word and is completely true. The term "fundamentalist" is also sometimes used for the same group, which is distinct from what have been called "mainline" Protestant groups.)

Evangelicals believe that all believers are saints from the time we become believers, with the term "saint" simply meaning "one who is set apart for holiness". This does not mean that they are set apart <u>because</u> they are holy. Rather it is understood that they are set apart so that they <u>will be</u> holy.

Pentecostal (or "Charismatic") and non-Pentecostal Christians also differ on whether or not God directly answers the prayers of believers or ever speaks directly to them. The former believe that He often does. But the latter believe that while God guides believers by His Holy Spirit in response to our prayers, He has already told us all that we need in the Bible. So for a person to claim to receive "special revelation" (whether in the form of "prophecy", "tongues" or "words of knowledge") in addition to the Bible is considered to be wrongly adding to the Word of God.

Claims of the special gift of healing are also a point of disagreement. Non-Pentecostal Evangelicals recognize that God does heal people, sometimes even in ways which can't be explained naturally, but deny that God anoints specific people as "healers". As evidence, they will point to the fact that so-called "healing ministries" often prove to be fraudulent, as a number of high-profile church scandals in the 1980's and 90's revealed.

From a non-Pentecostal point-of-view the Holy Spirit, who is described as dwelling within God's children, constantly applies what God has revealed in the Bible to their lives. So it is that we are "not under Law, but under the Spirit". On the other hand, the written Word, which is God's objective Revelation for us is the Standard by which we can determine when the Spirit

That Christianity is about the God and human relationship rather than about ritual may be seen in the "crucial" (pun intended once again) change of relationship which is described in chapter 6 of Paul's Letter to the Romans. Many Christians regard the New Testament passage of Romans chapter 8 to be the best passage in showing the glorious and unique message of the Gospel of Jesus Christ, especially verse 18 to the end of the chapter. British theologian J.I. Packer, for example, called Romans 8 "the high-water mark of God's Revelation". (By all means, read it!)

But Romans chapter 6 can be seen as the foundation for the Good News found in chapter 8. In short, the mind-blowingly wonderful message of this section of Paul's letter is this: <u>If anyone truly believes in the Gospel of Jesus Christ, from the moment that you believe you have permanently come under new ownership, going from being slaves to sin to being slaves to God and His righteousness.</u> This is clear from all of the past tense language found in verses 17-22, which continues the same past tense language found in the first half of Romans 6.[123]

---

is truly leading us and not something or someone else.

So it is essential to recognize the role both of the Spirit and the Bible. Unfortunately, it is all too often the case that one is emphasized at the expense of the other: the Spirit over the Bible by many Pentecostals or Charismatics or the Bible over the Spirit by many non-Pentecostals. Even more unfortunate, however, is the fact that many churches and individuals who call themselves "Christian" don't recognize either the Holy Spirit or the Bible as revealing the will of God.

123 *Romans 6:15-23 in the New International Version is as follows:*
    15 What then? Shall we sin because we are not under the law but under grace? By no means! 16 Don't you know that when you offer yourselves to someone as obedient slaves, you are slaves of the one you obey— whether you are slaves to sin, which leads to death, or to obedience, which leads to righteousness? 17 But thanks be to God that, though you used to be slaves to sin, you have come to obey from your heart the pattern of teaching that has now claimed your allegiance. 18 You have been set free from sin and have become slaves to righteousness. . .

Verse 23 is certainly a key verse for our proclamation of the Gospel to the world: *"For the wages of sin is death, but the gift of God is eternal life in Christ Jesus our Lord."* But verse 22 is priceless gold for believers:
> *"But now that you have been set free from sin and have becomes slaves of God, the benefit you reap leads to holiness, and the result is eternal life."*

What is really amazing is that this statement is not a conditional promise or even a promise at all. Rather it is a "matter-of-fact" assertion about what is presently true if you have come to believe in Jesus Christ as your Savior.

A preacher I know (Scott Berglin) once gave this analogy: Living the Christian life is like a soccer-player stepping over the line onto the soccer pitch (or field). If you have done what verse 17 says: *"But thanks be to God that, though you used to be slaves to sin, you have come to obey from your heart the pattern of teaching that has now claimed your allegiance."*, then you have become a true believer. And, if so, then you have permanently crossed onto the field-of-play as a player on God's Team. Yes, you will continue to struggle to play the game, as all of us do. But once we join God's Team we will never be off the field. And God will never kick us off His Team no matter how much we screw up! Rather, He will work with us individually by means of His Spirit and His Word (the Bible) so that we get better and better.

Sadly, many Christian preachers and teachers are afraid to stress this fully

---

> *19 I am using an example from everyday life because of your human limitations. Just as you used to offer yourselves as slaves to impurity and to ever-increasing wickedness, so now offer yourselves as slaves to righteousness leading to holiness. 20 When you were slaves to sin, you were free from the control of righteousness. 21 What benefit did you reap at that time from the things you are now ashamed of? Those things result in death! 22 But now that you have been set free from sin and have become slaves of God, the benefit you reap leads to holiness, and the result is eternal life. 23 For the wages of sin is death, but the gift of God is eternal life in Christ Jesus our Lord.*

(without reservations and qualifications). This is probably because they fear that it will lead to complacency. But Paul's rhetorical question in verse 15 actually anticipates this natural objection to his Gospel: *"Shall we sin because we are not under the law but under grace?"* The question is seen as rhetorical because of the answer that he himself gives: *"By no means!"*

The most amazing thing about the true Gospel that is taught in the Bible is that our Salvation is truly a totally free gift from God and is irreversible and, therefore, certain from start to finish. But such a message would naturally tend to make people think that once a person realizes that God has saved them, then they will believe that they won't have to work anymore. But, in essence, Paul's answer is that this is not the way Salvation works.

To show the importance of this issue, Paul had previously asked the same question (albeit in slightly different words) and given the same answer in the first verse of Romans 6: *"Shall we go on sinning so that grace may increase? By no means!"* Paradoxically, the Gospel Message is that Salvation is a free Gift, but it is one which makes us slaves. But we were already slaves, even though we weren't aware of this. We were slaves to sinfulness. But we now have a new Master Who knows what we need and will provide for it perfectly.

A totally free and guaranteed salvation by means of a free Act and Gift from God is the only salvation that could work for us. This is because none of us could ever merit God's favor and blessing at all, no matter how much we try. For we are born without merit and we will always have <u>demerits</u> whenever we fall short of perfect obedience. And even after we are saved, our obedience will still never merit His reward. This is because, as long as we live in this world our obedience will always be incomplete and sullied by our remaining sinfulness. Only a perfect obedience could merit reward from God. But, thankfully, Jesus Christ has provided this for us already!

Furthermore, once again we must recognize that even our obedience, along with our faith, is also part of God's Gift of Salvation. So, this brings us back again to the uniqueness of the Christian Gospel. Our Salvation from start-to-finish is entirely from God. And so all of the Glory is His.

The glorious Truth of the Gospel is that God gives His children everything that we need from start-to-finish: justifying us in Christ, calling us to relationship with Him, regenerating us so that we go from being "dead" to Him to being in a vibrant relationship, adopting us into His Family forever (rather than being Satan's forever, as the ambigram in chapter 4 illustrates), sanctifying us (so that we grow in holiness over time), and eventually glorifying us in Heaven. If we have truly been "born-again" as children of God, we have it all!

And contrary to what many think, far from causing us to become complacent, the more clearly and consistently we realize this, the more motivated we will be to live up to it. All those who are willing are "called up" to join The Greatest Team Ever! And being willing to accept God's call is all that is needed for us to join the Team. But if this is so, then is there really any doubt that we will be motivated to play our "position" the best that we can in the long run? If you have been playing baseball your entire life and the day comes when you are called up to play for the New York Yankees will you not be as motivated to play your best as anyone can possibly be?[124]

---

124 *Indeed it can be seen that, far from undermining the believer's motivation, assurance that one is saved actually proves to be our most powerful motive for persevering in the Christian life in the long run. A good way to see why is to compare your likely reaction to two different letters which you might receive: one from the Readers Clearinghouse saying that you may win millions of dollars if you respond and another from an estate attorney stating that a rich uncle of yours has recently died and has named you in his will and inviting you to the reading of his will. Many people will have little or no motivation to respond to the first. But who would fail to respond to the latter (assuming that the authenticity of this letter can be confirmed)? . . .*

Obviously, the difference is in the certainty of a pay-off with the latter. (That is, unless your uncle was angry with you and wants to punish you posthumously!) In the same way, the certainty that believers will be

So, while it is counter-intuitive (or contrary to what most would expect), the promise of God's saving grace is actually the most powerful motivator for believers to obey God. It is a promise which is absolutely certain because the One Who makes it cannot lie. Here again, Christianity is in contrast with every other religion and philosophy, which says in one way or another: if you follow this program, you will succeed. But there are two problems with this. First, how do you know that the program works? (You don't.) Second, even if the program worked, how could you know that you can actually follow it? (You can't.) By contrast, Christianity says that you will surely succeed because God will make sure that you succeed. All you have to do is trust Him.

The simple truth is that if salvation (or ultimate success by any other name which people have given this) was dependent on <u>anything</u> in us, then it could never be certain. This is because it is always possible that we might not be able to continue doing what we need to do and also that we may just give up! And this is so no matter how confident one may appear to be. The most self-confident Pharisee could never completely eradicate the anxiety that he might stumble and fall. So it is with all who are relying on their own efforts rather than trusting in what God has <u>already</u> done to save us through the sending of His Son Jesus Christ and what He has promised to do in the future in completing that salvation.

Relying on one's own efforts in any way in order to be saved (or ultimately successful in other terms) also tends to push a person in one of two bad directions: either to despair, whenever you can't fight off your inevitable anxiety over actual or possible failure, or to false pride and self-righteousness, when you believe you are doing as well as you can and, clearly, better than others. Only faith that God has already saved you and is

---

rewarded in the end actually motivates us to persevere in doing what God wants. On the other hand, having only an uncertain hope of reward is actually far less motivating, especially when obedience is hard or when we stumble.

now working out this salvation in your life can take away this pride and self-righteousness, as well as the anxiety that can lead to despair.

This is why the apostle Paul exhorted the Philippian Christians and us: *". . . continue to work out your salvation with fear and trembling, for it is God Who works in you to will and to act in order to fulfill His good purpose."* (Philippians 2:12-13) In other words, we are called to work because God is at work in us. And that our efforts are described here as being with *fear and trembling* doesn't mean that we should have the same fear and anxiety that unbelievers have. Paul has made this clear at many other points in his Letters (especially in Romans, chapters 6 & 8). Fear and trembling here may refer to that which a person has before he or she has truly come to understand the Gospel and put his or her faith in Christ, or to one who already has, but has not yet come to the full assurance that Christ has completely and permanently saved them. But God wants His children to know that they belong to Him forever.[125]

---

125 *Whether a person can be saved without having a full and infallible assurance that he or she has been saved has been a point of dispute since the 16th century. The continental European tradition of Reformed Theology has tended to hold that if one is not fully certain that he or she is saved, then he or she does not really have saving faith. On the other hand, the English and Scottish Puritan tradition has asserted that full and infallible assurance is not something which all believers attain, although this is something which God wants all of His children to have.*

That this is so is most clearly expressed in 1 John 5:13 - "I write these things to you who believe in the Name of the Son of God <u>so that you may know that you have eternal life</u>." Besides, all of the promises of Scripture become hollow if one cannot absolutely know for sure that they apply to me.

The Puritan tradition has been most beautifully summarized in the Westminster Confession of Faith, Chapter 18. It is important to realize that there is a difference between <u>knowing</u> that I am saved and <u>feeling</u> like I am saved. While it is true that God wants each of His children to know for certain that they are saved, it is also true that, even after coming to know this, we may go through times when we don't feel like we are one of God's children. But, as in other areas of life, we need to live based on what we know: that "it is well with my soul" (as a famous hymn expresses it), rather than what we feel.

It is also important to recognize that the possibility of attaining to a full and infallible assurance that one is saved must also exclude the possibility that anyone can be utterly convinced that they are saved when they aren't. This should be an encouragement to believers in sharing the Gospel. For we can be confident that even the most self-confident unbeliever we meet must know on some level of their subconsciousness that "it is <u>not</u> well with my soul." It is also part of what leaves them without excuse if they reject the Gospel.

Part 2
Not a Theocratic nor a Secular America, but a Pluralistic America (Another deficiency of Islam & Humanism)

We have considered how our basic beliefs about the nature of the universe, human-beings and God and about how we know right and wrong defines our worldview. And whether you consider yourself religious or not, your worldview functions in the same basic way for all of us, as a set of beliefs which cannot be proven but are assumed to be true and rarely questioned. And these beliefs, in turn, determine how you view yourself and everything in your life.

So, the question is: Which worldview should prevail in society? Most Christians in the past and many still today would say it's Christianity. Muslims have always said Islam. Humanists say it should be Humanism, Hindus Hinduism and so on. So, which is right? It will no doubt be surprising to many of you that the correct answer is: None of the above!

It is widely-believed by Christians that the United States of America was meant to be a Christian nation. It is true that the population of the nation at its founding was predominantly professing Christians. But this would only make it a nation of Christians, not a Christian nation in principle.

The rather surprising truth is that our founders envisioned a pluralistic society rather than a Christian one; that is, a Church State. This is mainly because most of our founders had come from Western European states which were Church States (with official and, usually, exclusive State Churches). And many of America's founders or their ancestors had actually fled their native lands specifically because of the persecution they faced due to this state of affairs.

While it can be seen that the separation of Church and State is implied in the

New Testament of the Bible, this understanding had actually been lost since the early stages of the history of Christianity. As a result, Christianity and politics had been wedded together for over 1000 years.[126] The result had been endless wars and other conflicts. So it was that not just our founders, but many of the settlers of the New World had come seeking freedom which they had been denied in the old world.

It is difficult for us today to understand the intensity of the sectarian strife which had followed the Protestant Reformation, not only between the Roman Catholic Church and the fledgling Protestant churches but also among the Protestant churches. Part of the problem was that, without a separation of Church and State, to disagree in theology and Christian practice meant being political enemies. And all too often political enmity had led to war.

Sadly, Catholics and Protestants were killing each other and Protestants were killing other Protestants ostensibly over theology and religious practice. Part of the reason for all of this fighting is that, when theology and politics are not considered separate spheres, the stakes of disagreements will tend to be raised, even to being viewed as the difference between going to Heaven and going to Hell in some cases. Not surprisingly, this makes peaceful cooperation more difficult and violent conflict more likely.

Indeed, this is also what we see throughout the history of Islam down to the present day. Whether Islam will learn this essential distinction remains to be

---

126 *Religion and politics remain inseparable in the Muslim world and with some other religious traditions. In fact, this is why there is such a thing as "the Muslim world". While there used to be a "Christian world" (or "Christendom") such can no longer be found. Some Christians bemoan this fact, but today's situation is actually a return to the situation of the 1st century And no clear mandate can be found in the New Testament for establishing Christian governments. In fact, Jesus confounded His contemporaries precisely because He did not seek political power, declaring that His Kingdom was not of this world (Gospel of John, chapter 18, verse 36).*

seen. There are some signs that many American Muslims want to live according to the American ideal of "liberty and justice for all", having seen (as our forefathers did) that it is superior to cultures from which many of them also fled. For in these cultures there is no separation of religion and politics and no tolerance of religious or political dissent, or, often, even of dissent in particular practices.

Fortunately for us, 18th century American Christians had begun to figure out the problem and came to realize that the solution lay in the relationship which the 1st century Church had with the Roman government under which it had emerged, as a spiritual community rather than a political movement. So it was that the ideal of the separation of Church and State was not a new discovery, but a re-discovery of what had been intended from the beginning of the Church's existence.[127]

Besides the New Testament precedent, it was clear to most people in the new nation that the ideal of a Christian nation was unrealizable in practice. After all, which form of Christianity would rule the nation? For in many cases it was believed that Christians in other sects were not even real Christians.

The only way the new nation could work would be if it had no established Church ("established" simply meaning the Official State Church, as still existed across Europe) and if "liberty and justice for all" was the law of the land. In theory this would include all Christian sects and all other religions as well as non-religious people. Of course, this would prove to be much

---

[127] *The 1st century relationship between the fledgling Church and the Roman government marked a major change from the theocratic model of Old Testament Israel. Indeed, confusion over this was one of the reasons the Jews rejected Jesus as their Messiah. They were looking for a political Savior, who would reestablish the Kingdom of Israel on earth. But Jesus was an altogether different kind of King. He Himself admitted to being a King, but One Whose Kingdom is not of this world and not of this time. So it was understood by His earliest disciples. Unfortunately, this perspective would become less and less common in the following centuries, eventually disappearing almost entirely by the Middle Ages.*

harder to put into practice. But the ideal was clear.

Our founders did not want a Christian America (although the Christians naturally did see a nation filled with like-minded Christians as the best situation). But it should also be clear that, contrary to what many Humanists today believe, they did not want a secular one either, in which religion would be excluded from politics. As important as their faith was to millions of Americans in the late 18th and early 19th century (before the Humanism "revolution" began to gain steam), it was literally unthinkable that people wouldn't bring their religious ideas into their public lives.

Humanists who want to exclude religious input in public policy and law always focus on the "anti-establishment" clause of the 1st Amendment of the U.S. Constitution. But they inevitably downplay, if not ignore altogether the "free exercise" clause. But even a rudimenatary examination of the period in which the Constitution emerged will unmistakably show that that the anti-establishment idea did not entail that religious influence be excluded from politics, but only that no particular religious influence would dominate. For, if it did, then the religious liberty of those who were not part of the ruling sect or religion would be in jeopardy. So it is that the purpose of the anti-establishment clause was to protect the free-exercise of religion, as well as the freedom of non-religious people.

In order for all people to have equal freedom no particular religion could be allowed to dominate. But the same must also be true about non-religious, or secular domination. Because if either religious people or non-religious dominate the rights of others would be lost. And it is not hard to see that freedom of religion is actually the foundation of all other freedoms (including freedom of conscience, speech, the press, association and economic freedom). This is because religious differences are always the biggest challenge to freedom and peace since they affect so many other issues and also because they arouse such strong passions. And this brings us back to our main point about the importance of worldviews.

All of this should make it clear that today's common notion that America was meant to be a secular nation is incorrect. One way to see this is to consider that it is precisely the public exercise of religion which most needed to be guaranteed by our Constitution. For, insofar as religion is exercised privately it is private and not generally in danger.

Furthermore, to believe that one should only practice his or her faith in private actually shows a fundamental ignorance of what religions are all about. Indeed, to practice one's religion only in private and not in one's dealings with others (and in one's interactions with the public in general) is actually hypocrisy! People who argue that religion should only be practiced in private are really only seeking to impose their perspective on everyone else. And this is just as wrong when done by secular people as it is when it is done by religious people. Secular tyranny is no less tyranny than religious tyranny!

The ideal of the secular State was the ideal of the Soviet Union and other Communist states, not the United States! Indeed, such an ideal was virtually unthinkable to our founders. For nearly all of them viewed ethics and morality (both on the individual and corporate levels) in theological terms, either as being based explicitly on the Bible or as mediated through divinely-designed Natural Law. The real danger they sought to safeguard against was the rise of the type of sectarian Church States which existed across Western Europe. (That this was the case is reflected in the fact that some European nations continue to have official State Churches to this day, though not with the power that they once had.)

So those who fear the rise of an American Theocracy should take comfort in knowing that the founders were firmly on their side. The same is true of those of us who see the New Testament and not Israel's Theocracy described in the Old Testament as normative for what God desires in this world.[128]

---

128 *There were many Christians in the early period of American history who still clung to the theocratic model. But, fortunately, they did not prevail, nor have other groups which emerged subsequently (like the Mormons). And to*

But the founders would also have been firmly opposed to secular dominance (which wouldn't even be fully advocated until about a century later, though the French Revolution did move in this direction). For there is another way. And that way is political pluralism. And pluralism, unlike Secularism, has the advantage of accomodating all groups.

How to coexist within a truly pluralistic society: Compromising on practices without compromising on principles whenever this is possible. However, sometimes, the freedom of one side or another will have to be sacrificed.

We have previously examined numerous issues in which there are serious disagreements between Humanists and Christians (and others). In many cases, however, compromises in practices are possible without compromising the principles of either side. This is because there will always be a lot of common-ground over basic principles of right and wrong and also a lot of agreement over what is true and, therefore, works in practice. Just because someone denies the True Source and Ground of morality and truth doesn't mean that they won't rightly accept that many things are good or evil and that many things are true or false.

Indeed, most people will accept much that is good and true and reject much that is evil and false despite rejecting God. This is because doing so is often necessary in order to survive in the world that God has made and also because they remain creatures made in the image of their Creator.[129]

---

this day there are a few Christian groups that see the Israelite Theocracy as the model for what God desires in this world. But they are very small in numbers and marginalized. On the other hand, this is not the case with Islam.

129 *That God reveals much about morality and truth through our created nature and in the way the world works, (both for Christians and non-Christians) is the basis for the correct belief by America's founders that Natural Law is the basis for the Rule of Law embodied in the Constitution. So, the claim of some that the rejection of Christianity and Biblical ethics leaves ethics without any foundation in Higher Law is incorrect.*

However, in some cases where we disagree, compromise won't be possible. For example, in the same-sex marriage debate there is no middle-ground of compromise possible. Either same-sex marriages will be recognized as equally-legitimate to heterosexual ones or they will not have the same societal standing. Of course, the United States Supreme Court ruled in favor of the former in its 2015 ruling in the case of Obergefell versus Hodges. But, contrary to the claims of many who hailed this decision, this ruling does not make it "settled law". For all Supreme Court rulings must be able to withstand subsequent challenges before they can legitimately be called "settled law". And, even after years of withstanding challenges, there will always be the possibility of a shift in the Court's perspective, as anti-abortion advocates still hope for with the 1973 Roe versus Wade decision.

On the marriage issue either those on the traditional side or those on the pro-LGBTQ side will eventually have to accept defeat. This won't take away either side's freedom to practice conscientious objection and non-violent resistance. But it will mean that the exercise of such freedom will involve sacrifices. As a Christian, I for one am willing to accept the possibility that the other side will win. But will you on the pro-LGBTQ side be willing to do this?

Chapter 12
Freedom, Capitalism and Socialism

Editorial note: The reader will notice that this chapter has extensive footnotes. Keep in mind that the main message is in the text, not in the notes. So try not to let the notes distract you from this.

Is anything really wrong with Socialism? If so, what?

One of the characteristics of Humanism has always been its preference for Socialism as the best approach to government. While most will decry the tyrannies which resulted from pursuing the Marxist form of Socialism, it is widely believed that these tyrannies were not an inevitable result of this system of government in general. Rather, they were thought to be the result of a defective version of it and/or of bad people seeking to implement it. (Surprisingly, many fail to recognize that Nazism was also an experiment in Socialism, forgetting that "Nazi" is an acronym for "National Socialist".)[130]

---

130 *Nazi Germany was really no different than any of the Marxist dictatorships in that it featured an all-controlling State. The main differences were that the Nazi's permitted a semblance of a private-sector (though it was still completely dominated by the government) and the Nazi regime also had a distinctly nationalist ideology. Marxism eliminates the private-sector altogether and also has an anti-nationalist ideal, in which the hope would be that the competing nations would eventually disappear and, even, that their governments would disappear as well, being replaced by a worldwide community of self-governing people.*

But to believe that people who are in charge of an all-controlling government would ever voluntarily give up their power at any point should be seen as a startlingly naive denial of human-nature. The reality is that the more powerful governments become, the more they tend to be corrupt and also increasingly draw power-hungry people, as is reflected in the saying: "Power corrupts and absolute power corrupts absolutely."

Believers in the virtues of Socialism point to high standards-of-living in Western European nations which embraced the socialist philosophy after World War 2. However, that the high standards-of-living are due to the form of government in these nations is debatable. There were certainly other factors, including massive amounts of money invested in many of these nations by America under the Marshall Plan, the lack of a need for defense spending due to American protection of these nations under NATO during the Cold War, residual wealth retained by these nations even after the war and the fact that the widespread reconstruction necessitated by the destruction of war has the effect of creating wealth. It could be true that the prosperity of Western Europe was actually in spite of a political and economic system which tends to undermine the creation of wealth compared to the Capitalism which reigned supreme in the United States until the late 20th century.

The ability of European socialist systems to maintain high standards-of-living is being severely tested in the early 21st century due to high levels of immigration of poor and unskilled people from the developing world, high and increasing amounts of government debt and sluggish growth-rates. Believers in Socialism often view economics as a "zero-sum game" in which the total amount of wealth doesn't change significantly. As such, "equality" becomes largely a matter of redistributing wealth from those who have it to those who don't.

Capitalism, on the other hand, is based on the demonstrable fact that human ingenuity and effort actually create tremendous amounts of wealth which did not previously exist. So there is no need to redistribute the wealth of the rich. This is because in a thriving economy the standard-of-living of those on all economic levels will rise. This is reflected in the analogy that "a rising tide will lift all boats".[131]

---

131 *This is just a short summary of what is known as "Supply-side Economics". But numerous books have been written in defense of it since the 1980's. This type of economics became prominent during the Ronald Reagan*

Furthermore, the Capitalism that ruled in America for its first 200 years or so (during which time it became the wealthiest nation in history) sought to maintain equality of economic <u>opportunity</u> and a vibrant economy through a minimal amount of government regulation and some incentives. But Socialism seeks equality of economic <u>outcomes</u>. Instead of a level playing-field, Socialism favors a level outcome in the game. Is it not clear that the only way to attempt to accomplish this would be through a major increase in

---

Administration. It was derisively labeled "trickle-down economics" or "voo-doo economics" by critics. But the economic boom of the 1980's showed that promoting lower taxes and less restrictions on businesses can provide much more than a "trickle" of improvement to those in the middle-class and the poor.

Some also claim that lower taxes inevitably lead to higher deficits. Indeed, deficits did increase in the 1980's (though not nearly as much as they did during the Barack Obama Administration). But this can be seen as being the result of big increases in defense spending and continuing increases in other areas.

It should be clear that the lowering of tax-rates, as well as reduced government regulations will tend to encourage business people to put more of their wealth into their businesses rather than just hanging on to it. After all, if increased business activity will tend to be less profitable because of higher costs due to high tax-rates and regulations, it stands to reason that most people just will not be as motivated to do as much business as possible, thereby creating fewer jobs and other economic activity.

Furthermore, unless governments prevent it (which, in itself would be a dangerous increase of government power), businesses will just pass along their increased costs due to the higher taxes and increased regulations to their customers. Ironically, then, high taxes and a high level of regulation of businesses actually hurts their middle-class and poor customers more than rich people.

Economist Arthur Laffer famously demonstrated that reducing tax-rates will often increase tax-revenues in economies with high tax-rates. The basic idea is that while having a zero tax-rate would result in zero tax-revenue, so would having a 100% tax-rate, since this would eliminate all financial

government power?[132]

That Socialism is favored by people with the Humanist worldview is not surprising. This is because it fits Humanism's assumption that people are not really responsible for the results of their actions. On this view, an ideal of economic equality (or "economic justice") would make sense. After all, on this view, wouldn't it be unfair for some to prosper more than others?

---

incentive for production and effectively eliminate the private-sector. So it was understood that there will be a bell-curve between the two extremes. Indeed, it is not hard to understand that increasing tax-rates will increase tax-revenues up to a certain point. But the downward pressure on production caused by high taxes (and regulation) will eventually lead to decreased economic activity and, thus, less creation of wealth and a reduced tax-base so that tax-revenue will also decline.

To see how lower tax-rates can lead to higher tax-revenues consider that a business which produces $10 million in taxable income and is taxed at a rate of 15% will generate $1.5 million in tax-revenue. But if a lower-tax and reduced-regulation environment helps the business to be more productive and produce 20% more income (or $12 million) it will generate more tax revenue even at a rate of 13% instead of 15 (or $1.56 million). Of course, the revenues would increase even more if the growth is greater.

132 *This view is expressed by the saying: "from each according to his ability, to each according to his needs". This saying was popularized by Karl Marx. While Marx didn't invent Socialism, he was undoubtedly its greatest popularizer. His version of Socialism, known as Communism, was a particular theory and approach to the development of a supposedly ideal and just economic system. But Socialism in general can be seen to be a reactionary movement among 19th century intellectuals to the economic inequalities which were becoming increasingly obvious in the emerging industrialized world, especially in America.*

These inequalities were a natural result of what happens when people are granted unprecedented freedom in the economic realm, as part of an overall environment of unprecedented political freedom. The so-called "American Revolution" may not have been the type of insurgency which would often be called a revolution subsequently (See note 134.), but its consequences were truly revolutionary...

On the other hand, Capitalism fits the worldview which Humanism replaced, Christianity, insofar as the latter holds that "workers are worthy of their wages". Thus, in the economic sphere justice would dictate that people should be rewarded to the level commensurate with the value of what they produce. So it is that NBA players, other athletes in high-revenue sports and successful actors and musicians are rightly paid extraordinary salaries because they produce extraordinary revenues (as do those who create successful businesses like Mark Zuckerberg or Bill Gates). But unskilled workers are much less responsible individually for directly producing wealth by their work. Furthermore, they are also much more easily replaced either by other people or, in many cases, by machines.

This is not at all to demean the value of unskilled workers as people! In fact, all people have equal intrinsic value as human-beings. But the value of people in the marketplace will vary greatly. Because of this it will often be seen that requiring businesses to pay unskilled workers artificially high wages pushes these businesses toward reducing the hours of their employees (so that they will often make less money despite being paid at a higher hourly rate) or by laying off employees and by just getting by with fewer

---

Never before was a nation as free as the United States, so free that it spawned an entirely new economic system, which came to be known as Capitalism. This system was producing unprecedented levels of wealth overall. But it also showed that when people, who by nature are not equal in ability, are given more widespread freedom than ever before, the economic results will have a high degree of inequality.

On the other hand, it should be seen that Socialism is a fundamentally different approach to economies, one which emerged as a direct response to the inequalities that Capitalism produces and seeks to eliminate the unequal outcomes of Capitalism. It seeks to do so chiefly by eliminating its freedoms where this is deemed necessary. So, to try to combine Socialism with a free-market economy, as many believe is possible, is to introduce a principle which inevitably undermines both the economic and political freedom which is at the core of the Capitalist system, as well as to the productivity and prosperity which that freedom produces.

people, or by replacing them with increased automation. And, in some cases, it has been shown to drive them out of business!

While the post-World War 2 history of the Western European nations seems to show that Socialism is compatible with political freedom, we have already noted that Socialism's driving desire to produce an outcome of economic equality (as well as other desired outcomes of equality) will inevitably require a steady increase in both the size and power of government. And where government increases, freedom necessarily will decrease, and not just economically but politically as well.[133] This is why Winston Churchill was deeply concerned with Great Britain's embrace of Socialism in the middle of the 20th century and famously predicted that all Socialist states must eventually adopt a State-security apparatus (like the Nazi SS and the Soviet Union's KGB) in order to protect the government's power to control both economic and political outcomes.[134]

---

133 *An illustration of this tendency can be seen with the "single-payer" government-run health systems which most Socialism-favoring political "progressives" see as the best possible system. But if the government becomes solely responsible for providing health-care then this will open the door for it to dictate what its citizens can or can't do in all sorts of ways in order to cut its costs, as well as giving it the power to determine the level of care which is considered appropriate, rather than allowing individual citizens, caregivers and insurance companies to determine this. And it should also be recognized that businesses usually must be responsive to their customers in order to stay in business. But governments have no such pressure.*

134 *The need to protect the government's power is also one of the reasons why socialists tend to favor strict limitations on the right of citizens to own firearms. There is no question that if the population is highly-armed it will always pose a threat to the government. Of course this is rarely stated. Instead, gun-control measures are usually promoted on the basis that they will reduce "gun violence". But this is dubious, as many American cities that have some of the most strict gun laws actually have the most gun violence. And even the term "gun violence" points to an unfortunate tendency we have seen in other areas to shift the focus away from human choice, in this case the bad choice by many to use a gun, to environmental factors, in this case the availability of guns. . .*

So, Socialism inevitably trends not toward a limited government "of the People, by the People and for the People" which was the ideal of America's founders, but toward an ever-increasing Government over the people. Furthermore, Socialism is ultimately based on the belief that none of us really owns what we earn, create or inherit. It really belongs to the entire society. Therefore, one's property ought to be shared with others as is deemed best by society. But who is to determine what is best? That would be

---

While opponents of gun-rights hate the saying, it is nevertheless literally true that "Guns don't kill people. People kill people." And, as for the availability of guns, short of a totalitarian government which outlaws all gun ownership and confiscates all guns (by means of the type of State-security apparatus that Churchill referred to), criminals who care nothing about gun restrictions will still be able to get guns, thereby putting citizens who abide by these restrictions or bans (like "gun-free zones") at a disadvantage. Ask any law-abiding resident who is unfortunate enough to have to live in the high-crime areas of dozens of American cities.

The unintended bad consequences of gun-control measures such as concealed-carry and open-carry bans is evident whenever there is a mass shooting incident or an attempt to kill multiple people in other ways (like suicide-bombers and those who use vehicles or knives). If people in the group targeted have guns these attacks can sometimes be stopped before they begin or, at least, can be ended quickly with minimal casualties. If not, then the body-count will be higher.

The June 2017 attack by an individual with a rifle on a group of Republican Congressional Representatives and staff practicing for a charity baseball game illustrates this. Since one of the Representatives happened to have an armed security detail present, the members of this detail were quickly able to engage the shooter so that he could not continue firing on those on the field and, indeed, was eventually killed. If not for this he may have been able to cut down most of the people on the field, who were essentially sitting-ducks, before law-enforcement people arrived.

A shooter facing an unarmed group will often be able to kill at will for a considerable period of time (as was seen in the mass shooting at an Orlando, Florida nightclub in 2016) because most people will

the rulers of society. So we see here how Socialism is contrary to the value and freedom of individuals and also requires "top-down" control. The fundamental contrast between the freedom of Capitalism and the control required in order to advance the Socialist ideal is why freedom-loving opponents of Marxism in the last century coined the expression "Better dead than Red."[135]

To illustrate the advantage of a free-market system over a government-run

---

understandably be too afraid to try to stop him. And unless there is a well-planned and highly-courageous group attack on him, even if people are brave enough to come at him, he will usually be able to shoot them. But if there is someone else who has a gun and starts shooting at him, he will need to focus his fire on that person, if indeed he is not taken out by him or her.

Like it or not, guns are here to stay. Evil people will find a way to get them or, even, make them, if necessary. And if a nation disarms completely then it will be defense-less against armed nations or groups which may wish to intimidate or dominate it. So governments must always have guns and other weapons. But if only those in government have fire-arms, as many Socialists favor (and, tellingly, as totalitarian governments always seek), then it truly becomes the Government <u>over</u> its citizens. And a government with the ability to impose its will on an unarmed citizenry with the threat of deadly force will always be prone to using this power for tyrannical purposes since there will be no danger of an armed resistance to keep it honest.

This is why the 2nd Amendment of the U.S. Constitution describes the right of the people to possess arms as being specifically for the maintaining of a "well regulated militia" as necessary for "the security of a free State". It cannot be reasonably claimed (as some do today) that the right for the people to own fire-arms was only for this purpose and, thus, is now obsolete altogether in an age of national armies and armed law-enforcement. For, regardless of how unnecessary guns may be for many today, by the late 18th century guns had already come to be considered as essential for other purposes, namely for the protection of one's family and for hunting. As such, the idea of taking away individuals' right to own them was unthinkable.

However, that a hostile power would seek to disarm the people was not at all unthinkable. So in an age prior to the establishment of a standing national army, asserting this right as the 2nd Amendment does was necessary

socialist one should consider that when people have a problem with a business they have multiple options: they can press the business to correct the problem or else they will lose them as a customer and perhaps be hurt in other ways due to bad customer relations (which is especially powerful in today's inter-connected world). This will often be a powerful incentive for businesses to better serve their customers. (This is one of the benefits of competition.)

---

to safeguard the ability of the fledgling nation to defend against possible future threats by hostile forces, including foreign powers, domestic uprisings, or (quite conceivably) a Federal Government seeking to take away the rights and freedoms which the Constitution sought to guarantee to the people and the states. Such possible threats could make it necessary for the people to take up arms once again. Indeed, this would subsequently prove to be the case, legitimately in several cases, but illegitimately in one: when the southern states did so against the Union.

It is not at all the case that ownership of fire-arms is mainly for taking on any government which one opposes. For this would actually be wrong from a Christian perspective. After all, there is no suggestion whatsoever in the New Testament that the early Christians should mount an insurgency against the Roman Empire, as oppressive as it often was in demanding allegiance and persecuting them and others.

Some regard "the War of American Independence" as a real "revolution" and have used it to justify many subsequent revolutionary uprisings by those with various political agendas. But many of the colonists were very concerned with the possibility that they may be participating in a sinful rebellion if they took up arms against the English Crown. In the end, many agreed to fight on the basis that they were engaging not in insurrection against England, but in a divinely-permitted separatist movement for independence from a remote government and for self-rule, in which it was asserted that "lesser magistrates" in the form of the colonial governments were better suited to rule. The war didn't begin as a war, but as a lawful effort to achieve independence. It only became so when Crown forces sought to stop it by force.

135 *This expression can be seen as the 20th century equivalent of Patrick Henry's famous 18th century proclamation: "Give me liberty or give me death!" Red refers to Marxism because it has always been the color associated with it,*

And if this doesn't work there is still the option of seeking remedy through consumer-rights agencies like the Better Business Bureau or, perhaps, regulatory agencies set up by various industries (like professional associations). Finally, if the problem still isn't solved there remains the option of seeking satisfaction through legal action.

But if one's problem is with the government (as it would be in a single-payer government-run health-care system) then he or she will only have the last option. And it should be clear that government agencies normally have much less incentive than most businesses to satisfy those who bring problems to them. They will also have less incentive to keep costs down. This is because they have no competition or need to show a profit. Rather, the operating expenses of government agencies come from taxes and other fees, which are required to be paid and are enforced with the backing of legal sanctions. And, if it ends up that you have to sue the government, you will be facing an opponent with "deep pockets" so that it is hard to defeat. Finally, even if you win you will actually be paying for part of your own settlement because of the fact that the government relies on its citizen tax-payers for its income.

Humanists tend to favor Socialism specifically because they reject a Higher Authority for right and wrong and believe that what is right and good is advanced by people working together. This is why former President Barack Obama expresses faith that "the arc of moral history bends toward justice".[136] This reflects the optimism which prevailed in the developed world up until the 1ˢᵗ World War. The advent of that war, which had been the most brutal and widespread ever seen, and the far more destructive World

---

including by many Marxists themselves. This being the case, it is rather ironic that red is today associated with the Republican Party, which still tends to be anti-socialist, especially among its more conservative members, rather than with the Democratic Party, which is quite pro-socialist and, even, pro-Marxist in some circles.

136 *This phrase apparently goes back to Theodore Parker, a pre-Civil War Unitarian minister. It's no mere coincidence that a Unitarian would express such optimism. For Unitarians have always been Humanists who reject historic Christian orthodoxy.*

War 2 should have been the "1-2 punch" that knocked out Humanist optimism forever.

But optimism dies hard. After all, one has to hope for the best. And without hope for a Higher Power bringing justice one can only hope that we can somehow achieve it. Even though, as we've seen, without this Higher Authority justice itself can only be arbitrary, a matter merely of human opinion.

This "desperate optimism" is why Humanists cling to the belief that human governments can be more than the sum of their parts in a good sense, despite numerous examples to the contrary, both in the past and present, and only rare exceptions. On the other hand, those who have the Christian understanding of human nature tend to see governments as magnifiers of the evil of individuals, with only rare exceptions.

So it is that those with the Christian worldview, in agreement with America's founders, favor limited governments with separated and balanced powers. But faith in the ability of governments as a force for good is why Humanists are so determined to solve the world's problems from the "top-down" instead of from the "bottom-up". This has always been the core of Socialism. And it is why obtaining political control is of paramount importance.[137]

---

[137] *It should be noted that the alternative to Socialism need not be an unregulated "laissez-faire" Capitalism. Rather it should be a Capitalism which is carefully (but not excessively) regulated by the government so as to maintain as level a playing-field as possible. It will do so by taking actions against unfair competitive practices or imbalances. And it will also promote equality of opportunity by providing social safety-nets for the truly disadvantaged (short-term assistance for many so that they can get back on their feet and back into the game, but long-term for those who are unable to do so due to real disabilities and/or age). But, unfortunately, while America's labor unions were originally organized in order to be a reforming influence on Capitalism along the lines I have just described, they often shifted to being advocates of Socialism, the inferior alternative. . .*

This is also why Humanists tend to favor unlimited immigration, and especially by poor people from the developing world. It is only natural that poor immigrants will tend to prize, utilize and depend on government benefits which they never could have received in their countries of origin. Thus, it is also naturally the case that they will overwhelmingly tend to skew toward candidates who promise greater government benefits. Of course, these will almost always be socialistic Humanists. So this proves to be a very effect way to increase the voter base for socialistic candidates, who will either be Democrats or independents who vote with the Democratic Party.

Ideally, then, if the demographics can be successfully turned, the supposedly optimum socialist regime might conceivably be put in place without firing a shot. Although there is certainly a degree of elitist arrogance in this, it is probably more a matter of naive optimism than hubris that so many Humanists still think that they can succeed where no one else ever has in

---

Furthermore, for a free-market system and a free society in general to succeed requires that there be a shared ethic which will cause people to be mainly self-policing. Without this the only alternative to chaos will be a Police State. Sadly, barring a major Revival, the latter seems to be where we are headed in the ethically-ambiguous post-modernist 21st century. That Capitalism requires an ethical population is a key aspect of the connection between the Christian worldview, Capitalism and political freedom. "The American Experiment" in freedom was successful to an unprecedented degree because it was based on the fact that the so-called "Protestant work-ethic" reigned for the first 175 years of America's existence.

It is also important to realize that the continuum of governments is not between Marxists on the Left and fascists on the Right, as many believe. For, both Marxism and fascism are actually totalitarian socialist systems. The real continuum of governments is between the anarchy of no government control on one side and all-controlling governments on the other (including both Marxist and fascist states). The desirable middle-ground is what America's founders set up: a free society (with a free-market) protected by a limited amount of government with shared and balanced powers under the rule of a Higher Law. The true continuum of governments is represented in a chart found at the end of this chapter.

creating a truly just and equitable society through government power.

It is very troubling for those of us who prize freedom that without a widespread changing of minds on a very basic level the Socialists may well succeed. But no human being or movement can be expected to cause such a change in people's basic thinking. Only a Higher Power could do this. So it is that this book is offered in the hope of such a Higher Power doing so, namely, The One True God Who reveals Himself in the minds of all (if you are willing to be open to this), in the world He has created and rules, and also in the Bible.

We need a real Revival the likes of which has not been seen since the Great Awakening in the colonies in the middle of the 18th century. Though such a Revival must come from above, it also occurs as a "grassroots movement" as more and more individuals are transformed on the inside so that the balance is eventually shifted.

It is the hope of this writer that such a Revival would occur. But this is mainly because it would mean that many more people will join us in the blessings of Salvation, blessings which we can experience now and, especially, in "the next world". We don't pray for this because it would produce a better society in this world, although it likely would in many ways. This can never be our priority. For this would be a worldly goal no less than the worldly goal of Socialists.

Furthermore, an optimum society in this world is nowhere promised in the New Testament.[138] Rather, our goal is what Jesus' Kingdom parables in the

---

138 *That earthly regimes don't last is reflected in the following observation: "The average age of the world's greatest civilizations from the beginning of history has been about 200 years. During those 200 years, these nations always progressed through the following sequence: From bondage to spiritual faith; From spiritual faith to great courage; From courage to liberty; From liberty to abundance; From abundance to selfishness; From selfishness to complacency; From complacency to apathy; From apathy to dependence; From dependence back into bondage." This observation,*

New Testament pointed to: creating citizens of the Kingdom of God which will be revealed when He returns, a Kingdom which when it comes in its Fullness will be nothing short of *"new heavens and a new earth"* (which we understand to be a transformation of the entire universe).

God's Kingdom was symbolically and uniquely represented in the Theocracy which God laid out for Israel during the Old Testament era. But this Theocracy was never fully-implemented and eventually collapsed. This was not because it failed, but because it was never intended to be the permanant Kingdom of God. It was only meant to be a picture of The Real Kingdom of God which God will some day bring, which will reign over all.

So it is that both the Old and New Testaments point us beyond this world. And so it is that the ultimate hope of this writer is that God might be pleased to use this and whatever else He wishes to transform others into citizens of real Ideal and Ultimate State which God intends for us: The Kingdom of Heaven, that which Jesus constantly pointed us toward. After all, it was He Who said: *"In this world you will have trouble. But, take heart, for I have overcome the world."* (Gospel of John, chapter 16, verse 33)

And two chapters earlier, Jesus said this:
"My Father's House has many rooms; if that were not so, would I have told you that I am going there to prepare a place for you? And if I go and prepare a place for you, I will come back and take you to be with Me where I am." (John 14:2-3)

---

which seems sensible both with respect to human-nature and human history has been variously attributed to Alexander Fraser Tytler or Alexis de Tocqueville. It also shows how individual responsibility and spirituality (or the lack of such) affects societies.

The Continuum of Governments

by Christopher Andrus
December 5, 2017

Anarchy	Pluralist, Free-market, Limited-government Democracies	Totalitarian Socialism
(No government)	*(Government of, by & for the People with "Liberty & Justice for all", whether religious or not)*	*Anti-religious/Anti-national (Marxism)* *Religious (Muslim, Christian, other)* *Nationalist (Nazism, Imperialist Japan, etc.)* *(Government over the people)*

Contrary to the conventional Left versus Right distinction, the real difference in societies is in how much government control exists versus how much freedom individuals and groups have. Socialist societies hold that it is the Government that ultimately determines both the rights of individuals and, even, what is right and wrong. This is the case whether such societies emerge quickly through revolutions (as with Bolshevik revolution in Russia) or through a gradual growth of the size and power of government (which has been known as "Fabian creeping Socialism" and has been the trend in the United States of America for almost 100 years).

Historically, most societies have embraced some form of Socialism because people will normally be willing to sacrifice freedom in the hope of having more security. But the United States of America was unique in being founded on the idea that both human rights and right and wrong are higher than any government, group or individual as part of the order of the universe as created by God. This Higher Law was understood to be conveyed both through Nature through the consciences and experience of humanity (Natural Law) and through God's revelation in the Bible. The only way to avoid both anarchy and the tyranny of human governments is to have a society in which most people are able to police themselves because they recognize and follow the Higher Law. Without this, societies will always move toward police states.

Appendix 1
A Response to a Hindu

A Hindu friend (Vijay Villiyil) shared the following with me:

Just heard of this wonderful piece of Sufi literature..and hence sharing. Amazing conclusions of the book (highlighted).

We are the birds in the story. All of us have our own ideas and ideals, our own fears and anxieties, as we hold on to our own version of the truth. Like the birds of this story, we may take flight together, but the journey itself will be different for each of us. Attar tells us that truth is not static, and that we each tread a path according to our own capacity. It evolves as we evolve. Those who are trapped within their own dogma, clinging to hardened beliefs or faith, are deprived of the journey toward the unfathomable Divine, which Attar calls the Great Ocean.

The seven valleys (see listed below) reminded me of the 7 Chakras of the yoga practice which needs to be opened for enlightenment. In Bible, the book of Revelation speaks of seven seals being opened prior to the return of Jesus Christ to earth.

The Conference of the Birds (Persian: Manṭiq-uṭ-Ṭayr, 1177), is a celebrated literary masterpiece of Persian literature by poet Farid ud-Din Attar, commonly known as Attar of Nishapur. The title, which is in Arabic, is taken directly from the Quran, 27:16, where Sulayman (Solomon) and Dāwūd (David) are said to have been taught the language, or speech, of the birds (Manṭiq Al-ṭayr).

Synopsis

In the poem, the birds of the world gather to decide who is to be their sovereign, as they have none. The Hoopoe, the wisest of them all, suggests that they should find the legendary Simorgh. The Hoopoe leads the birds, each of whom represents a human fault which prevents human kind from attaining enlightenment.

The Hoopoe tells the birds that they have to cross seven valleys in order to reach the abode of Simorgh. These valleys are as follows

1. Valley of the Quest, where the Wayfarer begins by casting aside all dogma, belief, and unbelief.

2. Valley of Love, where reason is abandoned for the sake of love.

3. Valley of Knowledge, where worldly knowledge becomes utterly useless.

4. Valley of Detachment, where all desires and attachments to the world are given up. Here, what is assumed to be "reality" vanishes.

5. Valley of Unity, where the Wayfarer realizes that everything is connected and that the Beloved is beyond everything, including harmony, multiplicity, and eternity.

6. Valley of Wonderment, where, entranced by the beauty of the Beloved, the Wayfarer becomes perplexed and, steeped in awe, finds that he or she has never known or understood anything.

7. Valley of Poverty and Annihilation, where the self disappears into the universe and the Wayfarer becomes timeless, existing in both the past and the future.

"When the birds hear the description of these valleys, they bow their heads in distress; some even die of fright right then and there. But despite their trepidations, they begin the great journey. On the way, many perish of thirst, heat or illness, while others fall prey to wild beasts, panic, and violence. Finally, only thirty birds make it to the abode of Simorgh. In the end, the birds learn that they themselves are the Simorgh; the name "Simorgh" in Persian means thirty (si) birds (morgh). They eventually come to understand that the majesty of that Beloved is like the sun that can be seen reflected in a mirror. Yet, whoever looks into that mirror will also behold his or her own image

Conference Of The Birds:

https://www.youtube.com/watch?v=5IgHxl310ms

"To Know Your Self is to Know God" (man 'arafa nafsahu faqad 'arafa Rabbahu) -Hadith

A Christian Responds

As nice as you & your fellow spiritualists are, Vijay, the differences in our understanding are becoming more and more clear. And it very much matters who is right. Here are the problems in the points you highlight.

First, we don't abandon dogma because we all live by dogma in the sense that we all have basic beliefs which we don't question and which are the basis for how we view everything else. So, to say that there is no dogma is actually dogma in itself!

Second, to say that love abandons reason is to assume a false dilemma between love and reason. If we abandon our reason in how we would try to love someone we will often fail to do what is really the loving thing. For example, it might seem kind to give money or, even, food to someone on the street or to support people who are caught up in homosexuality or transgender thinking. But if in doing so all that we do is to allow them to continue a self-destructive lifestyle then this is not really being loving to them. Rather, we must think about what we can do that will really help them.

Third, worldly knowledge is not useless. As much as I appreciate how you and other spiritualists like you recognize the reality of the spiritual realm, unlike those who have embraced today's dominant Materialism, Hinduism, Buddhism and all of the other Asian traditions make the same error that many ancients in the West made in assuming that the spiritual world is good, while the physical world is inherently evil. This notion was part of classical Greek thinking and also is found in Neo-Platonism and Gnosticism in the first centuries after the time of Jesus.

But God originally created both us and other spirits as good (but also free to become bad if we chose to do so) and He also created the physical world as good (but we corrupt it because we are both born as corrupted and also corrupt it by our own decisions). To deny the reality and importance of this world is to be too passive in this world, thereby allowing evil to be unopposed and also failing to do as much as we can to make this world a better place. This is why the Asian world had to catch up to the West in the area of technology and still lags behind it in its understanding of freedom and human-rights.

It is also wrong to assume that individuality is fundamentally wrong. God created us as individuals so that He could have a personal relationship with each one of us. The denial of the importance of individuals is also what all dictatorships or collectivist governments do (which includes not only Marxist ones, but also extreme nationalist states like Nazi Germany and Japan of the same era). Even religious dictatorships like those in the Muslim world make the same mistake of basing society on the idea that the every individual must sacrifice themselves for the common good. Indeed, we must sometimes do this. But to make this a universal principle is a sure recipe for oppression.

I would welcome you to share this with your friends, Vijay. And I always welcome response, whether it is in agreement or disagreement. Actually, I usually learn more from disagreement and believe that others do too.

In disagreement, but still respectfully yours,

Chris Andrus

The following is added to the original response for the benefit of the reader:

The most basic difference between Christianity and the Asian traditions is our understanding that there is a God and He will always be distinct from us. That The One True God is Tri-Personal (that is, the Trinity) and also became a man (the Incarnation) are the fundamental theological differences between Christianity and the other monotheistic traditions (principally, Islam and Judaism, but also including sects like Jehovah's Witnesses and Mormonism). Finally, polytheism is just an idolatrous rejection of The One True God.

Appendix 2
Suggestions For Further Study

The following books have been most helpful to me:

Lisle, Jason. The Ultimate Proof of Creation (Master Books, 2009)
> *This is the best critique of the evolutionary worldview that I have found. It not only deals with the key scientific issues, it is also very helpful with regard to the philosophical issues which are the main focus of this book. Lisle even has 2 great chapters on logical fallacies.*

Schlossberg, Herbert. Idols for Destruction (Wheaton, IL: Crossway, 1990)
> *This is the best critique of modern culture in America and the rest of the developed world that I have found. It isn't an "easy-read" by any means, but should greatly reward anyone willing to dig into it. In my opinion, it is one of the most underrated Christian books of the 20th century, although it does tend toward advocating that a Christian Theocracy is the most desirable society, rather than the pluralist ideal which America's founders sought.*

Keller, Timothy. The Reason for God (New York: Riverhead Books, 2008)

Sproul, R.C. Essential Truths of the Christian Faith (Carol Stream, IL: Tyndale House, 1992)
> *The Suggested Reading list on pages 301-307 will provide more than enough material for anyone.*

C.S. Lewis' Mere Christianity and J.I. Packer's Knowing God are somewhat older volumes, which are somewhat dated but are rightly regarded as classics that are still very helpful. The same is true of just about anything from Francis Schaeffer. And the same could be said for J. Gresham Machen's <u>Christianity & Liberalism</u> (Grand Rapids: William B. Eerdmans, 1923). The basic issue that Machen lays out remains the same.

A much older, but still very helpful work is <u>The Confessions</u> of Augustine. It is Augustine's own account of his conversion. Once again, the basic issue remains relevant today.

The video documentary "Evolution's Achilles Heels" is a great presentation of the scientific problems with Evolution and also provides reasons why 15 scientists abandoned it for Intelligent Design/Creationism. The website: AnswersinGenesis.org is also a good source.

The writings of Cornelius Van Til also lay out the basic issue between Christian faith and unbelief, although Van Til is notoriously hard-to-read. But, like the Schlossberg volume cited above, the effort can be very rewarding. Reading Van Til's writings directly, rather than the secondary material on him is preferable. Van Til is considered to be the founder of modern Presuppositional Apologetics, which this book seeks to advance. But, unfortunately, many subsequent presuppositionalists have tended to discourage doing apologetics and simply advocate preaching the Gospel, essentially asking unbelievers to presuppose that the Bible is true.

The author of this book prefers a "both/and" approach to apologetics and the proclamation of the Gospel, believing that some need the former, while others only need the latter. So, it is believed that many unbelievers must be called to recognize, first of all, that they already know that the God of the Bible exists (not some sort of generic "God", Romans 1:18-20), though they are both naturally-inclined and strongly-encouraged by a "post-Christian" culture to suppress this knowledge.

But knowledge which is suppressed is never eradicated entirely so that it must be re-established (either by being proven, as "evidentialist" apologists seek to do, or by accepting the authority of the Bible, as many presuppositionalists seek to do). Rather, one need only stop suppressing what he or she already knows by nature and experience but just doesn't want to accept.

So, unbelievers don't need to presuppose that the Bible is true or, even, that the God of the Bible exists. Rather, what is necessary is for one to simply stop living in Denial of The One True Creator God Whom he or she already knows to exist. Besides, it can be seen that <u>every human-being who has ever lived has actually presupposed the existence of this God at all times in order to function in the world that He has made</u>. If someone becomes willing to recognize this, then he or she will be able to see the Bible and its message of Salvation for what it is: God's written revelation to us.

Finally, I invite readers to check out my 2nd book: "Christianity From A to Z", which features 26 short chapters dealing with topics both timely and perennial. And I invite you to visit the blog from the author of this book: https://christianityistrue.org. Besides additional articles, there are some real-life dialogues with unbelievers in the comment boards there. Just click on "Replies" under the articles.

Appendix 3
Key Statements in Each Chapter

Chapter 1

If you have never really thought carefully about the question: "Why am I alive?" then you are not really a careful critical thinker on the most basic and most important level, regardless of your level of education.

In every society there will always be an enormous amount of pressure to accept the basic beliefs of the society and not to question them.

Germany's "Third Reich" did not spring up overnight in its fully-developed form. It was a gradual process of many steps, most of them small and easy to overlook, which occurred over many years. This is usually the way things change.

God is only your Enemy if you treat Him as such. Rather, He wants to be your perfectly-loving Father, His Son Jesus Christ your Savior and His Holy Spirit your Guide.

It is simply not possible to examine our lives without examining our most basic beliefs about life.

 . . . it is quite natural to be passionate about our most basic beliefs and also highly defensive of them and very hostile to challenges by people with different basic beliefs. This is so even for people who are not very aware of their basic beliefs, working on more of a subconscious level for such people.

We all have some sort of a belief-system that we are committed to; that is, a set of basic beliefs about ourselves, the world around us and whether or not there is a God or some other Higher Authority than us.

Chapter 2

. . . since Humanism had clearly rejected long-accepted fundamental aspects of Christianity, if one wished to keep up with the times but also retain some sense of Christianity, then it would be necessary for Christianity to be recast in a way in which it was not in conflict with the basic principles of Humanism.

Unlike many Christian approaches, I will not ask any reader who doesn't already believe this to presuppose that the Bible is true. Rather, my goal will be to get everyone who has not already done so to begin by accepting that the God Who makes Himself known in our minds and in the world around us must really exist.

To deny that God exists is like a pot saying to the potter who made it: "You don't exist.", or a child saying the same to his parents.

For most people, God's call to us in our minds is like a phone-call that we don't want to take; it's like a road that we don't want to take because we think it's an undesirable road and because we think the road that we are on is good enough.

The very nature of the God of the Bible means that there can be no neutrality toward Him. So if this God exists, and we say that He must, then we must view everything in relation to Him. So, to fail to begin with Him, as Humanism and all other religions and philosophies do, is to make the Huge Mistake of rejecting Him.

. . . this book is intended to be a concise and simple critique of Humanism and the other major non-Christian approaches, as well as a brief introduction to the Christian worldview.

The belief-system (or "worldview") that I had embraced claimed to tell me how it is that I am alive, but it had no answer to the question "Why?"

. . . if both Zen and modern scientists and intellectuals are correct, then all that we think and experience are merely passing fancies with only the illusion of meaning. In short, if this is the case, then we are all the victims of a cosmic joke of sorts.

I never really took seriously the teachings of the Catholic Church, much less did I actually consider them and, "Science forbid!", embrace them. I considered them outdated and irrelevant because that was what the culture I was living in told me.

I continued searching in every possible direction I could find other than Christianity. Until one day when God suddenly got my attention.

. . . out of all ancient religious scriptures, the Bible alone presents The God Who had just made me aware of Himself.

Chapter 3

. . . as awe-inspiring as the physical world is, is this all there is? Most people today have been convinced that it is. But there are many of us who have come to see that it isn't and have come to realize that we don't live in a universe that is ultimately impersonal.

. . . the main thing which has always divided us is that some of us live in a God-centered reality and some of us live in a no-God reality.

. . . we say that it is logically, morally and existentially necessary that the God described in the Bible does exist and, even, that every human being who has ever lived has known that He exists.

If you are determined to hold on to your view then you will always look for ways to do so no matter what evidence is offered against it, either by seeking to explain away what is offered or just by dismissing it.

. . . what I was really being "confirmed" in was the Humanism which was assumed by almost everyone I knew, including my school teachers, peers, family members and most of the "VIP's", the Very Influential People in society.

In order to understand other perspectives fairly and properly one needs to try to understand them on their own terms rather than imposing your terms on them.

It's logically impossible to know that the physical world around us is all that exists. There are two simple reasons why. First, there is the problem that this statement has two things in it: us and the world around us. We can't have perception and knowledge of the world without having both a world and perceivers/knowers of that world.

Russell's "argument" is essentially this: "Come on people, your belief that there is a God is clearly ridiculous and should be abandoned by all reasonable people even though it can't actually be proven that He doesn't exist."

The Humanist understanding of the universe is also known as the philosophy of Materialism (or also as Physicalism).

. . . it's one thing to have a strong and proper faith in Science and quite another to assume that since the scientific method proves to be the correct way to understand the physical world, then this world must be all that exists. This just doesn't follow logically.

Those who believe that previous generations were overwhelmingly ignorant compared to our own have a bias that's questionable at best.

. . . it has never been necessary to be trained in Science to have a basic understanding of how the laws of nature work in our everyday lives.

. . . if you don't know what the puzzle looks like overall, you will never be able to put the pieces together correctly. So it is also with worldviews.

The nature of the God described in the Bible gives us only two possible options. We can start with Him and view everything in relation to Him, and in a personal relationship <u>with</u> Him. Or we can reject Him and find another way.

One of the things today's Humanist cultural indoctrination does is to hide that it is an indoctrination in one particular worldview. The result is people who think that they have the only reasonable and scientific perspective.

Humanists and others who become Christians find that we lose nothing of value in making the switch. We only lose what isn't true and, thus, does not hold up.

. . . atheists who claim that they used to be Christians tend to show that they never developed a mature faith by the types of arguments they use against Christianity

Chapter 4

. . . if you turn the page upside-down you will see different words.

. . . it would take an extremely good puzzle-solver to assemble all of the pictures above properly in order to produce the correct big picture, even if the big picture is known. But it would literally be impossible if it isn't.

The severity of the cultural war polarization comes from the fact that one's worldview influences how one views virtually everything in life, often leading people with different worldviews to draw opposite conclusions when viewing the same situations or data.

Unfortunately, a very common reaction to differences over issues today is for people to say that "I and those on my side are right and those on the other side are wrong, either because they are ignorant or bad (or both)."

. . . all objections to what is in the Bible are based on the assumption that the God Who is described in the Bible (and is presented as speaking in it) cannot exist.

If you think you are a Christian only because your family has a Christian heritage or because you received some rudimenatary religious instruction as a child, then you are either a Humanist already in your basic beliefs, or, at least, you will have no strong objection to becoming one.

. . . as people become older and more experienced many of them turn to God.

. . . the general pattern of people becoming more conservative as they get older (which has been widely-recognized and measured for years) continues even in today's Humanism-dominated culture.

. . . to be sympathetic and, even, empathetic with bad people is neither "compassionate" nor loving. Rather, it is to encourage and sometimes enable or support those who are involved in behavior which is destructive to themselves, to others and, even, to society itself.

. . . the desire to punish those whom one resents is highly-destructive if the person or group has not been conclusively shown to be guilty and, therefore, deserving of punishment. . .

Since older people are more likely to be both religious believers and conservative isn't it reasonable that you should be willing to critically examine your own worldview and also become open to Christianity?

. . . the personal consequences of one's worldview are nothing less than life-defining. This is so no matter what point-of-view you currently have. And the worldview which one has is also (potentially, at least) of eternal consequence.

Chapter 5

If natural forces are all that exist and nature is amoral (that is, non-moral or morally neutral), then how can humanity be moral?

. . . concern for the preservation of humanity and other species, as well as concern for the environment, is Biblical. But it is inconsistent with the idea that we are just another species which emerged from mindless forces in Nature.

. . . neither might nor masses make right. If we are not moral beings who are under a Higher Authority, then it is all arbitrary.

To understand what the rule of law means one must realize what its alternative is: the rule of human-beings, whether it's a single human-being or a ruling few or, even, the rule of a majority.

. . . even those who rejected the Bible altogether as being of divine origin still held that humanity was under Higher Law in the form of "Natural Law".

Humanists tend to think that poverty causes crime. But Christians and other traditionalists see crime mainly as a problem of human character, saying that criminals cause crime and, also, that crime causes poverty in many cases.

Committing crimes is always a matter of choice. Indeed there are circumstances in which there are greater enticements to commit crimes, especially in the case of a starving person stealing food. But even in this case stealing is a choice, for there are always alternatives to stealing.

. . . the record shows that significantly more people are killed by murderers who have been spared the penalty of death than the number of innocent people who are wrongly executed.

It is one of the great ironies of the 21st century that those who ignore what Christians (and others) believe and assume other sinister motives for why we oppose the pro-LGBTQ movement actually are guilty of a very destructive form of prejudice and hate.

. . . the scientific and mental-health communities around the world were almost unanimously in agreement with the Christian point-of-view on sexuality until the 1970's. And it's not that the Science changed as a result of any significant new findings. Rather, what has changed is the political orientation of many scientists and their associations.

You who would condemn Christians because we won't affirm the choices that LGBTQ people make are, in effect, demanding that Christians agree with your point-of-view or shut-up or be penalized. This is just as wrong as when Christians have tried to do this to others in the past.

Today's false understanding of tolerance simply doesn't work in practice and inevitably leads to hypocrisy in which only certain views are considered acceptable.

Even if it is the case that some people are genetically pre-disposed to alcoholism, such people would still not become alchoholics if they simply refused to start drinking. And it's simply absurd to claim that it is ever physically necessary for anyone to do this.

No one doubts that we can change our physiques if we decide to start working-out. But it is now possible to observe that we can change our brains, too, by the choices that we make.

. . . the really good news is that many people diagnosed with mental-illness today either have nothing wrong with their brains, or, at least, nothing wrong with their brain-chemistry which can't be corrected by abandoning unhealthy patterns of thinking and behavior and adopting healthy ones.

. . . the spectre of being accountable to one's Creator at the end of our lives made it far less likely that people would ever consider taking their own lives.

. . . suicide, insofar as it is a deliberate act, is actually the ultimate personal decision that a person can make.

Suicide is surely the cruelest thing that one could ever do to those who care about the person who does it.

. . . the stunningly simple truth about sexuality is that it is always learned behavior, either learned normally (in monogamous heterosexual relationships) or not (in any other way in which sexual pleasure is sought).

. . . we all know that we have many real choices to make everyday. And we know that they are meaningful choices, which will either help us or hurt us. But this is only true because Materialism is false.

. . . what happened was that the Humanist narrative gradually became the dominant one, mainly due to the influence of the educational, media and entertainment establishments.

Chapter 6

As with the study of the past, what will happen in the future hinges on whether or not there is an Intelligent influence (or influences) on the cosmic level.

Since Materialism assumes that reality consists only of material objects along with mindless forces in space-time, those who hold to this view must deny that subjects really exist in themselves.

Consciousness and all that it entails is not just a "gap" in our understanding which Science just has not yet filled in (as many claim). Science will never be able to explore this side of reality. This is because Science, by its nature, can only study objects.

We can begin with what's inside our heads (that is, with how our thinking works). This is the Idealist approach. Or we can begin with what's outside of us (or, as an Idealist might say, what <u>seems</u> to be outside of us), the Materialist starting-point.

How does one go from a mindless reality of objects to the "world" (so to speak) of minds? This is a Big and unsolvable Problem for Materialism.

Thoughts that we have (whatever they are) may be seen to be associated with changes in our brain chemistry, but they are clearly a different type of thing altogether than the chemical changes which we observe.

. . . the process begins with deliberate choices which alter brain-chemistry, which, in turn, alter consciousness.

. . . the Materialist view really can't even explain why some sounds convey information (speech) while others (noise or purely instrumental music) don't.

Computers which we construct will never be anything more than what we make them precisely because they are not what we are: they are only machines. Indeed, we do have machine-like bodies (including our brains). But this is not all that we are.

. . . we as human-beings have the ability to make too many choices to enable us to completely replicate them. This can be seen in the area of facial expressions.

Some time ago there was a lot of excitement in scientific circles when it was thought that a Lowland Gorilla named Koko had successfully mastered sign-language so that she could now express what she was thinking. But these hopes faded quickly after there was an attempt to have a press conference with Koko.

. . . speech is the deliberate arranging of sounds which make specific connections with other things so as to convey information to others. And the only species we know which can do this is *homo sapiens*.

. . . to stay focussed on the narrow issues rather than the Big Picture is like the proverbial steward who was devoted to re-arranging the deck-chairs on the Titanic after it had struck the ice-berg!

. . . the real barrier keeping unbelievers from considering Christianity is the blind and false faith which most people today have in Evolution (both on the cosmic level and in the development of life), in Science as the only way to know things, in the Materialism worldview on which these beliefs are based, and in the entire Humanist belief-system, of which Materialism is a fundamental part.

Another very simple and basic fallacy of the 21st century, one which, amazingly, is believed by nearly everyone today is this: It is to believe that we can know what happened in the past and what will happen in the future based on what we understand about how Nature works now.

To project from the present either to the past or to the future requires that we account for all possible influences. If there is even the possibility of an over-ruling Power (which, again, could never be ruled out), then we can't do this!

. . . confidence in radiometric dating falsely assumes that we now know all of the natural forces involved.

. . . even if we have come to know all of the natural forces involved, can we really assume we know them well enough to understand all of their effects? Once again, this has proven to be a faulty assumption on many occasions in the history of Science.

Does the fact that you have never observed a "miracle" mean that such events are impossible? No, this simply doesn't follow. And does the fact that Science is the proper way to study Nature mean that Nature as we know it is all that can exist? Again, this simply doesn't follow.

All of this means that even though the process of induction is one of the foundations of proper Science essential for understanding how the universe works today, one simply cannot use induction in order to understand what happened in the distant past or what will happen in the future. For, strictly speaking, neither is subject to scientific examination.

It is undeniable that anti-theistic Naturalism is at the heart of all secular Science today. So the perspective being presented here is a fundamental challenge to today's scientific community. It is not a surprise, then, that it is treated as a serious threat.

. . . the rejection of Christian Theism, far from being a positive development in intellectual history, is actually The Largest Intellectual Error (or LIE) in human history.

Chapter 7

Humanists look at everything on the assumption that Humanism is true, Christians on the assumption that Christianity is, Muslims on the assumption that Islam is. Hindus, Buddhists, "New-age" spirtualists and everyone else does the same. This is known as "confirmation bias". And everyone does it.

If there is no materialistic explanation apparent in a particular situation, the committed Materialist will resort to an argument from ignorance rather than consider that a phenomenon he or she encounters might represent evidence that disproves Materialism.

We all interpret everything we encounter based on our current understanding of what is true and possible. There just isn't any other way to proceed in life.

. . . there are also many scientific problems addressed by scientists who have either come over to the side of Creationism or have at least become skeptics of natural selection and evolutionary Materialism.

. . . all religions and comprehensive philosophies are by nature exclusive. This includes the popular idea that all religions are just different paths to the same destination. If one holds this view he or she automatically considers wrong everyone who believes their religion or philosophy is the only true path!

Much of what people today think they know about Christianity is actually derogatory false stereotypes promoted by Humanists with an anti-Christian prejudice (Humanism being in itself a reaction mainly against Christianity).

The fact that Christianity is presented as the only true path is not a valid reason to reject it. The only thing that really matters is: Is it true or not?

. . . it may seem, at first, that a God Who would just forgive evil-doers would be the most loving God imaginable, kind of a Cosmic Santa Claus. But appearances can often be deceiving.

No one really wants a God who would just forgive everyone because it wouldn't be just. If this was really your ideal, then to be consistent with this you could not justify having prisons or, even, any judicial system at all.

. . . no one has ever proved that anything in the Bible is inevitably wrong. Indeed, many of the so-called errors can be found to have rather simple explanations.

You can decide that you don't like God because you don't like what the Bible says He has said and done. But you can't decide that He doesn't exist on account of this. That is simply irrational.

We just can't know that things would have been worse had Christianity remained the dominant viewpoint of the developed world. This is merely assumed as part of today's anti-Christian Humanist bias.

If the triumph of Humanism during the 20th century was such a positive development, then why is it that Humanists tend to have fewer children than Bible-believing Christians or other religious people?

. . . it does not reflect well on Humanism that pessimism about the future clearly has a much greater influence on the decision of Humanists to have children than it does for Christians and others.

The circularity of Humanist "reasoning" is well-summarized as follows: "I know my reasoning is valid because I checked the validity of my reasoning using my reasoning. Therefore, I know that my reasoning is valid."

Chapter 8

Far from God needing to prove His existence and goodness to us, those who deny God have to use the minds and breath that He gives them to deny Him.

God must be presupposed in order to be opposed. To claim that God doesn't exist is the ultimate case of Denial in the psychological sense of the term – that is, pretending that what you know to be true isn't true because you aren't ready to accept that it is true.

And all discussions about truth and goodness actually assume that there is absolute truth and goodness. This is because if one was to say that all such discussions are just differences of opinion it would effectively end the discussions.

. . . while we are born to know our Creator, we are also born with a natural tendency to rebel against Him. We do so by constantly suppressing our knowledge of Him so that we can deny that He is there, and by seeking to get along without Him in any way that we can.

<u>It is simply not necessary to prove the existence of someone whom one already knows</u>. And such is the case with our Creator for every human-being who has ever lived. But various arguments for God's existence are valid and remind us of Who He is and of His Glory.

In order for the cause and effect chain which we observe in the universe to exist, there must be a First Cause, which is un-caused, as its Source.

Without God right and wrong can only be arbitrary. And the same would also be true of human-rights.

As Germans in the 1920's & 30's needed to challenge the Nazi's and their evil views, so it is that peace-loving Muslims today need to challenge those in their religion who practice evil in the name of God (even as the Nazi's did).

. . . most of us have also been taught the Humanist belief that a return to Christianity as the dominant view will inevitably take us back to the "dark ages" of Medieval Europe, to rampant superstition and to theocratic rule. But, those of us who have turned to Christianity have come to see that this is not true.

. . . there is no choice except to go back to recognizing that reality is dualistic, including both objects (material things or bodies) and observers, who are more than material entities. So it is that human-beings must be seen as immaterial minds/souls/spirits joined to physical bodies. And this is precisely the view of Christianity.

If the Christian explanation is the simpler one (which we will agree is the case), then Occam's Razor cuts against the elaborate atheist and anti-theistic Humanist explanations, not the Christian approach.

That polytheists inevitably reject certain attributes of the Biblical God should be obvious for the simple reason that if they accepted all of the attributes of God described in the Bible (including God's One-ness) then they would have no conflict with those who believe in the God of the Bible.

. . . if we either are or can become equal to "God" in any real sense, then there would be no absolute distinction between God and us.

. . . if the universe is either Divine and Personal as a whole or just impersonal, our individuality as persons cannot be explained.

It is not hard to see that anti-individuality thinking will tend to lead to the idea that focusing on individuals and individual rights is wrong; or, at best, it is not of ultimate importance.

. . . our individuality not only implies the existence of other human-beings who are distinct from us, it also implies the existence of a God Who is also distinct from us.

From the Humanist, Hindu or Buddhist perspective our existence as individuals is either temporary or just an illusion. But Christianity, Judaism and Islam (despite crucial differences between them) all say that God made us individuals for eternity.

Chapter 9

. . . to hold that there is one true god but then deny that this god has certain attributes is also a failure to recognize God properly.

. . . the Gospel preached by the Christians of the first few centuries to their polytheistic neighbors was that they should abandon their false gods for The One True Lord, Jesus Christ, not three new Gods.

God the Father, God the Son and God the Holy Spirit are like perfectly-identical clones, although they manifest Themselves in distinct ways, most amazingly in the 2nd Person having become a real human-being.

Human nature is at its best when we care about others more than we do about ourselves. And isn't this the essence of love?

. . . when the Bible says that *God is love* it means that God is always outwardly-oriented, not inwardly-oriented. Before God created the universe this applied to each Person of the Trinity loving the other 2 Persons. But, most amazingly, God also created us to be the objects of His love, <u>if we are willing</u>.

If you really want to know what love really is (as the rock band "Foreigner" sang in the 1970's), the apostle Paul lists its characteristics in his first Letter to the Corinthians, chapter 13.

. . . one must become a Christian first before he or she can live the Christian life. This is always the First Priority and the main purpose of this book.

. . . there is one relationship which is always more important than marriage between a man and a woman. That is the relationship which we are all called to have with God (whether we have human spouses or not), which is also described as a marriage in the Bible.

. . . a person without God as his or her Father will always be alone in a more profound way, even if he or she is in a proper marriage bond. On the other hand, a person who knows God as Father will never be alone, regardless of his or her other relationships (or lack of these).

There is nothing more amazing than this: even though God knows all of our flaws and dark secrets, He is still committed to loving us forever.

. . . the Incarnation of "God, the Son" is neither a logical contradiction nor an immoral act.

When Joan Osborne asked "What if God was one of us?" in her 1995 hit song "One of Us" she was seemingly unaware of Christianity's central teaching that God did become one of us!

Chapter 10

. . . even though the credo of the Reformation was that we are saved by faith alone, it has always been understood that true faith will always lead to the doing of good works as opportunities present themselves.

The second perspective is known as Moralism. It is the view held by most people who identify themselves as non-religious (that is, secular Humanists).

Despite differences in terminology (especially with regard to the goal), the third conception is the most common one for serious practitioners of all of the major theistic religions of the world.

The problem with basing one's standing on having a particular kind of faith is that it could always be the wrong type of faith. Or, even if it is the right kind of faith, how can one know that he or she will be able to continue in this faith?

We all begin as truly lost sinners. And the definition of being lost is that you can't find your way out. So it is necessary that God must rescue us, just as park rangers must rescue lost hikers or else they will die!

Do you truly believe that God came into the world in the Person of The Eternal Son and that He accomplished the obedience that none of us could ever accomplish and also received the penalty for our disobedience in dying on a cross?

. . . atheists are right about all other gods and religions: they are cases of humanity making gods in our image, crafting gods or other ultimate authorities according to our desires. But Christians say that we only do this after we have rejected The One in Whose image we have been created.

. . . if one must constantly suppress his or her knowledge of God, then it is always possible that one can stop suppressing this and accept that He is real.

All other philosophies and religions must borrow much from God's general and special revelation in order to have any success at all in the world God has made and, thus, to have any credibility.

Anyone who truly seeks God's mercy will surely receive it, along with all of the blessings of Salvation.

While we observe the deaths of others, we won't actually experience our own deaths as such. We may experience the process of dying (if we don't die suddenly). But at the end of our lives in this world we simply pass on to the next stage of life.

It has been said that Christians can have so much confidence in our future in Heaven that it is as if we are already there. But, it seems more accurate to say that we ARE actually already there, just not from our current point-of-view!

So, while God, as a free Moral Being, could theoretically do evil, He just never does. This includes never lying to us or misleading us.

Chapter 11

If the Materialism on which Humanism is based was correct then there would be no such thing as freedom. What we do, say and think would only be what our brains determine that we will do, say and think.

No reasonable person would blame the author of a novel for evil done by a character in the novel he has created. So it is that God could create a story (and we say that history is His-story) with evil characters in it, but nevertheless not be responsible for the evil these created characters do.

. . . it is only because we are free that God can rightly hold us culpable for our choices, including the original choice to disobey Him, which all of us continue to do by nature.

. . . we are all free, but not completely free. <u>And the most freedom that we can possibly have is to be only under God's rule, not under the rule of someone or something else</u>. This is what happens if, and only if God sets us free. If God is truly our Lord we are truly free of the rule of anyone or anything else.

. . . submission to any organization or authority should never trump our universal obligation "to obey God rather than men". . .

. . . unbelief, regardless of what form it takes, is not really unbelief. Rather, it is <u>disbelief</u> in, or Denial of the relationship which God created us for and continuously calls us to.

True prayer is based on the one praying and God having a "speaking relationship". Without this, "prayer" is merely an act of ritual.

<u>If anyone truly believes in the Gospel of Jesus Christ, from the moment that you believe you have permanently come under new ownership, going from being slaves to sin to being slaves to God and His righteousness.</u>

. . . once we join God's Team we will never be off the field. And God will never kick us off His Team no matter how much we screw up! Rather, He will work with us individually by means of His Spirit and His Word (the Bible) so that we get better and better.

Our Salvation from start-to-finish is entirely from God. And so all of the Glory is His.

Christianity says that you will surely succeed because God will make sure that you succeed. All you have to do is trust Him.

Only faith that God has already saved you and is now working out this salvation in your life can take away pride and self-righteousness, as well as the anxiety that can lead to despair.

Which worldview should prevail in society? Most Christians in the past and many still today would say it's Christianity. Muslims have always said Islam. Humanists say it should be Humanism, Hindus Hinduism and so on. So, which is right? It will no doubt be surprising to many of you that the correct answer is: None of the above!

... when theology and politics are not considered separate spheres, the stakes of disagreements will tend to be raised, even to being viewed as the difference between going to Heaven and going to Hell in some cases.

... the purpose of the anti-establishment clause was to protect the free-exercise of religion, as well as the freedom of non-religious people.

... those who fear the rise of an American Theocracy should take comfort in knowing that the founders were firmly on their side.

Just because someone denies the True Source and Ground of morality and truth doesn't mean that they won't rightly accept that many things are good or evil and that many things are true or false.

As a Christian, I for one am willing to accept the possibility that the other side will win. But will you on the pro-LGBTQ side be willing to do this?

Chapter 12

Believers in the virtues of Socialism point to high standards-of-living in Western European nations which embraced the socialist philosophy after World War 2. However, that the high standards-of-living are due to the form of government in these nations is debatable.

Socialism seeks equality of economic <u>outcomes</u>. Instead of a level playing-field, Socialism favors a level outcome in the game. Is it not clear that the only way to attempt to accomplish this would be through a major increase in government power?

In fact, all people have equal intrinsic value as human-beings. But the value of people in the marketplace will vary greatly.

Socialism inevitably trends not toward a limited government "of the People, by the People and for the People" which was the ideal of America's founders, but toward an ever-increasing Government <u>over</u> the people.

. . . those who have the Christian understanding of human nature tend to see governments as magnifiers of the evil of individuals (with only rare exceptions).

. . . faith in the ability of governments as a force for good is why Humanists are so determined to solve the world's problems from the "top-down" instead of from the "bottom-up". This has always been the core of Socialism. And it is why obtaining political control is of paramount importance.

. . . an optimum society in this world is nowhere promised in the New Testament. Rather, our goal is what Jesus' Kingdom parables in the New Testament pointed to: creating citizens of the Kingdom of God which will be revealed when He returns.

Jonathan Trager, prominent television producer for ESPN, died last night from complications of losing his soul mate and his fiancee. He was 35 years old. Soft-spoken and obsessive, Trager never looked the part of a hopeless romantic. But, in the final days of his life, he revealed an unknown side of his psyche. This hidden quasi-Jungian persona surfaced during the Agatha Christie-like pursuit of his long reputed soul mate, a woman whom he only spent a few precious hours with. Sadly, the protracted search ended late Saturday night in complete and utter failure.

Yet even in certain defeat, the courageous Trager secretly clung to the belief that life is not merely a series of meaningless accidents or coincidences. Uh-uh. But rather, it's a tapestry of events that culminate in an exquisite, sublime plan. Asked about the loss of his dear friend, Dean Kansky, the Pulitzer Prize-winning author and executive editor of the New York Times, described Jonathan as a changed man in the last days of his life. "Things were clearer for him.", Kansky noted. "Ultimately Jonathan concluded that if we are to live life in harmony with the universe, we must all possess a powerful faith in what the ancients used to call 'fatum', what we currently refer to as destiny."
(from the film, "Serendipity")

"My God, the universe is random; it's not inevitable, it's simple chaos. It's subatomic particles and endless pings, collision – that's what science teaches us. What does this say? What is it telling us that the very night that this man's daughter dies, it's me who is having a drink with him? I mean, how could that be random?"

(Walter White musing about the coincidence of unknowingly meeting the father of his "business partner" Jesse's girlfriend on the very night in which he would later let her choke to death, "Breaking Bad", Season 3, Episode 10, "Fly")

"You'd best start believing in ghost stories, Miss Turner! . . . You're in one!"

(Captain Barbossa in response to the incredulous Elizabeth Turner, from the film "Pirates of the Caribbean: The Curse of the Black Pearl")

"You've taken your first step into a larger world."

(Obi-wan Kenobi to Luke Skywalker upon his first taste of the Force, "Star Wars, Episode 4")

"Oh how He loves you and me. He gave His life, what more could He give? Oh how He loves you. Oh how He loves me. Oh how He loves you and me."

(A popular Christian praise song. "He" refers to Jesus, Who is God's 2nd Person and became a man for us.)

www.ingramcontent.com/pod-product-compliance
Lightning Source LLC
Chambersburg PA
CBHW071346290426

44108CB00014B/1455